Nurturing Doubt |

Nurturing Doubt

**From Mennonite Missionary
to Anthropologist in the
Argentine Chaco**

Elmer S. Miller

University of Illinois Press
Urbana and Chicago

Manufactured in the United States of America

1 2 3 4 5 C P 5 4 3 2 1

This book is printed on acid-free paper.

Library of Congress Cataloging-in-Publication Data

Miller, Elmer S., 1931–

Nurturing doubt : from Mennonite missionary to anthropologist in the
Argentine Chaco / Elmer S. Miller.

p.   cm.

Includes bibliographical references and index.

ISBN 0-252-02155-X (cloth : acid-free paper). — ISBN 0-252-06455-0 (paper :
acid-free paper)

1. Miller, Elmer S., 1931– . 2. Ethnologists—United States—Biography.
3. Ethnology—Fieldwork. 4. Mennonites—Missions—Argentina. 5. Toba Indians.
6. Mennonites—Biography. I. Title.

GN21.M52A3 1995

301'.092—dc20   94-30791

CIP

Contents

Preface

Indeed, research in the field, by which every anthropological career begins, is mother and nurse of doubt, the philosophical attitude par excellence. This "anthropological doubt" does not only consist of knowing that one knows nothing, but of resolutely exposing what one thought one knew—and one's very ignorance—to the buffetings and denials directed at one's most cherished ideas and habits by other ideas and habits best able to rebut them.

—Lévi-Strauss

This book documents the transforming effects of field experiences upon a Mennonite missionary turned anthropologist. Recounted through a personal story, the experiences depict contemporary discourses involving anthropology, missionization, Mennonites, and indigenous people of the Argentine Chaco.

Primary attention is given to the close, but little explored, relationship between interpersonal encounters in the field that redefine a personal sense of identity and the manner in which such interactions get translated into professional knowledge associated with a discipline. This is particularly pertinent in anthropology, where fieldwork has constituted the discipline's raison d'être. The epigraph describes field experience as essentially an encounter with personal doubt about one's own myths and traditions.

My encounter with anthropological doubt of the sort described by Lévi-Strauss occurred, however, long before my initial field experience as a missionary. It began while I was still a teenager and involved questioning my Mennonite sense of identity. College and postgraduate work further nurtured my doubt so that I entered the field with serious questions about the missionary role I was about to assume. Five years of field experience in this role resolved my theological dilemmas in such a manner as to prompt me to change careers. Throughout return field trips as a professional anthropologist I no longer entertained doubt about my role, now the full-fledged ethnographer, but came to question increasingly the quality of interpersonal interaction I was able to experience given Toba disinterest in my new role. Doubt about the quality of ethnographic insight I was able to obtain, as well as the value of my scholarly work to the people concerned, led eventually to a reappraisal of my notion of ethnographic production itself.

The community in which I was raised taught its members that to doubt was a sin, and we all knew what happened to sinners. The deeply troubling tension generated by repression of the seeds of doubt in youth engendered a rebel spirit that appears to have remained with me throughout my life. Coming to recognize doubt as a *positive philosophical attitude* that expands intellectual horizons by strengthening the capacity to make mature judgments without excessive reliance upon authority was a long and painful process, one that influenced the way I have responded to shifting discourses throughout adulthood.

The story of that recognition, together with the persistent sense of myself as a pilgrim, with which I was raised as a Mennonite, is told in the following scenes. First, I recount my experiences with my ethnic and religious identity in childhood and youth that impacted significantly upon the way I subsequently dealt with alternative discursive forms in adulthood. The remainder of the book is primarily an examination of texts produced during fieldwork among the Toba Indians of northern Argentina, first as missionary and later as anthropologist, together with writings prepared for scholarly consumption. Since early 1959 I have traveled seven times to the Argentine Chaco, spending approximately seven years with the Toba.

Some of the texts consist of letters exchanged among colleagues and mission administrators, others are diaries kept for personal satisfaction, still others involve professional writings produced in the practice of anthropology. The value of the texts is in what they reveal *without conscious intention* about the relationship between personal field experiences and the discursive forms of a given discipline, shaped in turn by broader philosophical and epistemological transformations in Western thought throughout the latter twentieth century.

Although not the primary focus, considerable ethnographic insight is also provided on the Toba people, whose lives have become deeply intertwined with my own.

This work, then, is for those inquisitive about how personal encounters with specific forms of otherness get transformed into scholarly productions that move disciplinary discourses in particular ways. It is also for anyone who has questioned at one time or another his or her commitment to a given discourse. Each of us has experienced doubt in some form. Perhaps fewer among us know what it means to be a pilgrim in the sense of living in a community that conceptualizes itself as *called out* and *separated from* the world around it. It is this sense of *participation in* yet *isolation from* the broader community, whether nation or profession, that has shaped the manner in which I experience life and practice anthropology.

The story must be told in highly personal terms, it cannot be otherwise, since this is where doubt and pilgrimage are experienced. Such experience can only take place, of course, in communities of discourse that constitute the context for realization. The objective here is to demonstrate the manner in which such communities of discourse shape human experience that, in turn, serves to reconstitute and modify that discourse.

Acknowledgments

The following persons have contributed directly in one form or another to the production of this volume. Ken Kensinger discussed the idea with me from the start and provided helpful suggestions on various versions along the way. Pablo Wright responded to my initial efforts with valuable comments on both style and content. Dan Rose read an early draft and made recommendations that I have sought to incorporate. John Hostetler and Beula Hostetler also read an early draft and proposed thoughtful questions for consideration. Albert Buckwalter and Lois Buckwalter read several drafts and provided valuable comments and proofreading corrections. Albert graciously permitted me to cite extensively from his personal correspondence in act 1, scene 3 and act 2, scene 2 and to include a few of his photographs. Joyce Keener's enthusiastic comments and suggestions on an early version provided inspiration for revising the manuscript into its present form. Jon Church read the original draft, which sought to incorporate both personal experience and Toba ethnography objectives. His suggestion to write two volumes rather than one proved useful. Waud Kracke read a late draft and offered incisive recommendations both on content and style that have improved the text significantly. My daughter Lisa's suggestions on the final draft helped tie together the central theme of doubt by making implicit arguments more explicit, and my daughter Rosina helped prepare the index and promotional materials. Muriel Kirkpatrick prepared the maps and photographs for publication. Becky Standard's editorial skills preserved my style whjle clarifying the prose. I am sincerely grateful to each of these contributors. Responsibility for the final product is mine alone, but the suggestions and encouragement of family, colleagues, and students certainly has shaped this work in fundamental ways.

No one Toba individual has contributed specifically to this volume, but encounters with Toba worlds of understanding is what it is all about. I wish to express my warmest appreciation to every Toba person named in the following pages. Each one has shared in my pilgrimages over the years with open arms of comradeship and friendship.

Indian Reservation

PILCOMAYO RIVER

TEUCO

BERMEJO RIVER

RIVER

FORMOSA
PROVINCE

Tres Pozos
Pozo la China
Espinillo
Bartolomé
de las Casas

Miraflores
Pozo Toro
Colchón
Riacho de Oro
Legua 7
Lavalle
Diez de Mayo
Castelli
Campo
Pampa del Indio
Pampa
Alemani
Lote Cuatro
Argentina
Campo Medina
Pampa Chica
Raíz Chaqueña
Tres Isletas
Legua 15
Aguará
Legua 9
El Colorado
Legua 17

Formosa

Misión
Laishi

Puerto
Pilcomayo

PARAGUAY RIVER

BERMEJO R.

Sáenz Peña
(Barrio Nom Qom)
Quintilipi
Napalpí
Bajo
Machagai
Hondo
Martillo
La Reducción
Makallé

CHACO
PROVINCE

Resistencia

Corrientes

PARANA R.

Overture

Bermejito River, August 11, 1960

Upon our arrival late in the afternoon at a familiar Toba Indian community in the heart of the Argentine Chaco, my missionary colleague Albert and I discovered that most of the people we had intended to visit were called away unexpectedly to harvest a late growth of cotton. While drinking the familiar local *maté* tea around a campfire later that evening we learned from one of the senior elders that the Bermejito River was unusually low, making it possible to cross with our four-wheel-drive Jeep to Espinillo, home of the abandoned British Emmanuel Mission I had long yearned to visit.

The next morning we left bright and early with a local Toba companion who was raised in the Espinillo region. We followed wagon trails, cutting down stumps and brush along the way to allow the Jeep to pass. When we arrived at the river midmorning, Albert waded into the water to make certain we could cross safely. Although the water covered the wheels, four-wheel drive allowed us to proceed with no difficulty.

Beyond the far bank we encountered a Toba man from Espinillo who seemed to be awaiting our arrival. Upon inquiry, he informed us that he had come to show us the way because the old familiar trail was now abandoned. Despite more than a year of experiences in this cultural milieu, I was perplexed. The following conversation did little to resolve my disorientation.

"How did you know that we would arrive this morning?"

"I dreamed it last night."

Incredulously, "How did you know when to meet us here?"

Matter-of-factly, "Easy. In my dream the sun was there [pointing] in the sky."

Legua 17, June 13, 1959

Less than two months after settling into a routine of missionary visits to Toba communities scattered throughout the Chaco, I had my first serious encounter with faith healing.[1] While visiting a rural Toba community I was asked to accompany several local religious leaders to the home of an elderly man who lay dying on a cot in a typical house with mud walls and a grass-thatched roof.

We arrived in the midst of a chilly, damp drizzle. I learned later that a doctor at the local clinic had diagnosed the old man's illness as an advanced case of tuberculosis. The doctor voiced surprise that the sick man had managed to survive as long as he had. My companions helped him to his feet and led him outside to a chair, which they had hastily retrieved from the house. As we gathered around the chair I tried to block off the cold southern wind that seemed to pick up strength by the minute. Together we all laid hands on the man, an essential feature of the faith healing ceremony, and everyone prayed aloud. The prayers continued for probably fifteen or twenty minutes.

The longer they continued, the more disturbed I became over seeing this obviously very sick man subjected to the cold, damp wind. Emaciated and coughing up a great deal of phlegm, he appeared close to death, and I was afraid he would die on the spot.

During several lulls when the loud praying died down, the congregational minister asked the old man if he was healed. When he did not respond in the affirmative, everyone increased the intensity of prayer and shouted for the demons to leave. Since this was the first time I had ever participated in this type of faith healing ceremony, I was very uncomfortable and did not know how to act. No one seemed to notice my discomfort.

The prayers finally came to a halt and the elderly sick man looked at me imploringly as though expecting some word of wisdom. I asked if he had eaten recently. While he shook his head, a member of the family said he had not eaten in a week. I suggested that it might be a good idea for him to try some chicken broth. His family informed me that they did not have any chickens, nor money to buy one for soup. I then proposed that we take up a collection and contributed ten pesos to get it started. We gleaned twenty pesos in all, which was used to buy a chicken and other staples.

The following day I left the community and did not return for several months. Upon my return I saw the man attending the local church services. He was clearly improved. At the close of the service he came forward to tell me that I had cured him. On several subsequent visits I found him alive and he continued to express appreciation for having been healed.

His assertions made me very uncomfortable, not only because my doubts about faith healing were too strong to have contributed positively to such a "miracle," but also because word of my role in that event could travel widely. I was afraid others would expect my participation in faith healing ceremonies to help cure them when they were dangerously ill. I was not disturbed by their faith in divine healing, but I was conscious of my own skepticism; I certainly wanted to avoid the reputation of divine healer.

Pampa del Indio, September 17, 1961

While on a missionary trip to a small Toba settlement located at the edge of this central Chaco town, I was asked to travel inland to an isolated community to visit and help pray for a young woman who was very sick. There was no clear road and we traveled over rough wagon trails and across several streams. Finally we arrived at a house where the woman lay in apparent severe pain. Her side was swollen; she was feverish and perspiring heavily. In my inexpert opinion, she appeared to have an acute case of appendicitis.

After several prayers led by the local church leader, the woman expressed a strong desire to be taken to the church service at the edge of town. As the trip involved nearly eight miles of travel over rough terrain, I was highly reluctant to remove her, worried that the bouncing of the Jeep might cause her further damage, or even death.

I expressed grave concern about the risk of travel, offering instead to fetch a doctor from the town clinic. No one considered this a viable alternative. All were fully convinced that the only proper thing to do was to transport her to church, where all the faithful could pray for healing. It became apparent that I had no choice but to acquiesce to their request, so we helped her into the Jeep and, together with several family members, proceeded gingerly toward town.

When we arrived around eight o'clock in the evening the church service was already in progress. It continued for four and one-half hours, during which time various regional church leaders spoke about faith healing and the healing powers of the gospel through prayer. Throughout the service a number of the leaders stepped forward to pray for the woman.

In the final healing ceremony, which lasted for at least an hour, church leaders, shamans, and family members gathered around to lay hands on the woman in prayer. During the early part of the service the woman was moaning in pain, but as the singing, prayer, and preaching progressed, she grew increasingly calm. From time to time the praying would die down and the local leader would ask if she was healed. When she responded in the negative, they would continue to pray over her in increasingly loud and demanding voices.

By the end of the service she responded positively. Everyone seemed highly pleased, though exhausted.

I suggested that we take her by the clinic, where the doctor could check her over and witness the miraculous recovery. But they all disagreed, saying there was no need for a doctor now that she was healed. Besides, the woman wished to return home, so I drove her there.

In all candor, I fully expected the woman to die, but I heard later that she had recovered. When my wife, Lois, and I returned to the area some six months later, she was alive and healthy. She, too, expressed gratitude for my help, but I expect that she referred primarily to transportation. My low-key role in healing rituals was by now safely intact.

Sáenz Peña, March 1961

The Toba frequently arrived by train or by bus to visit at our home in Sáenz Peña, the second largest city of the Chaco province of northern Argentina. Late one evening we heard the clapping of hands at our front entrance, standard procedure for announcing one's arrival.

After offering our guest (a young male in his early thirties from Miraflores) the customary gourd of *maté* tea while Lois prepared something to eat, we conversed routinely about events in our respective areas. We spoke about the delay of the train and its frequent late arrival due to persistent engine trouble. Meanwhile, Lois had served the food she prepared and it was getting quite late. Although inclined to retire for the night, I was aware that our visitor had something in mind that he wished to share, but he was clearly reluctant to broach the subject.

After an extended pause in conversation my guest finally blurted out this story.

"My mother killed my brother," he said abruptly.

Since this was a family with whom we had visited when traveling in the area, not surprisingly the news came as a shock.

After I asked how this could have happened, he explained that it was unintentional. His mother, whom he now called a sorcerer, had picked up some watermelon seeds spit onto the patio in front of their home so that she could conjure them to kill her husband's brother, his uncle. By mistake she managed to retrieve seeds spit from the mouth of her son instead.

Consequently, after she had performed the sorcerer's ritual act, it was her own son who became deathly ill and died. While she recognized her mistake, it was impossible to undo the harm. Once a power object is sent, its purpose must be accomplished even if the person who sent it has a change of heart.

"But how can you be so sure of this accusation?" I inquired. "Did your mother confess?"

"No," he responded, "but my brother named his own mother shortly before he died and words uttered from a deathbed are infallible. There is no doubt in my mind, it must be true."

When I asked what retaliation might be taken, my guest shrugged his shoulders and explained. "It was an accident; she did not really intend to kill her own son."

Clearly she, along with the other members of the family, would have to live with her tragic mistake.

Sáenz Peña, September 1, 1959

The following dream was recounted to me by the church leader of a large community. On the way home from a visit to the community of his childhood and youth, Legua 17, he stopped by our house to "borrow" funds for return travel by train and bus.

At one point in our conversation, before requesting money, he asked me to read from Revelation 6, which depicts beasts and different colored horses speaking messages. When I had finished, he told me this dream.

> Around the middle of August I had a dream in which I saw four big, black horses come out of the east. Three of them passed by, but one fell on his side near my house. I went out to him and he was foaming at the mouth and had vomited. I tasted some of the vomit and it made me sick and dizzy.
>
> Soon a man in a long white robe with a long beard—just like the prophets of the Old Testament—told me to make the animal speak. I asked the animal to speak and he ordered me to cut a big circle of green grass around him and make a big fire so that he could go away in the smoke.
>
> I ordered the people to cut the green grass in a circle around the horse and to make a big fire with a lot of smoke.
>
> Just before the animal disappeared in the smoke he told me this: "You must go to Legua 17, brother." After that he went away in the smoke and I saw him no more. Therefore, I obeyed the dream. I went to Legua 17 as told.

Not only did this church leader obey the heavenly vision, but he also used the authority of the vision to lend authenticity to his request for funds from the missionary to return home.

• • •

Clearly these five episodes, representative of many other interactions with the Toba throughout the past thirty-five years, depict a discourse that most of us find strange, not to say incongruent. Faith healing, like handling snakes in worship services described in the film *The Holy Ghost People,* are recognized forms of behavior in our society. We know that such practices exist. But few among us have interacted meaningfully over extended periods of time with people who live with dream encounters and a world of spirits as a matter of daily routine. Most of us cannot remember our dreams, let alone call upon them for determinative action.

If I were writing for the Toba reader, the opening episodes would portray experiences from my Mennonite youth or from professional life at Temple University that would appear equally as incongruous to the Toba reader as these appear to North Americans.

My Mennonite upbringing framed significantly the manner in which I initially interacted with the Toba as a missionary. Those interactions, in turn, prompted me to question fundamentally not only my missionary role but the basic affirmations of Christianity itself as I understood them. The very religious interactions that the Toba appeared to find highly meaningful in an effort to revitalize their sense of identity as a people served to confirm my growing doubt about the exclusive claims of a Christianity I was being called upon to export.

The first two scenes document this doubting process as it relates to one form of Christian community and missionization. Recent research in Christian origins confirms the need to break the taboo against exposing the mythic nature of our Western Judeo-Christian heritage. Mack (1993:253) so argues, asserting that "for thoughtful people, the issues have to do with assessing the chances for constructing sane and safe societies in a multicultural world while understanding the conditions of predation and prejudice, power abuse, and violence." By revealing my own encounters with such exposure, I hope to contribute to the possible construction of the more sane and safe societies Mack has in mind.

After additional training in anthropology I returned to the field on repeated occasions to pursue research. These experiences, together with contemporary critiques of ethnography in the discipline, led me eventually to question the value of the ethnographic work I was producing, not only to the Toba who are of primary concern, but also to Western scholarship generally. Scene 3 focuses the critical attitude of doubt on the discipline of anthropology itself, which has often been quick to criticize missionary endeavors but not always equally alert to its own colonial role in Western ideological expansion. Thus, the doubting process continues.

Tortuous as this process may sound, doubt, or, in contemporary parlance, critical vigilance, constitutes the essential component of intellectual growth and development without which there would be no advancement of knowledge or greater understanding. It is the questioning attitude that makes it possible to recognize the extent to which cultural claims to truth constitute myths that require constant reexamination. Contemporary discourse in anthropology has called attention to the manner in which ethnographic productions have tended to serve Western colonial self-interest rather than the greater good of common humanity.[2] Thus, critical vigilance provides hope for greater insight into taken-for-granted affirmations that too often confirm cultural self-identities at the expense of human beings designated as Other. It is, in the words of Lévi-Strauss, "the philosophical attitude par excellence" (1976:26).

Closely related to the experiences of doubt portrayed here is the notion of pilgrim with which I was raised. The concept of being *in* but not *of* the world was one I struggled with as a child. Only in recent years have I come to appreciate its value. A pilgrim is someone in a strange land around people and practices that appear unfamiliar, even uncomfortable. In a multicultural world we must all become sensitized to the pilgrim's travail if we are to understand and relate meaningfully to one another.

Awareness of and sensitivity to the unfamiliar is what fieldwork is all about, giving modern anthropology its unique claim to disciplinary identity. Thus, anthropology represented a reasonable choice of profession for someone who had questioned his cultural roots and experienced extensive fieldwork in a setting as significantly Other as the Argentine Chaco. There was even a glimmer of hope that the transition to a new role would constitute an intellectual home where I could at long last settle down among supporting colleagues who understood the discomfort of persistent encounters with unfamiliarity. Scene 3 discloses not only that it didn't work out that way but that it couldn't given the nature of disciplinary discourse. But that is okay, since I have come to recognize the fundamental worth of the pilgrim stance in our late twentieth-century world.

Act 1 | Ethnic Discourse,
Seeds of Doubt

Scene 1: Growing Up Mennonite

I was born and raised in an eastern Pennsylvania Mennonite family that instilled a strong sense of responsibility to a "called out" community; that is, one separated from "this world" in deeds as well as ideals.[1] Two doctrines in particular served to mark this separation: "nonconformity" and "nonresistance."

We were taught that these doctrines were established on biblical foundations and were encouraged to memorize Scripture verses called upon frequently in church services. The one that comes immediately to mind in support of the first doctrine is 2 Cor. 6:17–18: "Wherefore come out from among them, and be ye separate, saith the Lord, and touch not the unclean thing; and I will receive you and will be a Father unto you, and ye shall be my sons and daughters, saith the Lord Almighty."

Separation meant wearing "plain" clothing that did not conform to "worldly" standards, such as capes, head veiling, and black stockings for women, and straight-cut suit coats without lapels or neckties for men. These rules were constantly reaffirmed by the regional bishop who visited the congregation to conduct Council Meetings designed to prepare one for Holy Communion. Those who did not follow the rules were discouraged from participating in the feet washing and communion services.

Nonconformity also meant avoiding "sinful" places like movie theaters, bars, or even the roller-skating rink, which we passed on our way to church and the grocery store. In my early youth it also meant not owning a radio or driving a flashy-colored car that demonstrated pride of possession. A song often sung in church services contained the affirmation, "I'm but a stranger here, heaven is my home." The notion of "pilgrims on this earth" was at the heart of the concept of separation from the world. It meant that the real home of Mennonites was in heaven rather than on earth, the home claimed by people of the world around us. *We* did not belong here, *they* did.

The related doctrine of nonresistance also had its biblical base. Matt. 5:39 was cited frequently: "But I say unto you, That you resist not evil: but whosoever shall smite thee on thy right cheek, turn to him the other also." Above all, this verse meant nonparticipation in military service and the affairs of state. One's allegiance was only to God, not to the state. Anyone who joined the military was excommunicated from the congregation and prohibited from taking communion. When I was twelve years old the son of a prominent church leader in our district chose to enlist in the army, asserting that he could see little difference between fighting among church members or fighting for his country. There were two disturbing ideas in this statement that haunted me. First, there was more fighting among church people than I cared to admit, and second, how had he come to think of this as *his* country? Could I ever make such a claim and still be a good Mennonite Christian? Deep inside I was beginning to hope that a way could be found. The official excommunication of this young man had a traumatic effect upon our community.

In my own family, the doctrine of nonresistance also meant refusing to vote in political elections, and of more immediate significance to me personally, refusing to pledge allegiance to the flag. One pledged only to God. This rule caused me some discomfort at our one-room, eight-grade school where taunts of "German-lovers," "yellow-bellies" ("turn the other cheek, Miller") and a general implication of being unpatriotic had to be confronted during World War II.

This brand of Mennonite tradition, however, was characteristic of a particular place and time. Although there are remnants of that tradition in Mennonite communities today, the Lancaster Conference Mennonite Church to which our congregation belonged has changed its doctrinal practice significantly, particularly with regard to nonconformity. Many congregations no longer require the prayer veiling and "plain coats" have largely disappeared. Even the concept of nonresistance conveys different meanings among Mennonites today than it did in the 1950s (see Miller 1985a). Not only is the war with Germany a distant memory, a country whose language and ethos remains associated with Mennonite roots, the peace position is much more tolerated and even respected by the larger society than it was prior to the 1960s.[2]

My attachment to the Mennonite community as a growing boy was slightly more tenuous than that of other Mennonite young people in eastern Pennsylvania for several reasons. First, I grew up at the edge of the rich "promised land" of Lancaster County rather than in the heart of it. Elizabethtown, while still in the county, was at the very border, and when I was eleven years old we moved across that magic border to Dauphin County, where the farmland was less rich and valuable. It didn't matter that our farm was only a few miles from the county line. In freshman year at Lancaster Mennonite High School I became consciously aware of a marginal status that required proof of identity and worth to the heart of the Mennonite community. I proved it that year by singing bass in the school quartet with three members of the senior class.

Especially after our move to Dauphin County we lived in an area where there were few Mennonite families, which meant that we attended elementary school with few if any Mennonite young people. Furthermore, the ministers of our church district were little known or called upon outside it. Most of my colleagues in high school, on the other hand, had attended schools where Mennonite students comprised the majority and churches were known regionally for their respected leadership. Thus, the experiences of these students were quite different from my own. My sense of Mennonite identity was not as neatly packaged as it appeared to be for fellow students, which only underscored a feeling of marginality.

Also, although my birth mother had been raised by a prominent Mennonite family, her family was not Mennonite, so I grew up with relatives from the Harrisburg area who were "of this world." Sometimes I was permitted to spend a week or two of summer vacation with these urban relatives, who always brought gifts to our house during the Christmas season.

My mother died when I was nearly three years old and my attachment to her kin became an exceptionally strong one emotionally, although I was unaware of this at the time. The gifts at Christmas and the occasional visits in summer became high points for me as a child but held special feelings of ambivalence, given my uncertainties about strong attachments to relatives who were obviously "worldly."

More importantly, the strict dichotomy between church and world that was supposed to be reinforced in the Mennonite community became blurred through my attachments to relatives who did not dress "plain," smoked cigars, attended movies, and participated in state and local politics. Although it was strictly forbidden, I once attended a movie with cousins while on summer vacation. I do not recall having told my family about it.

Despite these apparently anomalous relationships to the Mennonite community, Mennonite values were a central component of my socialization. I was highly conscious of identifying with a community that was isolated from a world that I knew very little about because I could not participate in it. My supporting institutions were family, church, and, to a lesser extent, school, while I had only a tangential sense of identity with the state and nation.

A strict division between state and church was formed in my mind so that what happened in the state was outside my control and of little interest to me personally. We did not receive a daily newspaper in our home, nor did we have a radio. My parents did not vote. School, while a source of conflict, nevertheless provided an avenue of intellectual stimulation and challenge, since I could always achieve self-confidence and payback on examinations and at spelling competitions. It was also a source of limited information about the unknown world, which I increasingly desired to discover.

After one year at Lancaster Mennonite High School I had reached the legal age when it was not mandatory to attend school. Since they could not afford to send me to private church school and they refused to allow me to attend public high school, my father and his second wife, who I consider my mother, sent me to live and work on a farm with a family who attended our congregation. While radios were frowned upon by the bishop of our district, they were not strictly forbidden. The family I worked for had a radio and I recall following the 1948 Republican Convention with fascination upon completing a long day's work in the fields. On at least one occasion the farmer found me asleep on a chair in front of the radio when he awakened the next morning to call in the cows for milking.

It was difficult to get answers to the many questions I had about the process of selecting a candidate for the presidency. When Harry Truman defeated Thomas Dewey during the following election, though local lore and, as it turned out, public discourse said Dewey was far ahead with an unbeatable lead, I became aware of limitations in the information I was receiving about the world around me, which I found intriguing, but knew so little about.

Opportunities to express my expanding inquiries about Mennonite faith and practice were provided in weekly Sunday school classes and in our newly established two-week summer Bible school sessions. In retrospect it is apparent that I must have driven teachers crazy with persistent questions and sometimes unsolvable philosophical dilemmas. An uncle who taught the young men's Sunday school class for a period of time told me shortly before his premature death from cancer that he used to pray to God for wisdom in order to know how to deal with my weekly probing.

One summer during my tenure as farmhand I advanced to the senior class in summer Bible school, which the newly ordained bishop from a neighboring congregation had agreed to teach. Finally, I expected more definitive answers to questions I found increasingly troubling. Were our church-going neighbors who did not practice Mennonite doctrines "saved"? How could we accept protection from state police and a national army while refusing to serve the state or the nation? Was not our "peculiar" dress a hindrance rather than a "witness" to people of the world? A more general question that perplexed me was how a loving God in total control of the universe could permit widespread suffering and injustice. The answer I was consistently given was found in the story of Job, but that story somehow never quite solved the problem satisfactorily for me.

To my great disappointment, the new bishop did not find my questions particularly interesting or challenging. Rather, he seemed to consider them a distraction from his plan of study. When I persisted, because I had already made up my mind on some of the questions (for example, I had bought a lapel suit and a necktie), the bishop indicated that I was a troublemaker who lacked obedience and trust in his elders.

This approach could conceivably have stifled my initiative had I not begun to attend weekly meetings at Youth for Christ in Lancaster, where I came into contact with young people who laid claim to the same apparent basic Christian doctrines that I was taught except for nonconformity to the world and nonresistance to evil. It was a shock to interact with both ex- and non-Mennonite Christian youth who dressed and in most respects acted like any other person of "the world," yet who appeared to be even more dedicated to spreading the Christian faith than I was. The already questionable reality of a *church-world* dichotomy with which I grew up began to wither further in these weekly sessions, where the dogmatism of ethnic tradition came to be replaced by dogmatism about a literal interpretation of divine revelation involving "plenary verbal" inspiration of the Bible, the Virgin Birth, and the premillennial return of Christ.[3] The primary emphasis at Youth for Christ was upon evangelism that called upon all "believers" to "witness for Christ," whether among the "unsaved" around us or in a higher calling to the "lost souls" of Africa, Asia, or Latin America (the three major areas of foreign Mennonite missions).

An advantage the Amish had over Mennonites in maintaining a more strict sense of isolation was that they did not allow automobiles or forms of communication that provided access to the outside world. The decision to participate seriously in Youth for Christ constituted a conscious act of rebellion against authority on my part since neither bishops nor parents approved of it. Together with several Mennonite buddies who also worked on farms, I drove to Lancaster every Saturday night to attend the weekly meetings, which gradually instilled doubt in us and eventually caused us to reject specific Mennonite doctrines. For the first time in my life I sensed possible relief from the burdens of being a pilgrim; perhaps now I could become familiar, even comfortable, with the world about me. The possibility of being both a Christian and a man of the world was part of the enticement to those Saturday night meetings of Youth for Christ.

The combination of growing dissatisfaction with responses from local church leaders to my doubts about ethnic doctrines and increasing fascination with more distant youth leaders, some of them ex-Mennonites who taught a doctrine of total commitment to Christ without the "baggage" of ethnicity that inhibited one's ability "to witness," came to a head for me one Sunday afternoon in June 1950 at Elizabethtown Mennonite Church.

At midcentury a spirit of revival was sweeping Mennonite congregations in Pennsylvania and Virginia that called for a "reconsecration of one's life to Christ." The visiting evangelists who spread this word tended to ignore traditional doctrines of nonconformity and nonresistance, stressing instead total surrender of one's self to the "call of Christ." Their meetings attracted large audiences in tents and churches. While attending one of these sessions that Sunday afternoon in June, I felt called to surrender myself completely to "Christ's service." My response involved a public stand and statement of commitment that would not leave me as we traveled home to milk the cows and tend the other animals. I performed the chores and sat through the evening meal in a sort of trance that sapped any desire to speak with others.

After dark I walked to the far edge of the farm where there was a small woodland and called upon God to show me what to do. It was an experience of intense emotional turmoil and physical exhaustion. I recall no sudden light nor voices, but I returned from that "encounter" with the clear indication that I should prepare myself for Christian service, probably mission work, by attending school somewhere.[4]

My immediate thought was the need for Bible study. Since I had not completed high school I did not initially consider college. However, when my father's cousin who was registrar and later dean of Eastern Mennonite College heard of my desire to prepare for Christian service, he arranged for a General Education Development test, which enabled me to enter the freshman class during the fall of 1950.[5] This decision disappointed my Youth for Christ friends, who strongly urged me to choose Bob Jones University or some similar theologically conservative Bible school or college.

However, my Mennonite roots were still sufficiently strong to lead me in the direction I chose. Furthermore, I already had some inclination that my interest in academic pursuits could lead far beyond Bible study. I had never been happy with the decision to quit high school. My parents had been concerned about the potential "worldly" influence of public school, especially since I had acquired two demerits for "mischievous behavior" during my year at the Mennonite high school. In retrospect, this parental concern appears to have been misguided since the powerful influence of Youth for Christ broke down the church-world barrier perhaps much more effectively than a public high school education in itself might have done.

It must be emphasized, however, that the break with Mennonite tradition involved much greater personal conflict and emotional struggle than this simple tale would suggest. The pain of causing offense to family and supporting friends was no easy burden to carry. Well do I remember the first time I chose to wear a lapel suit and tie to a church service in our district. When I descended the steps dressed for church, my mother went into such a shock that she was unable to accompany us.

My father and I went alone to the Saturday night service, which happened to be at the congregation we attended during the first eleven years of my life. En route I explained that my decision was carefully thought out and irrevocable. In fact, it had become a conviction. To me the "plain coat" had become a hindrance to Christian service rather than a symbol of obedience to Christ. Although he did not seem fully convinced, my father promised that he would try to explain my convictions to mother in a way that she might be able to accept.

Later, in a heated discussion with my mother's brother, the deacon of our congregation whom we all respected and held in high regard, he asked if I could expect to accompany Christ to heaven should he arrive and see me in lapel and tie. When I pointed out to Uncle Phares that he was making plain attire a point of salvation, he objected, insisting that "dressing plain" simply demonstrated willingness to obey the biblical commandment to "be separate from the world." The debate settled nothing but did cause a breach in our relationship that was never totally mended prior to his untimely death.

Thus, through my teenage encounter with an alternative religious rhetorical form, I learned that shifting discourse can be a highly traumatic and heart-wrenching experience. But I was not alone in making this shift. My Youth for Christ buddies, together with other Mennonite adults, including two ministers from our local district, decided to leave the Lancaster Conference Mennonite Church in order to practice their own convictions. They almost invariably chose an independent congregationalism that stressed fundamentalistic theology. It was no accident that the dogmatism of an authoritarian ethnicity was replaced by dogmatic stress on biblical interpretation involving a literalist reading of biblical texts.

One minister who renounced his Mennonite affiliation was a close personal friend and family acquaintance. He resigned from Lancaster Conference in order to preach the gospel on the radio, which was forbidden by the bishops at that time. With few exceptions, his entire congregation followed him to form an Independent Congregational church that through the years has assumed an increasingly fundamentalistic stance. Other individuals from the district also joined this church in protest against the authoritarian control of bishops. Two members who left their home congregations to join the newly formed group and sing in the radio quartet later became my brothers-in-law when I married their sister. This congregation subsequently provided financial support for our mission assignment to Argentina.

Not every minister chose to leave Lancaster Mennonite Conference of his own free will. Some were "silenced"; that is, ordered to stop preaching by the board of bishops. One classic example involved the husband of my father's cousin, who refused to follow the local bishop's demands to preach nonconformity in attire. This minister joined an already formed independent fundamentalist congregation on the outskirts of our hometown together with other members of his congregation. Other church members at the time were disciplined for selling dairy milk on Sundays. The story of such conflicts over the authority of bishops has been powerfully dramatized in the film *Silence at Bethany*.[6]

Thus, alienation from my religiously oriented family roots was but one example of a larger rebellion in the early 1950s against the traditional, authoritarian local Mennonite discourse. This rebellion, emboldened by itinerant Mennonite revivalist preachers during the 1950s who undermined the power of bishops by ignoring them, led in subsequent decades to a fundamental transformation of the Lancaster Conference Mennonite Church. Congregational decision-making came to replace the power of district bishops and contributed to the disintegration of "plain dress," which had persisted for nearly a century.[7]

My decision to enter Eastern Mennonite College was cautious in that it permitted pursuit of my scholarly interests in a familiar setting. I was highly conscious of having completed but one year of high school and uncertain about my abilities to compete with colleagues who had recently graduated. Therefore, I initially enrolled in a two-year Bible certificate program, but quickly transferred to the six-year bachelor of arts and theology program upon making the dean's list in my first year of study.

There is irony in the observation that much as Youth for Christ served to undermine my commitment to an ethnic discourse involving separation from the world, so six years of education at Eastern Mennonite College opened up a world of intellectual challenge and pursuit that led eventually to a questioning of Christian discourse in much broader terms.

Scene 2: Germinating Doubt in College and Seminary

My college experience opened up a world of understanding that I had not previously encountered. Courses in American literature, modern European history, the history of music, even biblical archaeology and ethics introduced me to a Western intellectual tradition that I found ever more intriguing. I was soon reading more than was required to satisfy my expanding curiosity. In the dorms we had no radio, movies were prohibited, and I was still unaccustomed to habitual reading of daily newspapers. Therefore, my growing familiarity with Western thought was acquired primarily through book knowledge. Only decades later did I become fully aware that, although educated in the 1950s, I was not a child of the period.

In college I discovered a keen fascination with languages while studying Spanish and New Testament Greek. This interest was further stimulated in seminary when I enrolled in biblical Hebrew along with advanced Greek. In contrast to the direct reading of God's will for one's life in the Bible that I had learned at Youth for Christ, the professors I regarded most highly carefully taught that one can only *interpret* God's will, never directly apprehend it. Studies in the Bible, New and Old Testament textual composition, and church history further eroded the simplistic view of the Bible taught in Sunday school classes and at Youth for Christ. It became increasingly apparent that a naive view of the Bible as authoritative for faith and action could not stand the test of serious scrutiny. The problem of hermeneutics, how the Bible gets interpreted, became the central focus of my attention.

Furthermore, the initial purpose for attending college and seminary, the goal that sustained me throughout those years of study, began to lose some of its charm. My studies of Christian missions uncovered for me a history of actions that were often far from admirable. The charming appeal of exotic places with "natives" eager to hear the good news did not jibe with the realities of mission expansion in an age of colonialism. Thus, by the time I finished seminary, seeds of doubt about a simplistic "go ye forth" approach to missionary work were not only sown but firmly germinated. A Bible verse we all knew from memory was "Go ye into all the world and preach the gospel to every creature" (Mark 15:15).

The role of doubt in shaping my intellectual development throughout my college and seminary years is epitomized by my unfolding struggle with the notion of biblical "revelation," which is a key concept in Christian theology. The basic idea is that God revealed himself to Abraham, Moses, and the prophets of the Old Testament and through the life of Jesus Christ in the New Testament. The nature of that revelation is conceptualized differently by various Christian churches, but some notion of God's revelation, "unveiling" of himself, primarily through biblical scripture, is central to all Christian affirmations and actions. Two appropriate biblical texts on this theme are "And the glory of the Lord shall be revealed, and all flesh shall see it together: for the mouth of the Lord hath spoken it" (Isa. 40:5) and the words of Jesus to Peter, "Blessed art thou, Simon Barjona, for flesh and blood hath not revealed it unto thee, but my Father which is in Heaven" (Matt. 16:17). The latter followed upon Peter's declaration that Jesus was "the Christ, the Son of the living God."

The notion of revelation with which I grew up was not a strict fundamentalist one that stressed doctrinal affirmations about the divinity of Christ and the inspiration of the Bible, although these "truths" were often affirmed. Rather, it was the idea that God had revealed himself to humans, entered history as it were, throughout two periods of divine revelation—the Old Testament and the New. The latter superseded the former, yet the former was considered highly important because it foreshadowed and foretold the latter. Together they constituted the total embodiment of religious knowledge that humans were expected to apprehend. Sermons involving Old and New Testament texts were generally allegorical in nature, with frequent references to sixteenth-century Anabaptist martyrs who died for the faith that we were being taught and permitted to practice freely. The ministers who preached these doctrines had no formal academic or biblical training; their illustrations were homespun or taken from sermon construction manuals.

Involvement with Youth for Christ and its strictly fundamentalist view of the Bible before entering college, however, made a deep impression upon me. The notion of a literal reading of God's will in the Scripture and of the imminent return of Christ to collect the chosen who would be spared the horrible fate of tribulation here on earth were doctrines that I came to accept at a deeper emotional level than the allegorical approach to biblical texts that I had experienced in childhood and early youth. This divergent discourse (alternative religious paradigm), which youth leaders explicitly defined as liberation from "the spiritual bondage" of ethnic tradition, legitimated my rejection of the Mennonite doctrine of separation.

However, rebellion against my Mennonite heritage did not consist of single actions here and there. Rather, it involved a long, slow process that gathered momentum over time. First there were the encounters with "unsaved" kin and neighbors who treated me with kindness and respect. There was the questioning of Sunday school teachers and eventually the bishop in summer Bible school that left me dissatisfied. Added to this were the itinerant Mennonite evangelists that undermined the hierarchical authority of bishops. The most significant factor serving to solidify my reaction against the authority of Mennonite ministers and bishops, however, was the teachings at Youth for Christ. My commitment to the doctrinaire tenets of fundamentalism instilled there was wholehearted and unreserved. It was the new authority that permitted a break with the Mennonite image of the pilgrim with which I was raised.

The drive to evangelize the world "out there" led me to street corner preaching, which I practiced into my third year of college. Upon entering college I even audaciously aimed, but failed, to convert an outstanding seminary professor to premillennialism. In the end, it was he who converted me to a nonmillennial view. The deeply held convictions that had led me to college in order to prepare for the mission field were not surrendered easily, however; the break with fundamentalist dogma involved a highly emotional struggle that left permanent scars.

Debate surrounding the Revised Standard Version translation of the Bible in which I engaged during college and seminary centered around the notion of revelation put forth in the King James Version. I understood the logic of those who rejected the new version because it was impressed upon me so effectively on Saturday nights in dynamic preaching at Lancaster during my latter teenage years. Encounters with Western humanism, however, together with studies in church history and biblical theology, led me to question that logic at its most basic foundation.

Perhaps most determinative of all in gradually undermining any notion I had of divine revelation tied to a literal inspiration of the King James Bible were my studies in New Testament Greek and Old Testament Hebrew. One seminar I specifically recall involved a word study of the Septuagint (the pre-Christian Greek translation of the Old Testament) in which the notion of interpretation in translation was driven home. In my study of the Greek translations of the Hebrew word *ohav*, "love," it was obvious that the translator had to decide in each context what Greek word to select. For example, was the sort of love under consideration erotic (*eros*), platonic (*philos*), or sacrificial/divine (*agape*) in nature? English conformed more closely to Hebrew in this instance since one word could serve fairly well as gloss for the Hebrew term.

While the problem of translation was not an entirely new idea, given my faint familiarity with the Pennsylvania Dutch dialect spoken by my parents but not passed on to me, the awareness that biblical texts contain the same problems of equivalency as any other translation constituted the formation of a *serious doubt* concerning the validity, not only of a plenary verbal view of biblical inspiration, but of the notion of inspiration itself.

I can still remember the table in the library where this discovery made its most dramatic impact on me. It was during Christmas holidays when students had traveled to their homes, the librarian had left for the day, and I had the library to myself. The major exegetical aids available in the library were lying open from one end of the long table to the other—Hebrew and Greek lexicons, biblical commentaries and concordances, books on textual criticism. I was wrestling with several crucial instances where the problem of translation was particularly acute when my Greek professor entered the room to express surprise that I was working so hard during vacation. I wanted to blurt out excitedly my discovery, but sensed that it would fall on deaf ears. The memory still lingers of his footsteps fading away down the hallway as I remained, alone, at the table.

The overwhelming sense of solitude I experienced that bleak December afternoon was not about the absence of people around me, but rather about the implications of what I later came to recognize as linguistic relativity. I knew I could no longer conceptualize biblical texts in the same way I had been, and was still being, taught. I also knew unquestionably that few, if any, of my fellow students would share the thrill, shock, and excitement of my conclusion.

Later I did attempt to share my insights with a major competitor for top honors in the seminar, but while he seemed to acknowledge their validity, he was not about to follow through on my decision to adopt a more relativistic approach to biblical interpretation than even our most open-minded seminary professors would allow. The sense of excited confidence that my conclusion was necessarily the only logical one, mixed with the lonely awareness that the implications could undermine ties with family and closest friends, was an emotion that is difficult to explain to anyone who has not experienced a sense of alienation from his or her roots. Knowledge can be bittersweet.

In addition to the germinating doubts about theological affirmations during my college and seminary years, my involvement with college choirs and quartets that toured Mennonite communities throughout the eastern seaboard further undermined confidence in my Mennonite upbringing. During my latter college and seminary years I also sang bass in the Mennonite Hour Quartet, a religious radio program aired on over four hundred stations throughout the world. Together with the radio minister we toured from coast to coast, as well as in various Canadian provinces, On these tours I came to confront cultural relativity, although the concept was not familiar to me at the time. The variety of "truths" claimed to characterize Mennonite tradition throughout the Northern Hemisphere astounded me.

My biggest shock was among Manitoba Mennonites. One town had seven different Mennonite affiliations, each one certain that it was practicing the tradition most faithfully. The touchstone for identity in the majority of these churches was not nonconformity, as I had been taught, but language. We gave the first English service in the history of one congregation, and it was obvious that many people felt guilty about it. Opening congregational singing, devotional reading, even our introduction were all in German.

After having sung the hymn "God the All Merciful" a member in the large congregation raised his hand to ask how many people present recalled singing that tune in Russia under the czars. These were descendants of Mennonites who had migrated to Russian under Catherine the Great and had migrated again to Canada after the Bolshevik Revolution. The question, which prompted scattered responses from elderly hands in the audience, reminded me that the tune we had sung was the Russian national anthem.

On tour we were consistently invited into Mennonite homes to spend the night. The families we visited in Manitoba could not believe that we were true Mennonites if we did not speak German. Even more astounding to them was the fact that I was studying theology with practically no knowledge of German. Not only was the Bible familiar to them in German, but also texts about theology and Anabaptist church history. Many insisted on speaking German to me in the expectation that I knew the language but simply refused to speak it. For them, to be Mennonite was to speak German.

The variety of ways that Mennonites expressed their commitment to faith from one region of the country to another, each one certain that its form of expression most authentically represented the *true* Anabaptist tradition, made a strong impression upon me at the same time that I was discovering linguistic relativity in biblical translation. The impact of these combined insights prompted me to question doctrinal dogma in a manner that neither one would have accomplished in and of itself. Although unaware of it in these terms at the time, I was becoming educated to the idea that "reality" is socially constructed. Later, at Hartford, Connecticut, and in the Argentine Chaco, the significance of this insight would be driven home with even greater force.

During my last semester of seminary in the spring of 1956 it became increasingly apparent that it would be inappropriate for me to accept the pastorate of a congregation given the theological doubts with which I was struggling. Furthermore, I wished to pursue my rapidly developing interest in biblical languages and textual criticism. The problem was where and how, given my lack of funds and ignorance about the types of programs available. Several weeks before graduation the general secretary of the Mennonite Board of Missions at Elkhart, Indiana, visited the campus and approached my wife, Lois, and me about the possibility of a mission assignment to the Toba Indians of the Argentine Chaco, with the promise of training in linguistics and anthropology at the Kennedy School of Missions in Hartford, Connecticut.

The offer had genuine appeal for several reasons: it allowed pursuit of further graduate study in our areas of interest; our assignment was to learn the language and provide support for a rapidly developing indigenous church in a context that did not call for proselytizing, which I found increasingly problematic; and the secretary did not seem particularly disturbed about my confession of theological doubts. While serving as a missionary in India many years before he had faced similar uncertainties in his confrontation with Hinduism. Elkhart was less theologically conservative than Harrisonburg, Virginia, home of my alma mater. It was reassuring to learn that my questions were, indeed, legitimate ones as far as one major Mennonite mission leader was concerned.

There was another reason for positive interest in the assignment. I was already acquainted with the Argentine Toba. The opportunity to travel there came as an unexpected bonus at a time when I had been at a total loss to know how to pursue my growing interest in critical studies of biblical texts.

My earliest memories of the Toba go back to boyhood days when our Mennonite congregation helped to support my father's cousin Sam Miller and family as missionaries in the Chaco.[8] Sam's father, David, our minister, read monthly letters to the congregation from the family in Argentina. I do not recall the images of Argentina that those letters prompted, but I do remember the excitement I felt at the opportunity to travel far and encounter new experiences of the sort they described in those letters. Sam and his wife Ella Mae were projected as role models for the dedication of one's life to Christian service. It was a model to which I aspired as I entered my teenage years.

Ella Mae recalls a visit to my parents' home for dinner in the early 1940s after she and Sam had been appointed to the mission board and shortly before their departure for Argentina. As they were about to leave, my sister and I went upstairs to empty our piggy banks and present a missionary offering for their journey. That experience made a deep impression upon her and she still recalls it with emotion today.

My deceased mother had wanted to be a missionary. It was no doubt the transmission of that desire by my parents together with the missionary emphasis at Youth for Christ that contributed most to my decision to enter Eastern Mennonite College and Seminary and my preparation to accept a mission assignment.

In college I studied Spanish with Professor J. W. Shank, who initiated the Mennonite mission to the Toba in the early 1940s. He often told stories about his Chaco experiences in his conversational Spanish classes. The stories, together with boyhood memories of letters from the Chaco, served to pique my interest. Although I had read Shank's *We Enter the Chaco Indian Work* (1951), which described the formation and early activities of the Mennonite mission to the Toba, and undoubtedly made connections between it and those early memories of letters from Sam and Ella Mae Miller, I had not considered an assignment to the Toba.

The decision to accept this mission was not made lightly, however. On the one hand, the high regard for missionary service within the Mennonite community where I was raised had provided my major motivation for entering college and seminary in the first place. My memories of the most interesting church services in childhood were those in which foreign missionaries participated and showed pictures of their work. We regularly took offerings not only to support the Sam Miller family in Argentina but other mission projects as well. Furthermore, my interactions at weekly Youth for Christ meetings called for an even greater commitment to missionary activity than had my Mennonite upbringing.

On the other hand, throughout seminary I had become increasingly convinced about the relative nature of "truth." Consequently, I found myself incapable of making the kind of exclusive claims it seemed obvious the home congregations providing our support would expect. Furthermore, the unknown world "out there" had become somewhat more familiar than the nebulous images projected in missionary letters and slides during childhood and youth. The idea that

I, with growing doubts about revelation and mission, might have something to offer that world was a bit intimidating. The luster of the highest "calling" had lost some of its charm.

However, at that point in time these concerns were more an uneasy awareness than a clear-cut conviction. Consequently, Lois and I accepted the secretary's offer with pleasure and proceeded to Hartford in September 1956. During the summer of 1957 we pursued further training in linguistics at the Summer Institute of Linguistics, University of Oklahoma, to help us learn the Toba language.

Scene 3: Training for Mission Assignment

During the 1956–57 academic year Lois and I studied anthropology, linguistics, literacy education, and Latin American history and cultures at the Kennedy School of Missions in preparation for our assignment to the Chaco. Since the mission school was located on the same campus as the Hartford Seminary, interactions with seminarians and professors allowed me to pursue theological questions with free rein. Topics that had begun to attract my attention throughout college and seminary years, such as Tillich's "Ground of Being" designation for divinity, Bultmann's demythologizing, and Niebuhr's neo-orthodoxy were encouraged rather than considered off-limits except for attack. The pursuit of these radically different notions of God and Christian commitment allowed me to place my theological doubts in an anthropological context for the first time. The concept of indigenous church growth involving a minimized role for Western missionaries was also widely discussed and encouraged. So much so, a critic might contend, that the mission school went out of business within a few decades.

Thus, at Hartford I was introduced to a far broader interpretation of revelation than I had imagined during seminary years that served to revitalize my interest in the subject. I became intrigued with the idea that the Bible was but one form of divine unveiling and that one could find in great literature and art the same sort of inspiration that one acquired from biblical texts. Nevertheless, while my notion of revelation was broadened, it was still tied to the notion of a divine purpose expressed to humans in various forms. It was this version of revelation that I took to the Chaco, but as we shall see, it was not the one with which I returned.

In addition to the liberating theological atmosphere that I found at Hartford, courses in anthropology had a profound effect upon my approach to the field. One course in particular, field methods in anthropology taught by Professor Paul Leser, stressed the importance of keeping a field diary and of writing down first impressions. Considerable attention was given also to strategies and techniques for establishing rapport and trust in the field, to what it means to be a "participant observer," as well as to the changing meanings of this concept through time. Among other assignments, we read carefully Malinowski's introduction to *The Argonauts of the Western Pacific* (1922), together with Kinsey's description (1948) of techniques for eliciting information from reluctant participants, such as those interviewed for his famous studies of sexual practices in the United States.

Many of the concepts and strategies discussed in this seminar proved highly useful during my years in the Argentine Chaco, particularly as they related to preparation for unexpected contingencies. In retrospect, however, it is obvious that Malinowski's approach to fieldwork automatically set up the image of the anthropologist as observer and recorder of "natives" who become defined as objects of study. There was no notion of social interaction in which the anthropologist/observer is also observed and analyzed, nor of negotiation about what is recorded and how it will be presented. Considerations such as these were not discussed at that point in time. It was simply taken for granted that the ethnographer had not only the right but the duty to speak for others considered incapable of speaking for themselves. This was the image of fieldwork I took to the Chaco in the late 1950s.

In addition to this practical course, my training in anthropology ranged from basic introduction to high-level theory. Professor Leser, trained in Berlin by the diffusionist theorist Fritz Graebner, was a delightful teacher. His classes were both intellectually stimulating and entertaining. In addition to German, he read French and English fluently and managed to follow the major journals in anthropology published in these languages, a feat possible in 1956–57 but highly improbable in the 1990s. This broad background of knowledge was brought into the classroom, where a wide range of theoretical topics were creatively presented and intensely debated.

Preferring evening seminars, Professor Leser became more alert as the evening wore on. The seminars were held in his living room next to the study, where we could always consult source materials in his extraordinary library. Many were the occasions when several of us returned home after midnight, mentally exhausted but exhilarated. Most students in the seminars had considerable training in both social theory and theology. The interactions communicated a much more liberal view of theology and missions than I had previously encountered, causing me to recognize that my pilgrim roots were still at work even in this more intellectually open atmosphere. We visited a variety of churches that year, none of which felt like home, including the Quaker Meetings. As the year progressed, my fascination with anthropology grew while concern about theological issues began to wane. Leser also introduced me to the basic anthropological journals that I began to read regularly that year and have followed ever since.

Another seminar that contributed to a subsequent sense of my ethnographer self was one on the history and culture of Latin America taught by Professor Benjamin Paul. Several elements of that seminar made their mark on me, not the least of which was the thirty-one-page syllabus. Professor Paul had a broad sense of the colonial and national history of the region as well as regional differences, but he also placed considerable stress on a Latin American "culture pattern." We read "Ethos Components in Modern Latin American Culture" by John Gillin (1955), with whom I would later study at Pittsburgh, together with a wide range of readings that focused on the distinct culture of the region.

The problem with the concept of *a* Latin American culture pattern, as I soon learned from experiences in Costa Rica and Argentina, is that the region is far too complex for such a generalization. No single notion of Latin American culture characterizes adequately the range of cultural activity. In the view of people living there, *ticos* (Costa Ricans) are as different from Argentines as North Americans are from Australians. I soon learned also in Argentina that I was a *provinciano* (person from the provincial interior), not a *porteño* (person from the port city Buenos Aires). The point is that the concept of *a* Latin American culture involves the construction of a generalized regional Other for North Americans that seriously misrepresents the ethnographic scenes encountered throughout the region. In this instance, personal experience contradicted what I had been taught in the classroom.

During that seminar Professor Paul urged me to construct an exhaustive study of bibliographic sources on the Gran Chaco Toba as a class project, which would become one of my most intensive scholarly pursuits. In addition to the excellent Case Memorial Library at Hartford, I researched the Human Relations Area Files and Sterling Library at New Haven; the Peabody Museum and Harvard University Libraries in Cambridge; the Museum of the American Indian Library; the Missionary Research Library and the New York Public Library in New York City; the Library of Congress; and the Newberry Library of Chicago in pursuit of Toba materials.[9]

Based upon my original research in North American libraries, I assumed that an exhaustive list of sources and secondary materials on the Toba might reach some fifty items maximum. When I completed this study as a Master's Thesis upon my return to Hartford during the 1963–64 academic year, the project was just the beginning of twenty years spent cataloging more than one thousand items in twelve languages.

The mental picture of Toba cultural history subsequent to colonial encounter that I acquired through this bibliographic study has significantly shaped my understanding of the people as I found them in the Chaco, thus contributing crucially to my ethnographic publications. One fundamental insight that left a deep impression upon me was the superficial nature of Toba interaction with Europeans until the midtwentieth century. The soldier, missionary, and governmental officials who confronted the Chaco aborigines throughout the centuries came to dominate and "civilize" rather than to communicate in any meaningful manner. Even explorers, whose interest and goals one might consider to have been somewhat more altruistic, or at least less "interested," depicted the indigenous population as exotic and strange (totally Other) rather than as human beings of the same order as Europeans. Thus, the image of Gran Chaco aborigines conceptualized by colonizers during the latter nineteenth century and the early twentieth was neither sympathetic nor supportive.

At the same time, all of these intruders into Chaco territory arrived alone, without family, so that the Toba were unable to observe normal daily interactions among Europeans until they settled in the region. Thus, Toba images of Europeans were equally warped.

I have argued that this long period of sporadic and superficial contact had a profound effect upon a Toba sense of self-identity vis-à-vis intruding Europeans. The connotations surrounding the Toba word for Europeans, *doqshi,* are certainly bound up in this view-from-a-distance that took centuries to formulate. As I have noted elsewhere (1989b), even today sustained personal relationships between Toba and "whites" (their translation of *doqshi*) are the rare exception rather than the norm. This fact certainly impacted upon the kind of interaction I was able to establish with the Toba upon my arrival in 1959, despite the fact that my role was largely predefined by missionaries who had preceded me.

The Kennedy School also offered excellent training in linguistics, taught primarily at that time by Professors H. A. Gleason and William Welmers. Dr. Welmers gave me a shock on the first day of class in descriptive linguistics when he entered smoking a cigarette. Before saying a word, he walked to an open window, took a deep drag, flicked the butt out the window as he exhaled, turned to the class, and said, "Let us pray." I had never met anyone before who both prayed and smoked, particularly at the same time. His class was both a challenge and a delight. We used Gleason's recently published textbook, *An Introduction to Descriptive Linguistics* (1955), which has remained a classic in the field.

Finally, Professor Maurice Hohlfeld's course in adult literacy education also proved invaluable in our efforts to produce simple primers and help the Toba learn to read and write in their language. His statement "Language is what people speak, not what they should speak" was famous among students. At the time the idea seemed more radical than it does today.

The contrast between an anthropological approach to knowledge with scientific goals and a theological one aimed at furthering particularistic beliefs gradually took on clarity during this year at Hartford, but only became deeply meaningful in the Chaco. Upon my return to Hartford after a five-year term in the Chaco, a fully developed awareness of identification with an anthropological perspective that sought to promote greater human understanding rather than beliefs and affirmations promoting specific religious affirmations led me to enter graduate school in anthropology and subsequently resign from the mission.

It was to build upon the linguistics foundation taught at Hartford that Lois and I entered the Summer Institute of Linguistics at the University of Oklahoma under the directorship of Professor Kenneth Pike the following summer. The linguistics training we received both at Hartford and at Oklahoma served us well, not only in our approach to the Toba language, but also in Costa Rica during 1957–58, where we were sent by the board to study Spanish. These experiences convinced us that some instruction in phonetics, phonemics, and grammar is essential prior to the study of any foreign language, particularly for adults. My greatest interest proved to be in phonemics, an interest I was able to apply in my study of the Toba language.

The year 1957–58 in Costa Rica was significant not only for the language skills acquired; it also enabled Lois and me to adjust to new time schedules, patterns of social interaction, and lifestyles. Professor Paul's seminar at Hartford had prepared us for many of the culture forms we observed in Costa Rica, such as a different perception of time, social space in conversation, and the overall slower pace of life. Many of the cultural differences we were most consciously aware of were connected with language, such as the distinction between the intimate and formal forms that establish social distance, the elaborate forms of address and attention to social graces, less attention to words of action and more to expressions of feeling and emotion.

However we found the generalizations useful only to a degree and some statements about the language that were stressed emphatically by our language professors in Costa Rica were simply misleading when learning to speak like a *chaqueño* (person from the Chaco) in Argentina.

Our interaction with a variety of missionaries at the language school in San José, some of whom were quite liberal in theology and mission philosophy despite the highly fundamentalist climate, also had a significant impact. We found ourselves increasingly attracted to the liberals. Most of our social interactions were with individuals who demonstrated sensitivity to Costa Rican culture. Upon observing attitudes and actions of an insensitive nature, we became even more determined to adapt to local cultural expectations rather than insisting that others adapt to ours.

We carried the same attitude to Argentina, where we established genuine friendships that have persisted and grown until today. Most of these friendships were established initially in Sáenz Peña, the northern city in which we resided, and among the rural Toba. Subsequently, we established personal relationships in other parts of Argentina as well, particularly in Buenos Aires.

Along with the formal training at Hartford, Oklahoma, and Costa Rica, Lois and I also received valuable informal preparation for fieldwork through correspondence with our future Chaco colleagues Albert Buckwalter and Lois Buckwalter, who graciously did their best to help us prepare for what lay ahead. In addition to logistical assistance with documents, housing, and transportation, their letters provided excellent insights into life among the Toba and what we might expect to encounter. Some of them foretold with uncanny accuracy events that we were later to experience.

One of Albert's letters sent to Costa Rica, dated October 3, 1957, was particularly instructive about experiences to come:

> You are already in a place where you are beginning to see the seemingly illogical ways of non–North Americans. But just wait, you haven't met the Toba Indians yet. They will tax your credulity to the limit, and even beyond. You will think that it is impossible that human beings be like this. But then you will suddenly come to your senses and realize that it *is* possible, because there they are!
>
> . . . Now you will find, to your dismay, that the more of the white man's world you can leave behind when you go out with the Indians, the more quickly you will find out what it is about North Americanism that is illogical to the Tobas.
>
> I say "dismay", because the Toba Indians are apparently among those

Indian tribes who upon contact with "civilization" do not become assimilated to the new ways, but in truth become annihilated. You will find a people occupying land good enough that if you were to farm it you could in several years time pay off the loan with which you bought an imported tractor and truck. But the Toba Indian starves for six months out of the year unless some white man takes pity on him and gives him credit during that period which the Indian all too often is not quite able to pay back during the working season. However, some actually come out of the working season with a neat little sum to their credit. But in a matter of weeks it is usually all gone. Perhaps you will feel dismayed when you observe that an Indian who wasn't able to pay his debts hands his brand new 15 jewel wrist watch to you and asks you to set it (he can't tell time)! Perhaps you will even feel anger when a government agent who is not a Christian comes to your colony of Tobas who are professing Christians and sets them all up with tin roofs, barbed wire fences, plows, cultivators, etc. on a credit basis, payable in annual quotas for ten years, and at the end of the first year one of the leading members of the church takes his profits and buys a brand new farm wagon, not even paying a cent on his debt to the government. Then the government man gets boiling mad and wants to know if the missionary taught them that, to which they answer "no"! Perhaps you will feel cheated when you give a small money gift to a hungry Indian family, and they go and spend it all for watermelons. Or perhaps you will feel hopeless when some good Indian brother, instead of spending his money for food, buys his wife a parasol which will probably be broken by his children within a week.

Perhaps you will hope that the Board doesn't find out about this when a witch-doctor who has learned a little of the Gospel vocabulary and has adopted the Bible as his main medicine for incantations comes to visit one of your Mennonite churches, and the Toba preacher asks him to preach. . . . Then, again, you might feel as though it is just plain treachery when you sell ten Bibles in a certain place, with the understanding that the people will soon pay the preacher who in turn will hold it for you until your soon return. Upon your return the preacher gives you only half of the money; he says he needed the rest, but he quickly adds that when harvest comes he will be able to give you the balance.

Or perhaps you are coming to the mission field chuck full of ideals about going indigenous, etc. You decide you are going to live with the Indians. But since you followed some other well-meaning missionary's advice about arriving on the field in the cool season in order to get established before the bugs and the heat come on, you also coincided your arrival with the slack season for Toba stomachs. You decide to live awhile with the Tobas in one of the northern colonies, because there you will find some oldsters who can't even understand Spanish; this should give you a chance to learn some Toba language. In the morning, the first thing, you are offered the maté (tea) which is shared by each in turn sucking on the same metal straw. A flea bitten dog brushes by your feet and lies down by the fire because the morning air is quite chilly at this time of the year, and you are trying desperately to keep from catching a cold. In spite of your heavy socks under your imported boots and your long underwear, as well as a poncho slung over your shoulders, you have to admit that your back is cold and your toes are stinging. For the life of you, you can't believe that a man could wear only cloth shoes without socks, with perhaps even a toe or two sticking out through a hole, and with his feet sopping wet from the heavy dew which he soaked up when he went out into the woods—and not die of pneumonia within a week. But there he is; he has a poncho thrown over his shoulders, but since his shirt collar is unbuttoned, you can see that he has on only thin cotton underwear. You can't help but think of the Christian injunction to share of your abundance, so you set to thinking on how to put your training into operation. But to just which one of the five men sitting around are you going to give your poncho? And what about the barefooted children, who don't have any underwear, and even one of the youngest ones doesn't have any clothes at all? And what about the one thousand others in the same colony who don't seem to have enough clothes? Why don't they take a blanket off the bed and use that as a poncho? You finally give up trying to reason, and end up by extending your poncho out over the shoulders as well of the one man who is sitting right beside you on the rickety bench, however, he doesn't seem to be particularly impressed by your generosity.

Well, you continue to sit and listen to the conversation which must be interesting to them, but to you it sounds like a hopeless jungle of back k's, back g's and glottal stops trying desperately to completely blot out the sounds which "civilized" people have in their languages! The hours pass. Long since you have quit drinking maté, fearing that you might upset your system by this foreign beverage, but they keep on going. About noon, you finally take mother nature's urge as the excuse for getting up and going out into the woods, just to loosen up your calcified joints a little. You do sort of wonder what they are going to have for breakfast, or dinner, or whatever they will call the meal, if and when it comes, since it is already noon, and no one has yet moved. You take up your belt one notch, and return to the sitting group. The maté, which had been left to rest for an hour or two, is again taken up. You drink some more, and much to your relief, you find that you don't feel quite so near death from starvation as five minutes earlier. Again you leave off with the maté before the others do.

About the middle of the afternoon, one of the women takes an ordinary wash basin, which was lying on the ground by the side of the mud hut and which you noticed earlier was being "cleaned out" by some lousy chickens and several terribly skinny dogs. She takes this basin, and with a little swamp water from a big tin bucket she washes out the basin in preparation for use as a mixing bowl. Some buggy flour is taken out of a bag that is almost empty and mixed with a little water in the mixing bowl to make a dough. Meanwhile, a black iron kettle with a little water in it is put over the fire to heat, after which the hot water is swished around inside the kettle with a gray rag; this is to clean it from the previous cooking. The kettle is then used to fry in deep fat the pancakes which have been made from the dough. When the whole batch has been prepared they are served in the wash basin. Each one helps himself by tearing off convenient sized pieces. After this some maté is served in cups with about three tablespoons of sugar per cup. This whole meal is amazingly satisfying, but you know that if you were at home, you would ask for another helping of mashed potatoes and gravy, and a little fruit for desert. But anyway, you join the Indians in thanking God for the meal for that day.

... All romanticism and love of adventure wear threadbare in a short time under the stress and shock of reality. ... For a North American to get in on the ground floor with the Toba, you are in for an extremely difficult adjustment. ...

Though the physical adjustment of living part time out with the Toba will tax you beyond limits that luxurious North Americans wouldn't dream of, not even in a nightmare, yet the spiritual adjustment seems to be the most far-reaching. However, if you come to the Tobas as a theological liberal, I don't think you will have as hard a time.

... Practically all of the missionaries, who have worked with the Tobas from the earliest times of Protestant missions among them, seem to have only words of depreciation and outright disdain for the Christian Tobas. ... To listen to his [a leading Toba preacher's] personal spiritual pilgrimage will make you cry with shame at the white man's blindness in the face of Toba sincerity. You will have to wonder that there are any Toba Christians at all.

In conclusion, Albert foresaw that "ministry" among the Toba would "transform your own lives about as much as or more than it will transform theirs."

It is difficult to reconstruct my reaction upon receiving this frank appraisal of things to come, but I do recall that nothing Albert stated caused us to reconsider our assignment. Perhaps I had been made aware of some of the cultural features in letters from Sam Miller and Ella Mae Miller and in conversations with J. W. Shank. Furthermore, classes in anthropology with Paul Leser had also prepared us for unanticipated eventualities. What strikes me as most interesting in retrospect was Albert's comment, which proved to be prophetically accurate, that the Toba would transform us as much or more than we would them. My hunch is that I did not really believe it to be true at the time. I do now.

It took nearly two months for Albert's letter to arrive in San José by airmail, underscoring the isolation of the place to which we were heading. In a letter dated January 1, 1958, I responded in the following manner:

Permit me to say . . . that I did not find [your] letter as "shocking" as you may have expected. I would hasten to add, however, that this proves nothing about our ability to adjust in the real situation. Already we have learned that it is one thing to be resigned to "strange customs" in theory and quite another to adjust in actuality. I am positive, though, that your vivid literary orientation is a definite help. . . .

Your comment about liberal theology was very interesting, and may I say, even a bit amusing. Don't misunderstand me, I found it amusing because it seems to me that you are exactly right. To be honest with you, I am not worried that my theology won't be liberal enough. Sometimes I do wonder if it is too liberal, though. No, I am not talking about the cultural aspects of our Mennonite heritage. I mean theology, the gospel, and the non-Christian world. I have just finished reading a book by Embree entitled *Indians of the Americas*. Books such as this make me wonder sometimes why I am a Christian missionary at all. If I felt that my contact with the Indians would only wreck personal security and initiative, I would be ready to throw in the towel before it became soiled. On a more positive note, however, I am quite certain that this need not be the case.

Our time at Hartford, Wycliffe, and here [San José language school] has given us ample opportunity to observe missionaries, both new and experienced. . . . One of the most disconcerting impressions I have gathered is the apparently unconscious ethnocentric superiority feelings of the missionary toward the people among whom he [or she] works. As if being a Christian (or more precisely a North American) puts one in a separate class from other people. Since this type of thing is more easily recognized in others than in oneself, perhaps we give the same impression. God grant that we do not, nor will. I am convinced that the more we work horizontally instead of vertically, the more we will learn from others, as well as contribute to them.

Albert's statement about liberal theology elicited some response from the regional secretary, and Albert later reported that he might not be willing to defend himself as such were he required to do so. His point, however, was that cultural background and worldview shape the way one interprets personal faith. As he stated in a subsequent missive (January 16, 1958), "our very understanding of Christianity is a part of our culture." Little did I suspect at that time the degree to which such awareness would ultimately lead me to question the nature of Christian affirmations themselves, with the result that we would resign from the mission and eventually sever our ties to church organizations.

My statement to Albert about wondering why I was a missionary merits further elaboration. It indicates the extent to which even before arriving in the Chaco Lois and I had disassociated ourselves from attitudes we found expressed widely among missionary colleagues in training. By the end of our year in Costa Rica, we were fully conscious of a distance from what the majority of our fellow students appeared to regard as the "missionary enterprise." We were not the first nor the only missionaries to feel uncomfortable with the label. The discomfort eventually led us to abandon the profession, not based upon actions of our fellow missionaries in the Chaco, whose dedication and cultural sensitivity we often admired, but because the philosophical premise on which it operates was one to which we could no longer subscribe. Encounters with missionaries committed to the mandate in Costa Rica contributed to that decision.

Enthusiasm at Hartford for indigenous church growth, which stressed a decreasing role for missionaries, also shaped the manner in which we conceptualized missions. During the post–World War II period of decolonialization the more culturally aware churches were becoming sensitized to the colonial image of the traditional missionary. McGavran's *Bridges of God* (1955), together with his later works on indigenous church growth, served as a basis for discussions about a dialogic approach to missions at Hartford. It made Lois and me consciously aware for the first time that the church was already planted abroad and that our role must be fraternal rather than domineering.

Mennonites, as already noted, do not consider themselves Protestant, but rather Anabaptist. The distinction is important because throughout the sixteenth and seventeenth centuries Mennonites found themselves pursued and persecuted by both Protestants and

Catholics, no doubt contributing to the image of the pilgrim associated with the Anabaptist tradition. Their brand of Christian faith, although expressed in many forms, consistently has stressed peace and commitment to communal values. It also influenced the approach to missions characteristic of Mennonite mission boards, particularly the one in Elkhart at that point in time, which may explain its somewhat unique support for indigenous church development among the Gran Chaco Toba at a time when the indigenization of missions was still in infancy.[10] Perhaps our identity with this tradition encouraged sensitivity to the notion of indigenous church autonomy, accounting also for our failure to identify more fully with many fellow missionaries in language school. Here again alienation from the enthusiasm for missionary expansion expressed by our language training colleagues reinforced the image of the pilgrim we had never completely shaken.

Albert's letters also communicated to us the disastrous effects of whites on the Toba. The following paragraph from one dated January 16, 1958, states clearly the nature of the problem.

> Concerning the contact with the Indians which wrecks personal security and initiative, I think that you won't be with the Tobas long before you will be convinced that contact has long since been made and the end results are near at hand. In fact, it hasn't just been contact, it has been a tight squeeze, a crush. The Gospel has come in just in time to ameliorate the death throes! Perhaps that sounds irreverent, if not just plain pessimistic, but if it appears to be the truth we ought not shrink from expressing it. If cultural contact might be restricted to a few chosen individuals, then I don't think the danger of wreckage would be so likely. But when the contact is an all inclusive type of thing in which a whole way of life is wrecked and made absurd economically, socially and spiritually, then what is there left for even a trained missionary to do in such a situation? You might say, that is the position in which we find ourselves. But all of this is an accident of history the cause of which is not always possible to fix. . . . The technological way of life is spreading over the face of the earth; people are clamoring for it. The nomadic way dies under the pressure; poor nomads who can't get the point!

While our training at Hartford had prepared us to anticipate negative effects of industrialization upon indigenous people, this was our first encounter with such a lucid assessment of its devastation. The impact was doubly powerful because it came from a practicing missionary who was soon to become a colleague.

My doctoral dissertation, written nearly a decade later, sought to demonstrate how the Pentecostalistic *culto* (worship service) served to revitalize traditional Toba culture rooted in foraging, enabling it to persist even in the midst of increasing interactions through waged labor with the broader Argentine society. However, I argued that the basis for this revitalization was precarious and that the *culto* actions and beliefs would not likely withstand more intensive interaction in schools, work, and military service, which would likely manage to incorporate the Toba increasingly into national life. However, incorporation has not occurred thus far to the extent I anticipated. Certainly I agree with Buckwalter that interaction with "whites" has wrecked personal security and initiative. The problem is that the interactions continue apace and the trick is to acknowledge traditional value expressions in the new contexts in which the Toba find themselves.

Evidence of the destruction of Toba culture was evident in a letter sent by the Buckwalters to home congregations, dated March 1958, in which a Toba chief was quoted as decrying dissention among the Toba over denominational affiliation. In the words of the chief,

> My dear brothers and sisters, we have always been at peace with one another before this new teaching came. We weren't fighting each other; we didn't think evil thoughts one of another; we got along together quite well. Now with this new teaching this person says he is better than the rest, while that person is saying that he himself has a greater power than anyone else to cast out demons and sickness. Therefore, it would be better for us to send these new teachers away and that we keep on as we were before.

Buckwalter's response was, "Amen, Brother, amen!" Perhaps this was one reason he had suggested that we would adjust to Toba life best if we came as "theological liberals." We would be less inclined to contribute to further factionalism in the religious community. The idea was appealing, given our experiences with a variety of mission enthusiasts at Hartford, Oklahoma, and Costa Rica.

Thus, the disruption and tension caused by interaction with whites was not limited to industrial and political contexts, it also pertained to missions and church life. The impact of missionization proved to be a double-edged sword, as my dissertation and subsequent writings on missionary actions sought to demonstrate.

By the time Lois and I arrived in the Chaco, therefore, we already had become deeply engaged with disparate discourses in contention for our allegiance. Both our ethnic and national senses of identity were precariously held as we approached a people and an environment that would forever change the texture of our lives. Most significantly, we had more questions than answers about the missionary role we were about to assume.

Act 2 | First Field Experience, Maturation of Doubt

After completing twelve months of Spanish language study at the Costa Rican Language School in August 1958, Lois and I made a brief return to the United States in order to visit family and pack bags for our assignment to Argentina. En route we stopped in Montevideo, Uruguay, to stay with the secretary for South American Mennonite missions, Nelson Litwiller, and his wife, Ada, until our baggage arrived by boat in Buenos Aires.

Having been born and raised in rural areas and educated in small, close-knit scholarly communities, our first introduction to genuine city life was San José, Costa Rica, where we came to rely on public transportation and a central public market. Montevideo, in contrast, offered the sense of a much older and more culturally elite city. Here the markets were located in local neighborhoods where families shopped daily for fresh bread, fruit, and vegetables.

In January 1959 we flew across the mouth of the River Plate to Buenos Aires, a city we fell in love with at first sight. Subsequent visits have only served to strengthen the bonds that tie us to Argentina's capital city. Its attraction is not only the active cultural life, the humane pace, the restaurants with their fabulous *bifes de lomo* (loin steaks), the open spaces, and parks filled with friendly faces ready to converse, but also the sense of age with modernity that visitors find intriguing and local citizens take for granted.

My fundamental task for the next three months was to pursue the paperwork required for legal entry and to get our baggage out of the customhouse. This initial introduction to Argentine bureaucracy was excellent training in cultural adaptation. The number of signatures required on our *cédulas* (identification documents) and import papers seemed endless. After standing in line to acquire an official signature, I would be sent to the post office for the appropriate fiscal stamp, where there was the usual line. I would then proceed to another office and line for new signatures, only to be sent back to the post office for a different fiscal stamp. Finally, in exasperation, I inquired as to the variety of fiscal stamps required and bought a dozen of each. There was perverse pleasure in watching the expression on the face of an official when he was about to send me off for another fiscal stamp but I quickly whipped out my stack and told him to take his pick.

A vivid memory of those early days in Buenos Aires is that of a customs official who asked why we wanted to immigrate to Argentina. When I explained that we planned to live and work with a church mission among the Toba Indians of the Chaco, he contradicted me firmly with the assertion, "We no longer have Indians in Argentina, they have all been civilized and incorporated into national life." I was soon to discover that his ignorance was shared by many Argentines, not only in Buenos Aires, but also in interior towns and cities where we traveled. Such ignorance is not limited to Argentina, of course. Many of us are blind to our own American Indian populations. Furthermore, North American colleagues in anthropology appeared to have bought the official line as well when I first spoke and wrote about the Toba. They frequently expressed surprise that significant indigenous cultural identity persisted in Argentina.

At that time the country was in the first few years of institutional normalization following the Perón era and the *Revolución Libertadora* (liberating revolution). The grass-roots populist movement identified with Perón contributed to the formation of an Argentine political consciousness that persists today. Most of the Argentines we met during those first few months in the capital city and provincial towns were affiliated with the Mennonite church that had been active in Argentina for forty years. These people, basically middle class, often commented that we were lucky to have arrived after Perón was gone, that creativity and independent initiative were stifled under his regime.

When we arrived in the Chaco and began visiting the Toba, however, we gained a different impression. Perón had given indigenous populations rights to the fiscal land they occupied and in other ways supported their self-interests. In the words of one Toba chief, "He treated us like genuine human beings." Thus, it is not surprising that they still remember him with affection. Furthermore, post-Perón Perónism was firmly established in the Chaco province by the time we arrived and it remains a strong political force to this day, despite the fact that local professionals often speak disparagingly of Perónism.

During our stay, political consciousness in Argentina was closely tied to the Perón legacy, eliciting strong pro and con reactions based to a large extent upon social class. In fact, Perónism's persistent domination in Argentine politics, often difficult for North Americans to understand, constituted the political environment for all of our Chaco field experiences.

Finally our documents were in order, the baggage was cleared by customs, and we were ready to proceed by a slow, narrow gauge, wood-burning engine train to the Chaco. A letter to folks back home announced our arrival as follows:

> Five minutes past midnight April 16 [1959], eight hours behind schedule and nearly two full days out of Buenos Aires, our train finally chugged into Sáenz Peña. The heavy rains had softened the track's foundation so that train speed was even slower than usual.

Albert Buckwalter met us at the station in his four-wheel-drive Jeep produced by Kaiser in Argentina and took us home to his wife and three children, where we lived for two months until our house was ready for habitation several blocks away.

Some of my earliest recollections of Sáenz Peña are of the pavement limited to main streets, which generally was covered with mud or ground owing to the many vehicles that tracked mud from dirt streets, the lack of stop signs or traffic lights, the low voltage street lamps, the lack of potable running water which required all houses to rely on cisterns needing to be refilled after a heavy rain had cleaned the roof and spouting, the warm welcome of friendly neighbors, the excellent bread baked daily, fresh tangerines and grapefruit. Above all I had to adjust to flatness. I had never lived in a place where the earth was so persistently flat.

At the time Lois and I arrived in Argentina the Mennonite Chaco Mission was in the process of radical transformation. The former missionary compound approach, established in 1943 at Aguará fifteen miles north of Sáenz Peña by my college Spanish teacher J. W. Shank, had been abandoned several years earlier with a view toward itinerant visits to the emerging indigenous churches throughout the region. The idea of indigenous church growth abroad was quite novel to North American mission boards in the 1950s and the decision to support the new itinerant approach constituted a remarkably venturesome act on the part of the Elkhart board. Our training at Hartford, Oklahoma, and Costa Rica was designed to prepare us to become companions and aides to indigenous leaders in their church growth and expansion efforts. The agenda had shifted from the missionary to the Toba; their interests and goals were to determine our actions.

The original mission was established on the principles of Protestant missionary activity widely shared by worldwide mission organizations throughout the latter nineteenth century and the early twentieth. These principles generally involved a four-pronged approach. Missionary families acquired land, often called a compound, where they constructed houses for personal use, together with other major buildings that attended to the health, education, and material and spiritual welfare of the people who agreed to join the mission.[1] In the case of the Mennonite missionaries, who modeled their compound at Aguará after the British Emmanuel Mission at Espinillo established in 1934, these other buildings involved a store, a school, a clinic, and a chapel.

Missionary personnel were assigned primarily on the basis of their ability to contribute to programs involving health, education, subsistence, and spiritual welfare. While all members of the mission were expected to share their religious faith, some were more prepared than others to teach school, practice medicine, or reinforce subsistence practices. The economic, educational, and medical programs were considered essentially "service" activities directed toward the support of the primary objective, which was to communicate the spiritual message associated with the chapel. I have argued that the separation of these activities into distinct domains reflected a process of secularization in Western society, which missionaries tended to transmit without conscious awareness.[2] In this approach it was missionaries who set the agenda, preached the sermons, baptized new adherents.

During the early 1950s it became increasingly apparent to the missionaries involved at Aguará that Toba discontent with the service activities, and disagreement among themselves about priorities of action, demanded serious reconsideration of the mission philosophy and objectives. A "missionary anthropologist" was called in to study the situation and to make recommendations to the Elkhart board about the future directions of the program.[3] On the basis of these recommendations, and in discussion with missionary personnel and program directors, the mission compound at Aguará was disbanded and the program completely restructured.

Thus, when Lois and I arrived in early 1959 only one missionary family remained, together with two missionary nurses who retired shortly after our arrival. Rather than continuing to instruct the Toba in agriculture, health care, and primary education at Aguará, Albert Buckwalter and Lois Buckwalter had moved to Sáenz Peña, the second largest city in the Chaco province. On weekends and during school vacations they traveled into the hinterland to visit the various indigenous churches that were springing up independently all over the Chaco. The primary task they envisioned was to help the Toba acquire legal authorization for the growing number of new churches with no official status and to translate the Bible into Toba with a view toward strengthening Toba faith and practice.

This experimental approach to mission work had the support of the home board, although there was some concern about its legitimacy on the part of individual members. Our appointment was intended to support and extend the activities undertaken by the Buckwalters. Thus, we were instructed to learn the Toba language and to provide Bible teaching and literacy education upon request by the Toba. With this assignment in mind, the mission board provided a house for us located near the Buckwalters in Sáenz Peña, together with our own four-wheel-drive Kaiser Jeep that made possible regular visits to the various Toba communities throughout the region.

From April 1959 until July 1963 Lois and I lived in Sáenz Peña and traveled regularly to visit some fifty Toba communities or settlements scattered throughout the Chaco and Formosa provinces of northern Argentina ranging in size from several dozen to several thousand individuals.[4] The terms *community* and *settlement* are utilized to distinguish the degree of social cohesion and mutual cooperation that occurs in each instance. Settlements tend to become communities over time. These represented the total number of semisedentary Toba populations that had formed geographically bounded social units throughout this century as a result of increasing colonization and restricted access to foraging resources.

The communities/settlements constituted traditional bands, or remnants thereof, confined to fiscal territory allotted to them originally by federal and, by the midtwentieth century, provincial authorities. They were organized into extended family plots where vegetables, and sometimes significant amounts of cotton, were grown. During cotton harvest, all except the elderly and youngest children migrated to regional farms to work in cotton fields for wages.

The ancient bilateral band remnants combined agriculture and seasonal waged labor with traditional hunting and gathering to subsist in a rapidly changing ecological niche. Some scholars have questioned whether the term *band* properly describes the named extended bilateral family units that roamed the Chaco.[5] No other term has been proposed, however, which can identify the family groups that were still recognized by senior Toba in the early 1960s. Elderly Toba spoke of long houses where the band leader slept inside the door to protect his kin.

The bands constituted segments of larger regional social categories, distinguished by dialect, that were named according to the geographical location in which they roamed and the primary food resources exploited. A shamanistic senior male leader headed the band. His primary responsibilities were to heal the sick, name the new babies, supervise hunting, and serve as spokesman for interactions with other bands and non-Toba populations. During warfare, he led the raids against enemies. According to a recent census, the Chaco province claims to have identified 23,000 Toba (Censo Indígena Nacional de la Provincia del Chaco 1987). Some additional thousands are located in Formosa province, not including the Pilagá, who form a closely related but distinct language group.

By the time Lois and I arrived in the Chaco these bands were sometimes thrust together in isolated territories that conformed only marginally to the regions they had previously occupied. As the Chaco became settled, largely by eastern Europeans during the early decades of the twentieth century, the Toba were confined increasingly to islands of fiscal land that could not be taken from them as long as they were occupied. These plots of land ranged in size from twenty-five acres to several hundred. Each extended family planted gardens but survived mainly from hunting, fishing, and collecting wild fruits and vegetables. In addition, members of the family unit worked for wages in neighboring cotton fields or sold animal skins or other local craft products to traders and tourists. Staple food items consisted of tortillas, soup of various sorts, and roasted meat or vegetables. A few families learned to cultivate cotton for sale to local store owners, but the quality and quantity produced was usually poor.

It was to these insulated rural communities and the few emerging urban settlements throughout the region that Lois and I traveled during our years with the mission. Most of our contacts on these visits were with religious leaders and their families, including traditional shamans, a few of whom were called chiefs owing to their role in bargaining with governmental officials for land and other resources. We also established rapport with families not directly involved in leadership who had long-established ties to the Aguará mission. Our most intensive non-Toba interactions involved the Buckwalters and the Kratzes, who arrived one year and a half before our return. We also established close friendships with several local families in Sáenz Peña with whom we visited regularly. One family in particular, the Perríns, has remained especially close to us.

Our entry into Toba life was well paved for us by the Buckwalter family. As a result, the Toba received us as family members immediately, an initial bond that persisted throughout our stay. Mutual expectations approximated actual interactions because we each had a fairly clear idea of how the other was expected to behave. Despite our extensive preparation, however, we could not anticipate the extent to which our interactions with the Toba would transform our lives forever.

During our initial stay with the Buckwalters we traveled by Jeep to several rural Toba settlements to visit and attend church services. Sometimes we went with Albert's family, at other times Albert and I traveled with Toba companions. It was a routine Lois and I soon developed ourselves once we had acquired a Jeep and our own home base. Most of the time we traveled on long weekends in order to participate in Saturday night and Sunday public church services. During the weekdays spent at home we regularly entertained Toba guests who visited from all over the Chaco. I did not keep a diary of those visits to our home in town where I tape-recorded Toba conversations and worked on the language, although I have other records and vivid memories of them. I did keep a diary of our trips to the country, however, which served to document the nature of our encounters with the Toba without consciously intending to do so. At the time I considered it merely a record of our weekly trips. In retrospect, it provides a commentary on the social relationships we established.

Scene 1: From a Missionary's Diary

From the time I completed the diary in 1963 until rediscovering it upon collecting materials for this book, I had not consulted it except when writing my dissertation in 1966. Thus, in the process of reviewing some of my earliest reactions to encounters in the Chaco I found my memory refreshed as I relived a period of life that has left a deep impression upon me. In addition to documenting the names of the people with whom we interacted, together with dates and times, it provides insight into what I considered important to write about, including items that amused or disturbed me. A significant change in diary content will be observed on later field trips when I returned to pursue anthropological fieldwork. The nature of that difference provides a commentary on the contemporary practice of ethnography.

The diary excerpts I cite have been selected to depict most clearly the range of activities and sentiments we experienced during our mission assignment. In some cases, particularly during the early years, I have reproduced the entire diary of a trip, editing for consistency, correcting misspellings, and translating into English the Spanish and Toba words and phrases that crept into the diary inadvertently as my familiarity with the languages increased and my usage of English diminished.[6] At other times I select only those portions of the entry that are of most interest. However, although it was tempting to correct comments and impressions that I would now state differently, the integrity of the original has been consistently preserved.

The majority of excerpts are taken from the first year because this was when my comments were the most fresh and insightful. Professor Leser, following the advice of Malinowski, had taught his students to write down first impressions, insisting that once one becomes accustomed to daily routine the powers of observation are diminished. This rule of thumb proved useful.

The idea here is to call upon the diaries as a text of fieldwork providing insight into the processes whereby field experience gets translated into forms of representation about others. By approaching the diaries as "holy writ," in the sense that Freud conceptualized dreams, my textual commentary constitutes a dialogue aimed at unveiling the experiential nature of the doubting process in the field. It is a process that did not end in the Chaco, but continued throughout my professional career in anthropology. In act 3 I will comment on a different kind of textual production, the more formal texts of professional ethnographic description and analysis.

Legua 15, April 17–19, 1959

First introduction to the strange sights, sounds, smells, hunger, and mosquitoes of the Chaco interior. The Albert Buckwalter family took Lois and me to this first regional Toba church convention attended by several hundred enthusiastic participants. Ate one cooked meal each day and slept on cots with mosquito netting under an open sky with a perfect view of the Southern Cross.

Some initial impressions: the length of church services (9:30 A.M. to 3:15 P.M. with no break); the beautiful singing in parts, despite the fact that no one reads music; the loud cacophonous group praying; the dancing, which raised so much dust it was difficult to breathe; the falling down in stiff body trances; the healing ceremonies with loud stomping and demands for Holy Spirit intervention; the scrawny dogs described twenty years earlier by Krieg (1939); the low tone of conversation outside the church around campfires in contrast to loud shouting inside; the presence of *maté* gourds and hot tea everywhere; our extremely warm reception by everyone; the sense of competition over which Toba community address to use for the new *fichero* [legal church affiliation permit], raising questions about what expectations are associated with its acquisition.

This initial entry was written several weeks after the church convention once I had acquired the diary. Subsequent entries were generally made en route. As it turned out, our first visit to a Toba church convention represented a historic event because we arrived when the members were in the process of selecting a mailing address for the Iglesia Evangélica Unida (United Evangelical Church), subsequently identified as IEU, newly registered with the Ministry of *Cultos* in Buenos Aires. This was the primary church organization that the Buckwalters had been instrumental in helping to organize. In Argentina, all non-Catholic church organizations are required to obtain a permit before holding services.

Members from Legua 17, another congregation affiliated with the initial Mennonite mission, wanted the permit to carry their address, whereas the group decided that the address would be Legua 15, the first established congregation. The address was later changed to the Toba settlement on the outskirts of Sáenz Peña currently named Barrio Nam Qom. While the diary calls this the first regional convention, there were apparently several earlier assemblies where the nature of the forming organization was discussed.

What this entry does not convey is the excitement of traveling into the Chaco interior for the first time: the dirt roads, which became mud when it rained (apart from city streets, one had to travel southeast over 250 miles to Reconquista in order to encounter pavement at that time); the dense forests with beautiful flowers and unfamiliar hardwood trees separated by open savannas; the sense of raw nature in its beauty and mystery, but also an awareness of danger (poisonous snakes, tarantulas) and discomfort (mosquitoes, heat—the strong sun, although past its hottest months, was still capable of packing a wallop); the unfamiliar fauna, such as three families of armadillo, rhea, and anteaters; the overwhelming awareness of bright stars and vibrant sounds of nature. When the rare vehicle was heard, it clearly represented an intrusion. We were generally too far from "white" neighbors to hear even their tractors; thus, no other motor sounds invaded our visits with the Toba in their rural habitat. My distinct initial impression of the people, subsequently confirmed, was one of open friendliness.

Having grown up in a rural Pennsylvania farming community, I was familiar with plant and animal life. But the domesticated plants (corn, wheat, barley, soybeans, garden vegetables) and farm animals (horses, cows, chickens, pigs, steers) I knew were no introduction to the wild plants and animals encountered in the Chaco interior. The Mennonites had taught me to dominate and control the physical environment; the Toba, in contrast, encouraged cautious respect for it. The forces of nature and of culture here seemed more on equal terms. This awareness had an impact upon my sense of self vis-à-vis nature, although I was not fully conscious of it at the time. It became apparent only in retrospect upon my return to youthful haunts, where I discovered a more cautiously respectful attitude toward the physical world about me.

To Bartolomé de las Casas, May 20–26, 1959

Left home at 10:00 A.M. rather than 7:30 as planned because Eugenio Martín arrived to visit and asked to travel with Albert and me to Formosa. We had to drive by his home in Legua 17 for a change of clothes and a poncho. Arrived in Campo Medina about 4:00 P.M. at the house and church of Aurelio López. Had service from 7:00 to 10:00 P.M. Afterward we sat around the fire, talked, and sipped *maté* until midnight. Conversation centered around Toba fights with the Mocoví and the uprising against *doqshi* [Argentines of European extraction] at Napalpí in 1924. The Toba consistently outsmarted other tribes and whites in these stories. They talked about the crackle of the burning *algarrobo* wood; old-timers said it announced a barbecue the next day.[7] Spent the night on the hard, uneven ground floor of the church.

At this early stage I was still concerned about time and scheduling. Clearly I was annoyed at the delay that Eugenio's request to accompany us entailed. Eventually I would learn to ignore my watch on these trips since it was totally irrelevant. I also came to accept the fact that where we traveled and who traveled with us was determined primarily by the Toba rather than by us.

The two Toba individuals mentioned here, Eugenio Martín and Aurelio López, show up frequently in my diary. Both were active Toba church leaders, although Aurelio had a much wider following than did Eugenio. Aurelio became the first president of the IEU and played a central role in its growth and development.

The Napalpí uprising would become a key point of reference for my doctoral dissertation seven years later. It was a topic that the Toba brought up repeatedly over the next five years, particularly in the Chaco province communities.

Awoke to sun peeping over the flap of my sleeping bag and the sight of frost on the ground outside. After *maté* (mine was so sweet I could not finish it) we left at 7:30 to visit Diez de Mayo, Campo Alemani, and Pampa del Indio. Listened to twelve sermons and spoke twice myself. Nothing but *maté* until 5:00 P.M., when we were offered a small piece of roasted meat. Sat around campfire where my back became frozen stiff while my knees and legs were roasting.

The ever-present *maté* merits comment, owing to its important role in social interaction as well as in physical survival. Its social significance for entree into Toba life and culture can scarcely be overestimated. Taking *maté* was one of our most ambivalent acts throughout the years with the mission. On the one hand, it was a lifesaver once we became accustomed to the hot straw and flavor; on the other, the risk of catching amoebas, which I did, from contaminated surface water, or worse, of contracting tuberculosis, was real and ever present according to all medical advice we were given. Doctors were uncertain as to the efficacy of the preventive TB shots we took upon our arrival.

The custom of drinking *maté* is practiced primarily in Argentina, Southern Brazil, Paraguay, and Uruguay, where the herbal tea is grown. The procedures for preparing and serving *maté* vary regionally, but it can be served everywhere sweet (with sugar) or bitter (plain) and with hot (most common) or cold water. The container in which the tea is served can be from the gourd plant, or made of wood or metal. The straw is metal. One person serves the tea by pouring hot water from a tea kettle into a gourd partially filled with crushed tea leaves. The water is poured carefully along the straw in order to avoid burning the leaves, which produces a bitter taste. The person being served drains the water from the gourd through the metal straw and returns it to the server, who replaces the water and passes it on to the next person in the circle. When one does not care for more, one says "thank you" and the server bypasses that person the next time around.

The tea itself is a stimulant that, with bread or crackers, satisfies hunger and thirst even in the hottest weather surprisingly well. Like other stimulants, once one is hooked it is difficult to abandon.[8]

> Ground was just as hard last night but I slept better (getting acclimated?). Only one church service today at Lote Cuatro. Heard seven sermons, one by a woman and two by a man who seemed to say much the same thing both times. Were offered rice and meat after church. It didn't matter that the plates and spoons were washed in cloudy water, our first meal in three days was scrumptious. During the service several women became emotionally involved, chanting at the top of their lungs and falling into a stiff trance on the dirt floor. Spent the night on a big estancia where Francisco Francia works. The ground is not getting any softer!

Until I acquired an air mattress some years later, I always slept on the ground when traveling with Albert or alone with the Toba. It was an adjustment I never made satisfactorily, as the diaries indicate from time to time. When I traveled with Lois we slept on cots, which we carried with us. Whether on ground or on cots we always slept under a mosquito netting, except for a few of the coldest nights when the temperature could approach freezing.

This second encounter with dancing and trance made a great impression on me. As a child I had been to several camp meetings where people got "happy," but the dusty floor where the perspired participants fell and the unison breathing with loud shouts of "glory" or "hallelujah" left me mesmerized. It soon became a routine that I would take in stride. I have written extensively on the Toba trance, which they call *gozo* (joy), curiously and perhaps not coincidentally comparable to the camp meeting term *happy*.[9] It follows a heavy rhythmic dance in which the participants inhale and exhale in unison and involves a falling to the ground in a rigid position with no visible sign of breathing. Other dancers gather around the body to bring it back to life. When the person revives, he or she usually stands up and recounts a message received during the trance state. As Reyburn noted with regard to preaching content (1954b:48), the admonitions received in trance often pertain to cultural conflicts with the broader society.

The big *estancia* (ranch) where we spent the night proved to be a tragic site for Francisco Francia some five years later when he was killed within its borders. We learned of this during the first year after our return to the United States in late 1963. Having tracked an animal he had wounded across a fence line posted No Trespassing, he was shot by a hired hand. It was a personal loss I took hard despite the distance of time and space. Francisco was the proud father of twelve children, whom he provided for admirably. He was also active in the church and demonstrated his positive leadership skills.

Not only did Francisco believe that he had the right to cross the line since he sometimes worked for the estate, but he also had an inner cultural moral obligation to complete the kill of an animal he had wounded. The ranch was an enormous stakeout of land, largely underdeveloped, which cut off Toba access to traditional hunting and fishing resources. I do not know what happened to the hired hand who killed Francisco, but I have been told that he was detained for a brief period and released. No compensation had been awarded the family when I returned to visit them in 1966, an example of why the Toba complain about lack of justice.

Awoke to the tune of Toba prayers on the other side of the smoky, dying fire.[10] The hard *quebracho* [Schinopsis balansae] and *algarrobo* woods burn forever and generate a unique smell that has thoroughly saturated my clothes and sleeping bag.[11] After *maté* we left with Eugenio, Aurelio, and Francisco around 7:30 A.M. and drove all day over rough dirt roads, arriving at the home of the preacher Guillermo Flores in Bartolomé de las Casas, Formosa, around 6:00 P.M. We sipped *maté* until 11:00 P.M. to the tune of stomping Pilagá dancing in the distance. I wanted to go visit but Albert said that would be misunderstood, since this group considers the *nomi* dance part of an old life they have left behind.

Most of the conversation was in Toba, but the snatches of interspersed Spanish made it clear that they were complaining bitterly about government administration of the colony. Mainly I sat still during the five hours with back frozen and legs toasted again and took my *maté;* at least I am learning to drink the hot stuff without flinching! Bread, water, and *maté* comprised the diet again today. No wonder the Lord said, "Not by bread alone"! Even a little butter and jam would help. Shortly after arrival Guillermo announced that his family was hungry and had no food. Aurelio said that "we" had bread and oranges in the Jeep and asked me to get some for distribution. Despite the fact that the four-day-old biscuits were getting hard, I eyed with dismay the dwindling supply we had bought and loaded in Sáenz Peña.

The comment about smell recreates distinct memories even thirty-five years later. It is a smell we associated with the country and with the Toba. In fact, when our friends in Sáenz Peña entered the Jeep after our return from a trip to the interior, they invariably commented on the "Indian odor" in the Jeep. They also noted it at our house if they approached the room where Toba visitors slept. While diet and personal hygiene no doubt contributed, it is my impression that smoke from the ever-present wood burning fires contributed most to this distinct olfactory sensation.

My culture shock at Aurelio's audacity to ask me to get "our" bread and oranges was more unnerving than this citation suggests. The trick of sharing and figuring out precisely who had control over what items at any given point in time was never fully settled in my mind. It should be pointed out, however, that Aurelio made more demands on the goodwill of others than did most Toba with whom I became acquainted. As head leader of the IEU, he expected support from those he served much as a traditional shaman demanded compensation from persons he healed.

The diary fails to record my disappointment at having to suppress my curiosity over the Pilagá *nomi* dance about which I had read. The fact that young women were supposed to have selected paramours for sexual encounters after the dance piqued my curiosity. I wanted to know if the practice was still followed but couldn't ask, an early frustration with my role that I soon found ways to overcome.

Complaints against local officials is a theme we have grown accustomed to over the years. It was repeated on nearly every trip, and as recently as our last visit in 1988. The major accusation is that the Toba are inadequately compensated for their labor, loss of land, and other resources, and are generally treated with disrespect.

> Awoke again to the loud and lengthy prayers of our Toba brethren. Reminded myself to ask for a shovel to smooth out the ground in the future before retiring![12] Sleeping with our heads toward the fire, we were cozy despite the chilly temperature. During the night Aurelio was called upon to pray for a sick child in a neighboring hut.[13] My morning trip to squat for a bowel movement in the bush proved an adventure as hordes of mosquitoes attacked my exposed bottom. One variety is black as coal and very large, another sits straight up and stings like a bee. Could they be malaria carriers? The intelligent scoundrels also found their way inside my mosquito netting and between the cracks in my chair. My poor butt feels like a war zone.[14]
>
> The conversation today centered around discontent and animosity aimed at reservation officials and the local police. They complained of cheating and exploitation and spoke of a plan to take over the administration of the reservation themselves. Although our travel companions were sympathetic, they told us later that the plan was unrealistic and doomed to failure. It fascinates me that the rebellious and discontent are associated with the church, while the non-church people boycott the meetings and apparently defend the government officials. Here, at least, the recently organized church represents social action and revolution, while the outsiders constitute the status quo.
>
> Two church services today, the first lasted nearly four hours during which 80 percent of the men stood without noticeable discomfort the entire time. The evening service was approximately two hours long. Today's diet consisted of *maté,* three oranges, and three small pieces of five-day-old bread. Before retiring Albert slipped me a piece of chocolate candy.

The observation that church members were the radicals while non-participants were the conservatives proved to hold true in the long run for most Toba communities. Yet they were radicals only in terms of reacting to governmental control and domination. They were conservative in the sense that they sought to hold on to traditional practices and values. The developing indigenous church, especially the IEU, helped them do that.

> Slept on the same spot, poorly, as it warmed up during the night and the blankets inside my sleeping bag were too heavy. Shed my long johns in the bush under the attacks of mosquitoes. We had planned to return home this morning but Guillermo had announced a baptismal service. We were told it would take place shortly and we could soon get on our way. However, the people did not gather until 11:00 A.M. First, a representative had to be chosen for the new northern church zone. This called for fifteen speeches, all basically stating their support for the appointment of Guillermo.
>
> After three hours, during which we all stood in the hot sun, everyone marched to a nearby lagoon where ten adults, including the local chief, were baptized by Aurelio and Guillermo, with the assistance of Eugenio and Francisco. We returned to the church for preaching and communion. An announced feet-washing service was called off and we were free to begin our 250-mile trek home over dirt roads at 4:30 P.M.
>
> Thirty minutes out of the reservation we stopped at a local store and bought some cold cuts and fresh bread. Having deposited our three companions in their respective homes along the way, we arrived home at 6:00 A.M. tired, sleepy, dirty, and HUNGRY. Mrs. Buckwalter's breakfast of bacon and eggs, bread, jam, and fruit was the most delicious I had ever tasted.

Little did I appreciate at the time the fact that I was witnessing an archaic council of elders at work in which everyone spoke with unanimous voice on an action already agreed upon by all. I have experienced similar discussions since, but nothing quite like this one. Overly anxious to get started on the return trip, I failed to appreciate the judicial process at work.

The public services seemed to drag, although this first encounter with Toba baptism in a lagoon where initiates were immersed once backwards was a dramatic introduction to Toba baptisms.

The extraordinary amount of time spent in church services was typical of visits to Toba communities during our mission assignment. Generally the longer the services, the more the Toba expressed their appreciation. Sometimes I thought they would never end. Physical stamina, generally taken for granted, was clearly viewed positively. In this instance the men were on their feet the entire five and one-half hours. By the time this first extended trip was completed I had no difficulty accepting Toba expressions of Christian faith as genuine and no worries about the kind of syncretism involved. The implications of this acceptance eventually put to rest my struggle with the concept of revelation.

By the last day I was clearly ready for home cooking and a bed. Therefore, the thirteen and one-half hour return trip over dirt roads was not as formidable as anticipated. I did feel a bit guilty about the return to excellent food and a comfortable bed, wondering what fate awaited our Toba traveling companions.

To Legua 17, June 13–14, 1959

The first trip Lois and I made to the country alone. We left after lunch and had to detour via Quitilipi since the more direct route was covered with water. Arrived just before evening service to a full church with many standing outside looking through the holes in the mud walls. The spirited meeting lasted about three hours. Afterward we visited with Chief Ramón Gómez while he provided a history of political and religious activities in the community.

Slept in a brick house built by Mennonite missionaries in the late 1940s on cots we had taken with us. We had forgotten mosquito netting, but fortunately it was cold and there were very few. Also forgot matches and *maté,* which were soon provided by the chief's daughter, along with some firewood. After a four-hour church service, we sat and drank *maté* with the chief and several young men who had sung and spoken in the meeting. When everyone retired for a siesta, Lois cooked up some soup. At 4:00 P.M. the evening service started and was over shortly after 6:00, although a number of young people who had danced during the service had fallen to the ground and were still in a trance state when we left. A request for passage to Sáenz Peña proved to include three adults and two children rather than the single male we had imagined, but it was a pleasant trip and everyone was in good spirits.

Chief Gómez was both a supporter and a thorn in the side of the mission over the years. It was a place where Sam Miller and his wife, Ella Mae, had dedicated a great deal of energy. I recalled the name Chief Gómez from their letters to our congregation over a decade earlier. To my surprise, I liked him immediately. We always got along well, although he later expressed displeasure that Chief Soria had given me my Toba name, which was adopted quickly all over the Chaco. I suspect that he was chagrined at not having named me first, a name which he insisted would have been more in keeping with my missionary role.

Comments showing concern about people's moods ("in good spirits") appear frequently in my missionary diary while no such remarks appear in the subsequent ones I kept as ethnographer. Perhaps I initially identified more closely with the people and their concerns because I was with them most every day. Or perhaps I was concerned to be a success on our weekly sojourns, seeking to evaluate my contribution in terms of Toba expressions of sentiment. I am not sure what motivated the comment, but it is clear that I was pleased when they were content and upset when they were in turmoil. Such statements were more prevalent during the early years than later when I became more acclimated and aware that Toba moods had very little to do with my presence or absence. Perhaps inclined to overevaluate my role during the early years, I gained better perspective in later ones.

The request for rides was a constant theme on nearly every trip to the country and we were often able to accommodate. In addition to a convenient ride to town to visit friends or attend to business, many used the occasion to visit further and prolong the interaction initiated in their community. Some stayed at our house, while others stayed with the Buckwalters or family members living at the edge of town.

I sometimes had the impression that the ideal life for many Toba would have been to travel constantly from one community to another visiting and participating in church services. Yet it apparently hadn't occurred to me that this was precisely the life we led. How idyllic it must have seemed. In retrospect, we might have given more attention to the role models we set by deed rather than word.

To Miraflores, June 19–21, 1959

Left S.P. [Sáenz Peña] at 6:30 A.M. with the Buckwalter family in two Jeeps, picking up the Cressman sisters [Mennonite missionary nurses] in Tres Isletas.[15] We arrived at Mariano Naporichi's house about 2:00 P.M. Continued on to Chief Agusto Soria's (Do'oxoi) where the church is located, but he wasn't home. After a brief visit with his family, we drove over to greet Chief Juan Alegre, rival of Do'oxoi. He wanted us to pray for the healing of a sick granddaughter who seemed at the point of death. They asked for medicine, but we did not know what to give. The nurses had chosen to remain with their acquaintance Mariano rather than accompany us. The chief offered to take the child to church the next day for healing. Spent the night with Mariano under a big *algarrobo* tree. During the night it started to rain, but, fortunately, soon quit.

Spent most of the morning with Mariano family and neighbors drinking *maté* and conversing. Had chicken noodle soup before driving over to Do'oxoi for church service. During the afternoon service, from 4:00 to 6:00 P.M., Chief Alegre's granddaughter died. Afterward Do'oxoi fed us roasted goat and attempted to teach me Toba. Spent the night in the church next to his house.

Church service from 10:00 A.M. to 1:30 P.M. was packed with people. There was intensive dancing and many people fell to the ground in trance. Left for S.P. after church, arriving at 10:00 P.M. Do'oxoi sent a side of dressed goat home with us.

Observations: the people in Miraflores are very friendly and the countryside is lovely; fewer mosquitoes and sand flies; newer land; more food; greater isolation and community spirit.

Miraflores quickly became a favorite spot for both Lois and me to visit. Our attachment to the people there was strong from this initial trip. One of our very favorite persons was Chief Agusto Soria, or Do'oxoi, known widely for his healing prowess. He named us and often expressed concern about our infertility during those early years. He also gave our two daughters Toba names in 1972. A primary source on shamanism, he volunteered to train me in its logic during mutual visits, the significance of which I only came to appreciate during ethnographic field trips in 1966 and 1972. Fortunately, he seemed pleased to share his knowledge with an apprentice. It is a pity I did not recognize the enormous opportunity to learn more of Toba tradition, especially shamanism, during this first field experience when Soria was most intent on instructing me. By the time I became interested, he had lost some of his enthusiasm and power, although I did learn a great deal from him in 1966.

The death of Chief Alegre's granddaughter seemed to have no effect on participation in church service the following day. However, it was the only occasion I recall when Alegre attended the *culto* at Soria's. The child was nearly dead when we visited the previous day and I never heard that Alegre blamed the church for his granddaughter's death, although such accusations were not uncommon. Some years later Alegre did try to initiate his own *culto,* but it never got off the ground.

To Miraflores, July 21–22, 1959

Albert and I took this trip with regional church representatives Aurelio López, Bailón Domingo, and Eugenio Martín to visit with

Mariano Naporichi, also a representative. The only one missing was Guillermo Flores of Bartolomé de las Casas. The issue for discussion was Aurelio's idea of forming a regional center with funds to support indigenous preachers, which Mariano strongly opposed. Eugenio supported Aurelio; Bailón was neutral. The discussion, always intense and sometimes heated, raged from 8:00 P.M. until after midnight, when Albert was asked to state his opinion. His comments provided a calm basis for airing the difficulties associated with raising and managing funds. Finally at 2:30 A.M. everyone agreed it was bedtime. The ground is just as hard in Miraflores!

Awoke to indigenous prayers. After *maté* and further discussion, Aurelio agreed to give up the idea of a center where money could be collected. Everyone seemed satisfied with this conclusion and we traveled over to report to Chief Do'oxoi, who expressed relief and strong support for the decision. We shared oranges and bread from S.P. with everyone. During our conversation I witnessed Do'oxoi's wife making baskets from the *caraguata* cactus plant. She offered one for Lois. Drove Aurelio and Eugenio to Legua 17 and arrived home tired and hungry at 10:00 P.M. Bailón and Eugenio's brother had dinner with us and spent the night, leaving the next day.

This entry introduces a theme that reverberates throughout the diaries and reflects on the role of the missionary in local church organization and development. Little did I realize at the time the extent to which the notion of a center where funds might be accumulated for dissemination among indigenous church leaders would become a political hot potato. It now became apparent why feelings had run so high at the April meeting in Legua 15 where the idea of an address for the IEU was hotly debated. The thought of a center where funds might be accumulated never entered my mind at the time. To me it was simply a postal address where the Ministry of *Cultos* could stay in touch with the religious body. However, it now became clear that many, including Aurelio, had greater expectations for it. The collection and use of church funds continues to be an unresolved problem for the Toba.

The strong objection of Mariano (the person present with most experience in a mission) and Chief Soria to the center idea is of interest in retrospect since it was one of the few topics on which they agreed. I quickly learned that Soria kept a close grip over church activities in "his" community. He foresaw at once the dissention that the collection of funds would engender. A more cynical observer might suggest that he was not about to let preachers acquire a salaried position when he had never gotten one. Such a salaried person might well have represented a threat to his authority.

This was my first introduction to the persistent rift between shamans and preachers, although in this instance it was more implicit than explicit. Soria was clearly opposed to Aurelio's idea and he had support in Mariano. It was also my initiation into the mediating role that the missionary played when contention over church actions developed. I noted at this early juncture that Albert performed the role exceptionally well.

To Pampa Argentina, August 7–10, 1959

Albert and I left S.P. around noon, stopping in Legua 15 to pick up José Durán. We offered to take José Carmelo with us as well, but he could not leave because his wife was expecting a baby. Encountered a lot of mud on the way and eventually got stuck at the entrance to Carlos Rodríguez's house. Despite everyone's help in pushing, it was finally a shovel that got us out. Albert and I spent the night on the ground in a wagon shed where a dog snuggled up against my sleeping bag for the long winter's night; José slept in Carlos's house.

Spent the A.M. on Bible translation with José and Carlos's son Francisco. Trudged to the church midafternoon where no one arrived until we were about to leave two hours later. Eight people eventually showed up and there was preaching until 7:00 P.M. Returned to the Rodríguez house. Another son, Pacheco, arrived at 9:30 and we talked and sang until nearly midnight. We decided to move our sleeping bags outdoors despite the cold to a smoother spot.

The Rodríguez family had been among the first to join J. W. Shank in the Mennonite mission at Aguará. They had been with the British Emmanuel Mission at Espinillo prior to its demise in the late 1940s. Francisco had worked early on with Albert in Bible translation. Pacheco later moved his family to the settlement at the edge of Sáenz Peña, where he also served for a period of time as Albert's translator. He and his wife occasionally traveled with Lois and me on our visits to rural Toba communities, where we often taught new songs to local singers.

Handed over the rice and potatoes Lois had sent along before heading out for church. The local preacher had announced communion but did not want to serve it himself, since it was always done by the visiting Pentecostal minister. When Albert refused to perform the ritual, saying the preacher was himself qualified, the problem was solved by asking our traveling companion José to take over. A few refused to participate, apparently because it was not blessed with official hands. There was also an afternoon service which lasted until 7:30 P.M.

As we were about to leave for home after the service, José announced that he intended to take his niece along back with us. Since we had already agreed to take Pacheco, Albert insisted that there was no room. José then decided to walk his niece home, which set back our return nearly two hours. On the way out we twice got stuck in the mud, once when the motor stalled as we were pushing mud. All passengers stripped up to their knees and pushed until the Jeep started. The generator decided to get temperamental and finally left us without power of any sort after we had dropped Pacheco and José at Legua 15. We got out sleeping bags and slept along the road until I managed to get a hop into town at 7:00 A.M., where I acquired a fresh battery and returned with the other Jeep. We both arrived home at 10:00 A.M. sleepy and hungry.

By now I had become familiar with the texture of time associated with trips to the Chaco interior where weather, vehicles, and roads were unpredictable. Any notion of a fixed schedule was out of the question. We simply learned to do what everyone else did—take things in stride. There was always another day.

Drivers on Chaco roads were accustomed to picking up stranded fellow travelers and giving them a ride to town. We did the same when there was space in the Jeep, which was seldom due to constant Toba companionship. Most of the interior roads we traveled had no buses, while the main ones had bus service once a day when it didn't break down. Assisting fellow travelers was a means of participating in a kind of solidarity among those who traveled the interior on a regular basis. Our light blue Jeep with a red top developed something of a reputation for pulling trucks, even tractor trailers, out of the mud when its four-wheel-drive tires had solid dry ground on which to pull.

Disagreement about how many people the Jeep could carry was never totally resolved, since the Toba were always convinced that there was room for one more. Not only were our senses of personal space different, we had concern about broken springs and shock absorbers that made little sense to the Toba. The room the Toba occupied at our house in town could conveniently sleep four when the cots were extended or at the most, six. Yet there were occasions when fifteen or more individuals slept there, not on cots, of course, which were conveniently placed outside the room.

In this case I imagine that Albert's objection to another rider was based partly on the fact that the person was a single female in a crowded carload of men. José was clearly disappointed and annoyed that his niece could not travel with us, although he never said so. He appeared to take plenty of time to accompany her home, which left us stranded by the road in the middle of the night when the generator gave out.

Albert's approach to mission work was to consistently encourage indigenous participation at every juncture. In this case he wished to underscore the point that the local preachers had all the authority they needed to perform communion. Churches affiliated with foreign missions relied on personnel ordained by denominational officials to enact this ritual, whereas the IEU empowered its own preachers without external authorization.

To Bajo Hondo, August 16, 1959

Took this trip in our Jeep with the Buckwalter family. Arrived at Luciano Ramírez's place at 10:00 A.M. as church service was getting under way. It ended at 1:00 P.M. We waited until Luciano had his hair cut and then all piled in to head for a Mocoví settlement several miles south, visiting with them for several hours. They spoke and understood Toba.[16] On the return trip we stopped to visit with Camilo Sánchez who is supported [financially] by the Pentecostal church. Had prayer and singing in his church until 7:00 P.M., when we returned to Luciano's house where his wife had a delicious chicken soup waiting for us. The evening service included communion and lasted until 11:00 P.M. We arrived home at 1:00 A.M. Luciano's service was almost exclusively in Toba while Camilo spoke entirely in Spanish.

External funding for indigenous leadership has been a thorny problem, both for the Toba and for missionaries, throughout the history of Protestant missions in the Chaco. Prior to the Buckwalters' move to town and the decision to encourage indigenous leadership rather than serve in an authoritarian capacity, the Mennonite mission at Aguará had provided funding for various types of social services. I quickly came to agree with Albert that if the church was to be truly indigenous the Toba should be totally in charge of their *cultos*, including the collection and control of finances. This was sometimes interpreted as closing our "bowels of compassion" by those who recalled the original mission policy. Of course, we did provide transportation and food for those traveling with us to various communities as well as food, shelter, and sometimes travel "loans" (seldom paid back) for those visiting us in Sáenz Peña. This constituted a significant form of reciprocity for Toba sharing with us in the country.

The notion that preachers should be financially supported grew out of the Protestant practice of providing minimal salaries to indigenous leaders to work as extensions of the church.[17] Since they were only a few miles apart, the contrast in style and leadership between the indigenous IEU church where the language was Toba and the Pentecostal-funded one held in Spanish was apparent. The former congregation relied on no external authority to dictate polity, while the latter depended on the Pentecostal church headquartered in Buenos Aires for legitimacy.

In recent years several European mission organizations have brought in significant funding for Toba churches, including the IEU. Some of these funds support preachers, but others are dedicated to church building and repair as well as to community development. In each instance unresolved tensions developed over the funding.

To Legua 17, September 13, 1959

Chief Ramón Gómez had arrived at our house last evening with a request that we drive him and Luís Escalante from the edge of town to Legua 17 today for a big communion service. We had planned to go elsewhere, but changed our plans accordingly. On the outskirts of S.P. we found Luís and a large group of people from both L. 15 and L. 17 in high spirits because they had been granted land. The owner of Quinta 8 had died and left the land to be parceled out to indigenous people. They were excited, saying, "Now we are 'real' Argentines!" Bricks and tin for roofing were also promised [but failed to materialize]. We proceeded to L. 17 together for the lengthy communion service and returned with Luís and several of his kin late in the afternoon.

This citation significantly documents when Quinta 8, later to be named Barrio Nam Qom, became official Toba property rather than merely land for squatting. I observed the evolution of this plot from seasonal squatter space when we first arrived to the formation of a permanent community by the end of our mission assignment.

The Toba expressed desire to become "real" Argentines in this instance meant possessing an official title to land at the edge of town. It demonstrates the extent to which the Toba failed to identify with the broader society, a failure which, unfortunately, was not resolved with the acquisition of title rights to Quinta 8.

Although public discourse by religious organizations and political institutions calls for the incorporation of the Toba into national life, such discourse ignores the fact that they had been incorporated de jure into the subordinate position of wage earners over a century ago. What the Toba appear to desire, however, is recognition and acceptance for themselves as a people with unique cultural values and knowledge. Such desire, becoming increasingly a demand, lies at the heart of contemporary Toba interactions with white society.

To Miraflores, October 2–4, 1959

Lois and I stopped at Aguará to pick up Hilario Cabrera and his brother Marcelino. Hilario decided to take his wife and three children, which left us with a load of eight, more than the Jeep could comfortably handle. Arrived after dark at Mariano Naporichi's house, drank *maté*, and conversed until nearly 1:00 A.M. Rain threatened our out-of-doors sleep on cots with mosquito netting, but it stopped after a few drops.

Up at 7:30 A.M. Big discussion over *maté* and tortillas with Mariano about Albert's translation of the book of Mark into Toba. He criticized the choice of expressions and thought that the Bible would lose its mystery and charm. Later we took a long walk over land he soon expected to claim rights to, stopping by Antonio Leiva's house for a swig of *maté*. When we returned, we were offered a delicious goat soup. Mariano also spent a lot of time criticizing Chief Soria and his brother, saying they were dictatorial and did not understand the gospel. The chorus "I Have Neither Silver Nor Gold" went over big and we had to sing it at least twenty-five times until everyone had learned it well from memory.

Lois, Hilario and wife, Mariano, and I went over to visit with Chief Soria around 3:00 P.M. His nephew was at the point of dying and we were asked to pray for him. Later a packed church service lasted for nearly four hours. We sat with Do'oxoi until 11:00 P.M.; he spoke about fighting with whites in 1904, 1924, and 1942. He also spoke of the church and economics, asserting that the church should be voluntary and no one should collect funds for serving God. We were about to set up cots and sleeping bags under a tree but he suggested we move inside the church because it was going to rain. When the rain arrived at 3:00 A.M. we were pleased to have taken his advice!

Chief Soria arrived at our cots at 7:30 A.M. shortly after we had roused. He explained that it would likely rain all day and we should not plan to return until tomorrow at the earliest. He wanted a meeting with Mariano and Antonio Leiva, which was later held at Cabral Naporichi's [brother of Mariano] house, where Hilario and family had spent the night. The major item discussed was the possible move of Hilario and family to Miraflores. The rain let up midmorning and after praying over Mariano's sick wife, we left before noon for home. We had to push mud much of the way, arriving before sundown.

The conflict between the Naporichi and Soria families is one that appears frequently in the diary. The Naporichis, associated with the original Mennonite mission in Aguará, had moved to Miraflores with the express purpose of helping to build the church there. In the process they also acquired land. They were *l'añaxashic* (southerners) rather than *piguempi* (northerners), as the Soria group was called. In addition to differentiation based on language, the southern group had more contact and experience with white society. Somewhat more acculturated, they criticized the northerners as backward and improperly instructed in the ways of the gospel. Chief Soria was not about to permit an uppity southerner to interfere with his leadership of Miraflores. Hilario Cabrera, married to Antonia Naporichi, a sister of Mariano and Cabral, later moved to Miraflores, where he became the most successful cotton farmer in the region.

Mariano's complaint about Albert's translation of the Bible is significant, perhaps less for his criticism of the choice of words and phrases, a problem Bible translators face frequently, than for his observation that putting the Bible into the vernacular would cause it to lose "mystery and charm." Chalk one up for the Latin Vulgate.

It was on one of these early visits to Miraflores that Soria gave me my Toba name, although this event is curiously ignored in the diaries, which raises a question as to what motivated the selection of topics for entry. Clearly this was an experience that impressed me deeply because I recall it to this very day. After staying close by my side and observing me intently for the entire day, he named me in the evening when the family was gathered around. As we were all drinking *maté*, he looked at me intently and dramatically announced, "*'am Toqos*" (You are Toqos). He seemed highly pleased with my response, "*aŷim Toqos*" (I am Toqos). Toqos was his paternal uncle who was remembered as a courageous warrior, having fought to keep Argentine soldiers out of the Chaco in the late nineteenth century. Everyone present seemed highly pleased with the choice. On a later visit Chief Soria bestowed an even greater honor on Lois by designating her *Potaxauai*, the name of his long deceased mother. It was a clear expression of his esteem for her that he often expressed in other ways as well. These names remain with us today.

To Bajo Hondo, October 11, 1959

Due to rain and wet roads we decided not to travel far this weekend. We left 8:30 Sunday A.M. barely arriving at Luciano Ramírez's house through numerous mud holes. His family told us he was at Camilo Sánchez's church. We arrived there during the Sunday school hour![18] The teacher read almost entirely from printed materials and the class was 98 percent Spanish. Even Camilo's preaching was almost exclusively in Spanish. The lesson, curiously enough, was about Melchisedec in Genesis 14. After church we visited for awhile and sang choruses until 2:30 P.M., when we returned to Ramírez's place, where we were served potato and noodle soup. Later we walked over his farm and saw his crops and the big piece of land he plans to put into cotton.

The evening service started around 7:30 P.M. The people arrived slowly, but by the time they all got there the church was nearly full. Camilo Sánchez and a few officials from his congregation also arrived. First we all had Holy Communion Ramírez style; then came the sermons. I was highly disappointed that I could not preach in Toba since I expected that Sánchez would probably again preach in Spanish, which he did. Since it was known that we would take one of the men to the clinic in Quitilipi who had hurt his foot, everyone said farewell quickly after the service concluded and we were on our way by 11:00 P.M.

Luciano accompanied us to our home, where he spent the night and the next day. During the day we went out to Quinta 8 to explore the Escalante land deal. Although they were highly pleased with it, one wonders what they gained. At 7:30 P.M. Ramírez went over to the Buckwalters' house, where he spent the night, planning to return to Bajo Hondo the next day.

Impressions. The big talk these days is unity, the idea being to downplay denominational differences. Ramírez would like to travel around spreading this doctrine.

In retrospect, it is clear that despite the call for unity the desire for financial support from denominations was too tempting to turn down. Ramírez himself, who enjoyed the freedom to preach in Toba and direct his congregation the way he pleased, was here implicitly soliciting external support for itinerant travel to promote the IEU. When both Albert Buckwalter and I clearly expressed no encouragement for the idea, he abandoned it. Other Toba preachers also voiced interest in support from our mission board for their activity. Our consistent negative response was prompted by commitment to the concept of indigenous church initiative rather than dependence.

By now the routine of visits to rural Toba communities and return visits to our house was becoming well established. My comment about whether the Toba had gained anything with Quinta 8 was certainly mistaken since it has become a major center for sedentary residence and a Toba entrée into broader national life.

To Legua 17, October 17–18, 1959

Yesterday Clemente Gómez with his wife and children arrived at our house to visit and expressed a desire to travel with us for the weekend to wherever we were going. Together we decided to travel today to Legua 17, leaving shortly after a good noon meal. We went directly to the house of Marcelino. In the late afternoon we walked over to the church, where we visited a long while with Chief Gómez. The people were slow to arrive, but by 9:00 P.M. the meeting was in full swing. We arrived back at Marcelino's around 10:30 and spent time around the campfire drinking *maté*, getting the latest local news, and finally eating a maize mixture. Lois and I ate from the same plate but still had difficulty finishing it. Fortunately, we had a small mosquito netting along; with the cot they offered us we made out satisfactorily for the night once we got to bed after midnight.

Up at 6:00 A.M. and glad to be out of the uncomfortable "trough." Had sweet *maté* and bread with oranges. Arrived at church around 8:00 A.M.; the service started shortly thereafter and lasted until 12:00 noon. Afterward we went to the house of Vicente Molina and had prayer with him. He was so weak he could barely stand on two feet, but said he was healed, he only needed food. The irony of our praying for him in a raw wind while he stood on damp ground in bare feet with a temperature struck me. During the morning service the people gave their offering to the tune in Spanish "I Have Neither Silver Nor Gold"!

We left around 1:30 P.M. and drove the Clemente family to Quitilipi, where we dropped them off with friends, giving them cash to get the remainder of the way home by bus. On the return to Sáenz Peña we passed a tractor with double trailer that had overturned in the ditch. There was plenty of help around, so we continued our journey. Had dinner at Asturia Hotel.

Impressions. We simply must seek to provide more help for the Toba in their *economic* and *health* needs.

Clearly we were still getting adjusted to traveling with the Toba. Since we didn't have enough sleeping equipment to provide for the Gómez family, we didn't take any for ourselves either. As it turned out, they stayed with kin. We learned in time that no one traveling with us expected us to take cots for them. It is of interest to note my concern about economic and health needs. This became a point for debate about mission philosophy as discussed in the following scene.

To Legua 15, October 24–25, 1959

Lois and I picked up Pacheco Rodríguez and family at Quinta 8, arriving at José Durán's around 3:30 P.M. He was not home, but arrived shortly. Church began at 5:00 P.M. Afterward he was in a talkative mood as we sat and drank *maté*. He told some traditional tales, one that involved the destruction of the world by fire. At one point he got around to asking about the brick house built by missionaries that was not occupied, except when we visited, now that the Cressman sisters had retired and left for Canada. I opened the house and left him in charge of the medicines which the nurses had taught him to dispense, along with several other items he coveted. This seemed to make him feel better. Spent the night inside wishing we were out, owing to the heat.[19]

Unfortunately, I did not recognize at the time the significance of those tales. It was a rare occasion when tales were told in our presence in the country, particularly by a preacher. I do not recall what prompted José to recount them here, although I had obviously demonstrated a greater interest in traditional lore than had my predecessors. When I later became interested in tape recording tales, which I was only able to do at our home in town, I forgot about José's contribution here and the opportunity was lost. I never did manage to record the story of the destruction of the earth by fire, although it appears in the Toba folktale literature.[20]

When the Mennonite mission at Aguará was abandoned, much of the land and equipment was turned over to the families who lived there. This precedent was in Jose's mind and we saw no reason to disappoint him, having discussed the matter previously with the Buckwalters. He later moved his family into the house, but it did not prove to be as comfortable as he had imagined.

Church started at 8:00 A.M. and lasted until 1:00 P.M. The place was packed, with a lot of dancing and trances. One young man who had recently returned from a stint in the army danced with such frenzy that he fell to the floor in a trance that would not quit. He lay there for over three hours stiff as a board with no observable movement whatsoever. The shamans in the group, both men and women, hovered over him shouting for his "resurrection" while touching his chest and navel with their right index finger. Eventually he began to twitch and stagger to his feet. We were told later that he had a vision telling him to remain with his people.

This account of an extraordinarily long trance not only documents the extent to which a return from trance was equated with resurrection, but it also demonstrates how trance provided a crucial mechanism for confronting deeply personal and family decisions, such as this one urging the vision recipient to return to the community rather than extend his military service. It confirms Reyburn's comment, already cited, that trances tended to deal with conflicts faced in adapting to the broader society. Trance experience and interpretation occurred frequently during our weekly visits. I probably mentioned this one specifically because it was unusually long and caused concern among the leaders. I was about to go for a doctor when the young man revived.

To Legua 7, November 14–16, 1959

Albert and I left Sáenz Peña at 6:45 A.M., picking up Aurelio López at the crossroad near Aguará where he had arrived by bus. He wanted to stop with the Hilario Cabrera family, who offered him breakfast. This took nearly two hours. Finally we were on our way to L. 15 to pick up José Durán and Luciano Ramírez. José took another hour to get ready and we did not leave until nearly noon.

We arrived at the Fisherman's Club in Bermejito, where we stopped for a snack of biscuit, cheese, salami, and oranges. Upon leaving we took a wrong turn and had to return to the club for better directions. Finally as we proceeded along trails, no roads, we arrived at a Russian's house, who told us to wait because Bernardino López was about to arrive to show us the way to his house. When he arrived it was decided to have a service at the Russian's house before leaving. The service lasted until 10:00 P.M. and we did not arrive at Bernardino's place until midnight. We hit the ground at 1:00 A.M.

Delays were apparently still an annoyance to me at this juncture. We had left early with the obvious intention to arrive at our unfamiliar destination during daylight. Due to the delays we were obliged to travel unknown trails through thick forest in the dark, which is what we had tried to avoid. People, in this case a *gringo* (light-skinned

European), were always looking for an opportunity to call a church service.

Bernardino, affiliated with the Grace and Glory Mission, had invited us to visit him on his trips to Sáenz Peña. We were asked to visit Toba churches regardless of denominational affiliation, and Toba of all denominations visited us in town. They consistently expressed approval of our blindness to denominational affiliation. However, not all denominations working with the Toba agreed with this action, particularly given the fact that the independent indigenous IEU, with which we were associated most closely, was gaining prominence throughout the region. One foreign missionary registered a protest with our regional secretary.

Up at 6:00 A.M. After *maté* and soup we headed out on an hour and one-half walk to an outdoor meeting that was already under way when we arrived around 9:00 A.M. The service led by Bernardino was long and drawn out, finally winding down at 3:30 P.M. Both Bernardino and Aurelio preached several times and a large portion of the crowd spent the entire time standing! At 4:00 P.M. we started our return trek in exhausting heat. Upon return a group gathered around to sing while Buckwalter attempted to teach Bernardino to read in Toba. Later Bernardino played his guitar and we sat around the campfire while the mosquitoes had a heyday. Retired around 10:00 P.M. exhausted and hungry. Spent a miserable night fighting mosquitoes that kept finding their way into the net Buckwalter and I shared.

Talk about an exhausting day. Toba stamina during these long services continues to impress me, although this represented an extreme case. At this time I no longer complained about the hard ground, although the mosquitoes continued to attract my attention.

Bernardino's desire to read the Bible in Toba was unique. Few demonstrated interest or requested help in reading the translated text.

Up at 5:30 A.M. After *maté* and farewells we left at 6:30, stopping en route to buy some bread and oranges. Saw several deer and a huge tarantula. Visited with a Toba family in Fortín Lavalle that had recently moved from Aguará. They offered us roasting ears and noodle soup. It was incredibly delicious. We then drove north to see the new ferry at the Bermejo River. Headed home in an afternoon of oppressive heat, dropping off our companions along the way. Later in the evening after we were home it rained hard and cooled things down.

Aurelio López and I at his home in Campo Medina.

Aurelio's daughter and family in Campo Medina.

José Durán's daughter roasts corn at their home in Legua 15.

Widely respected chief/shaman Agusto Soria of Miraflores. (Courtesy of Albert Buckwalter)

Famous storyteller Carlos
Temai of Legua 15. (Courtesy of
Albert Buckwalter)

Grandpa Naporichi with grandchildren in Miraflores.

The author with church leader Saiuan in Pozo Toro.

An elder Toba layman drinks *maté*.

References to the Chaco climate and fauna appear frequently during this first year. Encountering tarantulas was not unusual, but one so large caught my attention. Later, when Jim Kratz brought the 16-gauge pump gun my uncle had sent for me, I was able to hunt deer and other animals with the Toba.

The heat, oppressive in the open, can be devastating in the forest where breezes rarely penetrate. As usual, the rain brought relief because it was normally accompanied by a refreshing wind from the south. This wind, called *nte* in Toba, is considered dangerous in winter months because it can carry disease.

To Bartolomé de las Casas, November 28–December 1, 1959

Threatening clouds postponed our departure until 8:30 A.M. When it appeared that the rain had passed us by, Lois and I proceeded to Legua 15 to pick up José Durán and head for the river, which had risen and was moving swiftly. Mr. Gloss, the *gringo* boatman, said he was afraid to take us across given the high water. While we ate lunch he changed his mind and decided to make a trial run without the Jeep. After letting the motor cool, we loaded the Jeep and headed across. Three-quarters of the way, as we angled upstream, the engine stalled from overheating, leaving us drifting toward shore!! When we hit the bank, Gloss lassoed a post he had sunk the first time over, which only temporarily halted our drift downstream! As Gloss held the post with his back, Lois, José, and I quickly threw down planks and I managed to drive the Jeep off into the murky edge of the river. Thank Kaiser for four-wheel drive! When the weight was removed, it was easier to contain the ferry while the engine cooled.

After this trip, without doubt the most unnerving of our entire experience in the Chaco, we learned not to attempt long-distance journeys when the weather was unstable. It was also adventuresome to initiate the ferry rather than wait until the operator had the routine more firmly established. The prospect of floating off toward Resistencia was more real than I care to remember. Today the trip can be made on paved road and a bridge.

We proceeded on our way only to encounter a lagoon with a broken-down bridge. The slats nailed over sunken tree trunks only grabbed about one-half of the tires as I eased across within a whisker of plunging into the lagoon. We arrived at Riacho de Oro around 4:00 P.M. to find the preacher away (not our day!). We decided to press on to Bartolomé since we had no acquaintances there other than the preacher. One man asked to ride with us and we waited nearly an hour while he prepared. He turned out to be a valuable asset as the road was cut and we had to travel through farmyards and semi-trails. Once we descended a steep bank, crossed a stream, and climbed a steep incline on the other side. I had to make three attempts before the wheels bounced precariously over the top! The closer we arrived to Bartolomé the more mud we pushed. It had rained hard all day and drizzled en route. We barely pushed and shoved our way to Guillermo Flores's house, where the whole patio was under water. At 11:30 we set up our sleeping bags under an *algarrobo* tree. One-half hour later we had to sprint for the church as it began to pour! There were no guaranteed dry spots under the leaky roof and we ended up with damp sleeping bags and wet faces.

Next to floating downstream, the most unnerving moment was crossing that makeshift bridge on a hot, still afternoon in completely unknown territory with no help in sight. We chose to cross the lagoon with its broken-down bridge rather than return to the river's edge and take our chances on the ferry. Only later did I discover that had I properly engaged the four-wheel drive, travel across the bridge and up the bank of a stream would have been far less treacherous.

Awoke to the coughing and wheezing of other folks who had sought refuge from the weather. It rained all day. As we sat in the house of Guillermo and family the water forced us farther and farther inward until there was only a tiny island left for the smoky, damp, wood fire. There was no food, and the rain prohibited action to acquire any. We passed out biscuits and oranges, sang songs, studied Toba, and sat on our damp butts. About 4:00 P.M. it stopped raining and shortly after people began to arrive for church service. The entire service was a mixture of Toba and Pilagá, which only confused my attempts to speak and understand the language. A long, drawn out healing service continued well into darkness. Before setting up our cots in the mud under the house roof this time, we passed out our remaining biscuits and oranges.

Monday morning I accompanied Guillermo on horseback to the administration headquarters. Everything was covered with water. Met the administrator, who did not appear friendly. In the P.M. we tried to escape, getting stuck in the Flores patio on the way out. The entire family worked strenuously to help us on our way. Finally we made it to the highway, where we headed to Fontana for food and gas. We tried to retrace our tracks for Riacho de Oro but lost our way in the mud. Finally, we dropped off our guide, who continued on foot, and we headed around the long way home via El Colorado. We spent the night in a room at the bridge, sharing it with José.

We left early the next day, arriving in S.P. at 1:00 P.M. The closer to home we got, the more dust and heat we encountered. José spent the afternoon and night at our house, where we had a good meal and siesta. I gave him funds to travel by bus to L. 15 the following day.

Wet sleeping bags, a horse ride through mud to headquarters of the administration, spending the night with our traveling companion in a local pension, mud at the beginning, and dust at the end of a trip were all unique experiences not to become part of our normal routine. After this initiation, all subsequent trips were a breeze.

To Quinta 8, December 6, 1959

Heavy rains canceled the trip to L. 17 that Lois and I had planned with Luís Escalante. Instead, Albert and I headed out to the newly established and ever-growing settlement at the edge of town for our first church service there. Escalante led the meeting, which drew less people than I would have expected. Afterward we walked around the various lots and visited with families installed there. We also helped to fill out baptismal cards for new members. Returned to our house for dinner with the Buckwalter family, visiting until 11:15 P.M. when the lights went out.

This initial urban settlement in our adopted city, currently called Barrio Nam Qom, has become a major contact with the white world, both through foreign religious organizations and through contacts with municipal government for jobs, education, and health care. Upon my return visit in 1966 the more or less permanent population had grown to over five hundred, and in 1988 it approached one thousand. Every plot currently has running water, thanks to a Protestant Swedish mission in town. There is also a school on the lot, and plans in 1988 called for the construction and staffing of a clinic. In addition, several other settlements of Toba had been established nearby.

One of our missionary activities in association with the IEU is documented here—helping to fill out baptismal cards for new members and replacements when they were lost. All were officially signed and distributed by Toba *culto* leaders and given to any adult who asked for one. The request was made to the local church leader in control of the membership cards. His signature, along with that of the member, appeared on the card. We simply helped to fill out the congregational and official registration information when the card supply ran low. Today these are printed for each congregation.

To Pampa del Indio, December 11–14, 1959

Lois and I left the house at 7:30 A.M., stopping to pick up Luís Escalante at Quinta 8 as planned, but he was not home. It was 10:00 A.M. before he returned and we got away. Passed by L. 17, where Luís decided to stay and visit. We stopped by to invite Eugenio Martín to accompany us, but he was also away. Finally, we continued on our own. Arrived at Aurelio López's place around 4:00 P.M., but neither he nor his family were home. A neighbor went to search for them and they appeared promptly. After visiting a short while, we went over to the church to pray for a sick man who had been carried there on a bed. Later we went to visit Vicente Núñez, who was also not home. Upon return we discovered that the sick man had died. Had a service from 9:00 P.M. until 12:15 A.M. To bed on cots with mosquito netting at 1:00 A.M.

Community leaders often arrived at our home in Sáenz Peña to request that we visit them. Sometimes we returned with them. At other times we invited folks along for one reason or another. Occasionally individuals asked to travel with us when it was known we would travel to a specific community. In this instance we thought that Escalante intended to travel with us all the way to La Pampa. Thus, it came as a surprise when he decided to stay in Legua 17. It also seemed strange that no one else wished to accompany us. There was always someone who wanted to travel at the slightest opportunity. When we were asked to transport a sick couple active in the church at Pampa Chica back to Legua 17 upon return, it became apparent that folks there must have known about this and therefore allowed space in the Jeep. We were more amused than annoyed at these less than subtle manipulations because we accepted the fact that our purpose in traveling was to serve Toba needs rather than our own.

As suggested in the Overture, praying for the sick always represented something of a dilemma for me. While I did not consider prayer inefficacious, the notion of laying on of hands with the expectation of a miracle was over and beyond my standard of faith. I was particularly uneasy when the sick were removed from the protective walls of their homes into the heat or cold so that church leaders could lay on hands and pray for healing. When the person's condition did improve I was, of course, pleased but uncertain that the prayer in and of itself was the determining factor. In contrast to Toba preachers, I consistently recommended clinics and medicine. For that reason I always felt uncomfortable when someone claimed to have been healed because we laid on hands and prayed. I was pleased with the result but disquieted about my low level of involvement. Prayers, as this instance demonstrates, did not always effect healing.

Up at 6:30 A.M. After *maté* we headed for Campo Alemani. The roads were terrible and we traveled slowly as the Jeep was loaded with Aurelio's family and relatives. Visited with Aurelio's brother-in-law after his return from town. Ate green watermelons twice during the day. Had church service from 4:00 until 6:00 P.M. and then headed back to Medina. Had another church service at Aurelio's place from 9:00 P.M. to 12:30 A.M. Huge crowd, excellent singing. Finally shut eyes in exhaustion at 1:30 A.M.

Green watermelons were always a problem; they gave me stomachaches. The Toba could not wait until they became ripe, so they picked them green. In fact, they seemed to enjoy them in unripened form.

Sunday was another big day. Traveled to Cuarta Legua for church, arriving around 9:45 A.M. while the service was in full swing. Later we all headed for a lagoon where a baptism was to take place. It was a trek of well over a mile. At least five hundred people attended; the service was impressive. Fifteen persons were immersed in baptism by Aurelio, thirteen adults, including an elderly woman, and two young boys. The singing was super and the mood upbeat. Afterward everyone returned to the church for preaching and communion. Around 3:00 P.M. it was over and we shook five hundred hands, some several times. Had a good talk with Nieves Ramírez and Antonio Núñez. On the way home we visited with Domingo Sánchez. Returned to Aurelio's place for another church service, which lasted from 9:30 to 11:30 P.M. To bed at 12:30 A.M. Everybody bushed.

During this first year, it seemed that we spent practically the entire time with rural Toba in church services. Many times the last thing I wanted to do was drive off for another service. Although I attended many baptisms, always by immersion in a lagoon, I never actually baptized anyone because it seemed important to support Toba leadership in this important symbolic act. As already stated, when missionaries were in charge of services they did all the baptizing, which for the Mennonites was by sprinkling rather than by immersion. Perhaps this memory prompted the indigenous leadership to do it themselves in the way they preferred. The Toba baptized not only new initiates but also members who had strayed from the fold or for one reason or another wished to reaffirm their commitment to the *culto*.

This was a particularly long and exhausting day. It is a pity I did not comment further on my conversation with Nieves Ramírez, who later became the first, and to date only, Indian congressman in the provincial assembly. He remains an active politician in defense of indigenous interests and rights as he understands them.

> After visiting a while Monday morning, we agreed to take a local couple active in the church along back to L. 17. We loaded the Jeep with bananas, fruit trees, flowers, and squash, along with clothing, because the couple plans to stay there for an indefinite time. On the way we stopped in Pampa del Indio at the clinic, where I spoke with the doctor in charge. He told me that the couple with us has syphilis. We arrived at L. 17 shortly after noon and visited for a while with Chief Gómez before heading back to S.P. with Luís Escalante and his aunt. By midafternoon we were home, ready to stretch out, eat up, and sleep in.
>
> Observation. The Church of God Pentecostal is having a lot of difficulty attempting to set up a Bible school and central office in La Pampa. There is much dissention about where it should be located and who should receive training and funds. The whole purpose of the operation seems to be lost in the desire to get funded. I am glad we have no such financial deals to manage. We must continue searching for ways to share our resources and knowledge without making the Toba dependent upon us.

The fact that active members of the church had syphilis disturbed me, but at the time I had no idea how prevalent venereal diseases were, particularly near towns and cities. In this case the treatment was effective because both recovered and the man later became an active church leader in a responsible position.

In retrospect, I am intrigued with my final comment about managing finances. We were undoubtedly less removed from the problem than this comment would suggest. Certainly our time and facilities, including the Jeep, were at Aurelio's disposal when we traveled with him. The extent to which he considered these Toba resources remains unclear to me.

To Bajo Hondo, February 21, 1960

Lois and I left at 7:30 A.M. and returned after midnight. Luciano Ramírez had a three-hour service, although only two handfuls of people showed up. Everyone is out harvesting. Went to visit Camilo Sánchez in the afternoon, who complained about the Pentecostal church, claiming their leaders do not like indigenous people. Returned to Luciano's place for evening service. It was agreed that Camilo and Luciano would combine their services when we visit in the future.

Gave our full donation to the mosquito blood bank, although no one seemed impressed with our reluctant generosity. Perhaps the mosquitoes were—they came back for more often enough!

During harvest time we would arrive in Toba communities to find them abandoned except for the very young and old. To this day, when people return from urban centers to participate in cotton harvest, this period is one of travel and festivity among the Toba. It appears to reenact olden times when Toba gathered to celebrate the *algarroba* harvests.

These one-day trips tended to be more exhausting than the extended weekend visits. Complaints such as Camilo's about other white church leaders working with the Toba always made me uneasy since I was uncertain whether the individuals in question were aware of how the Toba felt about them. Perhaps we were equally uninformed of our own failure to meet Toba expectations.

To Miraflores, April 8–11, 1960

Lois and I had planned this trip, but owing to leadership tensions in the community it was decided that Albert and I would go with several Toba church leaders. Luciano Ramírez, Luís Escalante, and Aurelio Villalba accompanied us. Left Friday A.M. and returned Monday P.M.

Went first to Chief Soria's, who attempted to explain why he had silenced Antonio Leiva, the preacher from L. 17. Late in the evening we continued on to Mariano Naporichi's place, who expressed his sorrow for Antonio since the latter had been rejected. Spent the night back with Soria in the church building, where the mosquitoes were impossible.

Saturday A.M. we talked with the chief's brothers and others opposed to Antonio. Chief Do'oxoi agreed to talk things over with Antonio, with the result that the latter was reinstalled as church leader. Afternoon service lasted from 1:30 until 6:00 P.M.! A lot of people, spirits high. Spent the night at Antonio's house under a tree with a breeze that scattered the mosquitoes.

Two services Sunday, 10:00–2:00 and 5:00–8:00. Had feast of turkey at Mariano's after evening service and slept there. Left Monday A.M. for S.P.

The role of the missionary in mediating leadership disputes is again documented here. While the diary mentions neither Albert's nor my role, by now we functioned as an effective team. His style was laid back while mine was more interventionist, particularly during the early years. We never really designed a strategy in this regard, but simply followed our own hunches in any given situation. Extensive discussion and patient listening constituted crucial strategies for conflict resolution.

While Antonio was pleased with his reinstatement on this occasion, we will see in a later diary entry that he complained about not having the support, meaning I think, both from the congregation and the missionary, to provide the pastoral leadership required. The superimposed legitimacy he wanted we could not provide given our role as colleagues rather than overseers.

To Legua 17, April 18–19, 1960

Lois and I took Albert, Aurelio Villalba, and friend with us to a huge Monday night meeting with eight hundred present. It was cold and the dancing started early. Everyone in high spirits.

The highlight of the trip was a political meeting Tuesday that lasted from 11:00 A.M. until 4:00 P.M. in which there was almost unanimous support for dumping Hilario Tomás as general chief. The idea was to name no one to the post until a "nonpolitical" person could be agreed upon. Evening church service lasted from 7:30 P.M. until past midnight! Again, much enthusiasm in preaching, singing, and dancing. Arrived home 2:00 A.M.

This represented our first anniversary trip to the Chaco interior. Note the more brief, succinct entries.

It is difficult to conceptualize what a "nonpolitical" chief would be, since the position itself is political. This was a rare occasion when political representation with the provincial government was discussed openly in church. Today the mixture of political issues and the *culto* is more common than it was in the early 1960s. Hilario Tomás had been appointed to his position by state officials. The pervasive conviction expressed was that he no longer represented the interests of the people. This was by far the largest participation at any church meeting in all our visits to Legua 17. It represented a significant step in the politicization of the IEU and its leadership.

To Pampa Argentina, April 30–May 2, 1960

Lois and I left early Saturday A.M., picking up Pacheco Rodríguez in Tres Isletas. We had planned to meet Chief Juan Pablo in Castelli, but we could not find him. Had to detour owing to bad roads and arrived at 3:15 P.M. Stopped first at the chief's house, but he had not yet returned. Continued on to Carlos Rodríguez's place, where we put up for the night. Walked to church for evening service, but only a few attended. Upon return we talked until late about Juan Pablo, whom Carlos claims is using the church for his own personal aggrandizement.

Sunday A.M. we all went to church, which was well attended. Visited with Juan Pablo in the afternoon before an evening service in which only the visitors spoke. Afterward the chief gave his version of the situation in soft but compelling terms. There is no question that he is in charge here. Slept under a tree at his house.

Left Monday A.M., picking up Pacheco and his brother Francisco at Carlos's house. Took Francisco to Castelli for his weekly TB shots. Arrived home early afternoon and promptly went to bed with a high fever.

It will be recalled that the Rodríguez family had been with the Emmanuel mission in Espinillo and with the Mennonites at Aguará. Thus, they had a more missionary notion of how church life should be practiced. Not having the "benefit" of this instruction, Chief Pablo managed the community, including the *culto,* in the manner he saw fit. This resulted in tension between the two families, much as existed in Miraflores between Chief Soria and the Leiva and Naporichi families.

The preachers wanted the chiefs to back off on church matters, limiting their leadership to "political" concerns involving representation with government over land rights and other resources. The chiefs, on the other hand, who were all strong shamans, felt proprietary about every activity involving the community. The tension between more senior traditional and younger church leadership was characteristic of communities where a strong chief/shaman was active.

In this particular instance, I listened to Chief Pablo's complaint that church leaders were interfering in his legitimate exercise of leadership in the community. I explained what I understood to be their complaint but made no recommendation to him about what to do about it. In turn, I also communicated to the Rodríguez family the concerns of Chief Pablo without comment. Both expressed appreciation for my involvement. Church activities did pick up after this visit for a period of time, but I am unaware to what extent my intervention contributed.

To La Reducción, May 28–29, 1960

Lois and I went to Bailón Domingo's place for a good afternoon visit before church, which lasted from 7:30 to 11:00 P.M. Slept in a solid grass-roofed house, fortunately, since it rained during the night.

After *maté* and *tortas* we left midmorning for Juan Acosta's with a Jeep full of people.[21] Service, lasting from noon to 3:30 P.M., seemed to drag. Bailón was in charge of communion. Afterward we visited for a while before returning to Bailón's place by dusk. We took his son and daughter-in-law and four kids to Machagai, arriving home around 8:00 P.M. to discover that we had guests from Miraflores. They had spent the previous night and the day on our patio waiting for us! Lois cooked a meal for all of us and we visited until late.

La Reducción was the reservation administered initially by a federal and later a provincial agency in charge of Indian affairs. It is where the 1924 uprising occurred at Napalpí and the cite of my first field trip as an anthropologist in 1966. The families we visited headed two of the regional churches.

Since we always locked our front gate when traveling to the country, we had mixed feelings when Toba individuals climbed over the wall to stay in our backyard during our absence. On the one hand, we were glad they felt at home and had a place to stay while attending to business in Sáenz Peña; on the other, it appeared that the lock had little meaning if it could be freely ignored. Also, we generally arrived home exhausted and ready for a good bath and rest, which had to be postponed when visitors were waiting to be entertained. As time progressed, we became accustomed to finding guests waiting for our arrival, although they expressed discomfort if their stay involved more than one night before our return. Our friendly, accommodating neighbors next door understood our work with the Toba. They often advised them as to when we could be expected and assisted them in other ways.

Our own cultural need for privacy was slowly eroding, but it never disappeared completely. Mosquito nets and sleeping bags provided the only privacy in the country until the Kratz family brought us a tent when they arrived the following year. Our visits with the Toba at our home in town were always in our backyard or in the room where they slept. The house remained our own private domain. I invited Aurelio inside for the tape recording mentioned in the following entry; he seemed disoriented and Albert questioned the wisdom of this decision.

To Quinta 8, Legua 17, and Legua 9, July 13–17, 1960

Aurelio López arrived in the A.M. and the two of us traveled to Quinta 8 for a long afternoon and evening visit. The evening service included special prayers for a young couple who could not have children. Thursday was spent recording a life history of Aurelio on my recorder.[22]

Lois, Aurelio, and I left Friday noon for L. 17, stopping on the way to visit in Aguará. When we got to L. 17 Antonio Leiva had also arrived from Miraflores, so a big meeting was called for Friday night. It was well attended and spirits were high. A special meeting was called for Saturday A.M. to discuss the problem of church leadership at L. 17. Aurelio López dominated both meetings and the threat of division seemed resolved, at least temporarily. Saturday we took Eugenio Martín with the three of us to L. 9 for a service there. It rained and we fought mud on the way back to L. 17 for a late service. Sunday everyone was present and the discussion was intense. Eugenio Martín claimed Chief Gómez had designated him *dirigente,* but the people clearly supported Francisco Pablo. The resolution named Francisco preacher, with Eugenio assigned to travel around to fulfill his duties as regional representative. Sunday eve we returned to Quinta 8 for church, arriving home near midnight.

Here was a typical Toba resolution to leadership conflict. Each competitor was assigned a position of responsibility. In this instance Aurelio intervened; neither Lois nor I spoke, nor were we asked.

Eugenio Martín's claim to congregational leadership, based upon the designation of Chief Gómez, apparently carried little weight because Eugenio was simply confirmed in the position of regional representative, which he already held. The congregation got Francisco, whom they wanted. Clearly Chief Gómez had lost much of the authority he had exercised in prior years. It is of interest to note, however, that he apparently had named Martín, just as Soria would name his son, *dirigente* after Leiva died in Miraflores. The shift in power relations from chief/shaman to *culto* leader confirmed by congregational participation is nicely documented here. Although not fully aware of it at the time, I was witnessing the transformation of leadership from an authority system based on charisma to a democratic system based on community voice. Voting for Toba representatives to political office in the 1980s further supported this trend.

To Aguará, Legua 15, and Miraflores, July 29–31, 1960

Lois and I left at 8:30 A.M., stopping to visit in Aguará and L. 15. Took José Durán and son along with us, arriving at Chief Soria's around 4:00 P.M. Visited with him and his brothers for about two hours and returned to Mariano Naporichi's, where we conversed with him and his brother Cabral. Returned to the chief's place and slept in the church building. During the night it was cold and damp.

Our visits were always the most successful when we touched base first with Chief Soria. This instance represents a good example of our travel directly to Soria's house upon arrival, despite the fact that we had to drive out of our way to return José Durán to the Naporichi family, with whom he was acquainted and where he wished to spend the night.

Saturday was bleak and dreary. Visited with the chief all morning. Church from 2:00 until 7:00 P.M.! Went to Antonio Leiva's after service for beef soup and visited until around 10:00 before returning to our bedroom in the church. During the night it rained.

Still cloudy Sunday, but no rain. People arrived late. Church from 10:00 to 2:00 while Mr. Crovato (the provincial director of Indian affairs) waited in the wings. He had announced a meeting for 11:00 A.M. to distribute tools and equipment. In the P.M. we drove over to Hilario Cabrera's, who had now moved to Miraflores from Aguará. While there some folks came by to say that Crovato had left in a huff, angry that he had to wait until the service was over. Changed a tire and went by to greet Mariano Naporichi, who gave us a chicken to take home. Left about 5:30 P.M., dropping off José and son at L. 15 and stopping in Aguará to bring news and greetings from the Cabrera and Naporichi families.

Note. Mariano claims that the Soria family in Miraflores steals meat, that July 9 was a "feast of stolen meat." When asked to speak in church, my text was the Ten Commandments with particular attention to number eight! People are angry with Crovato and the administration for what they consider failed promises to assist them in agriculture.

Complaints about white administrators were common, yet the disrespectful treatment of Crovato was extraordinary. The cup of frustration appeared to have run over. Clearly the Toba were sending a message by not inviting him into the *culto*. Not only was he obliged to wait for hours until the service was over, but when he did promise equipment and seeds for the community they complained that he offered too little too late. This example of misunderstanding with the Indian Agency in Resistencia was characteristic of many we observed at the time.

I was never able to unravel the story of stolen meat. To me the accusation seemed totally out of character for Chief Soria, although I was not well acquainted with all of his children and their families. This topic reemerged when I returned on an anthropological field trip in 1966. The picture presented at that time is much less one-sided than it appears here.

To Espinillo, Pozo la China, and Tres Pozos, August 10–15, 1960

Albert and I took this trip with Pacheco Rodríguez. Left Wednesday A.M., arriving in Castelli to repair his Jeep, which was acting up. Waited two hours for a soldering job. Saw Chief Juan Pablo while waiting and other people from Pampa Argentina. Arrived at Carlos Rodríguez's around 7:30 P.M., who appeared with his son Francisco an hour later. Hit the ground at 11:00 P.M.

Our interactions with the Toba in rural towns demonstrated most clearly the nature of the anti-Indian prejudice with which the Toba had to deal. With but few exceptions, townspeople eyed them with caution and distance, often expressing perplexity at our easy interaction. Self-assured and confident in his rural community, Juan Pablo appeared meek and ill at ease in Castelli.

Up at daybreak. After *maté* and a brief stop to greet Juan Pablo, who had returned from town, we headed with Carlos for Espinillo along trails and across the Bermejito to Valentín Moreno's place. Since he was in Castelli and only women were home, we proceeded on toward Pozo la China. On the way we visited the site of the old Emmanuel mission, which is now in ruins. Had an excellent fish meal with a Morales family and slept under a huge *algarrobo* tree.[23]

Readers will recognize this trip from the Overture. I did not write here about the person who met us because of his dream and only wrote about that later after our return to Sáenz Peña. This represents but one clear example of where I repressed in the diary the very experiences that obviously stimulated doubt, not only about my religious faith, but also about faith in rationalistic Western assumptions concerning the nature of reality and the limits these place on the sort of communication the Toba find meaningful. The question does arise why emotions are sometimes recorded when most entries describe actions and circumstances.

> Left early for Pozo La China and the home of Pancho Pellegrini, who was overjoyed to tears to see us. They had had no services for over a year since their preacher had died and he was seeking authorization to hold services. Left around 11:00 A.M. and drove by Espinillo, where we fixed our second flat caused by the large needles. Traveled on to Tres Pozos, arriving 5:00 P.M. at the home of Andrés Díaz. During the night a strong south wind blew up and scattered the fire to kingdom come, removing the recent oppressive heat. Started the night on top of the sleeping bag and kept crawling downward throughout the night until all the blankets were on top of me by daybreak. Over fifty degrees F drop between dusk and dawn![24]

At the time I was fascinated by the extent to which the old Emmanuel mission philosophy of controlling religious services continued to dominate the people in Espinillo. There appeared to be great interest in conducting their own services, but a reluctance, even fear, to do so. Clearly they were seeking legitimation to hold services but uncertain about how to obtain it. The IEU sounded attractive, but they did not appear convinced. At least the old Emmanuel mission had funds to carry out activities, which is more than the IEU offered.[25]

> Chief Jesús Bachorí arrived in the A.M. for a big discussion about the United Evangelical Church and how it operates strictly under indigenous leadership. He wanted to know what precisely is Buckwalter's and my role. We said to visit and assist, not to lead. He seemed cautiously impressed. We left for Pozo La China, arriving at 4:00 P.M. A number of people had gathered for a meeting, but left thinking we would not arrive. We were given a fire, *maté* and straw, a tea kettle, and a place to stay near the old church. Pancho killed a sheep and we ate roast sheep and soup. Excellent. During the night it rained, but we were under a spot where the roof did not leak.

Chief Bachorí was an impressive old-time leader who evinced authority. Clearly he was checking us out to determine whether he wished to lend his support for the establishment of a congregation under the auspices of the IEU. Had Aurelio López been with us he would certainly have pushed for this. Carlos Rodríguez, however, took a more passive attitude. Despite the commitment expressed in the following paragraph, no congregation was established at that time.

Had two services this Sunday, both led by Carlos. The people affirmed their commitment to start up the work that had been abandoned. It was a beautiful sunny day and we went walking in the P.M. to find *toue,* a wild plant the Toba use for salt.

Up at 3:45 A.M. in freezing cold with a heavy frost. Left 5:00 A.M. for Pampa Argentina, picking up a small lame deer on the way, which we left with the Rodríguez family. Arrived home 4:30 P.M.

While I had heard about it previously, this was my first opportunity to encounter *toue* used for salt by the *dapicoshic,* northern Toba known for collecting honey stored in the ground. The plant is pulled from the ground and left to dry. When the leaves and stem have dried, they are burned. A little water is added to the ashes to form a black ball, which is then rubbed off to provide salt for soup or other food.

To Miraflores, September 9–11, 1961

Lois and I took Quintana [layman active in the church from Quinta 8] with us, stopping to pick up Mrs. Luciano Cabrera in Aguará. Dropped off Luciano's wife with her brother-in-law Hilario Cabrera and family, then on to church service at Chief Soria's place. Afterward, we returned to spend the night with Mariano Naporichi, who spoke mostly of his plans to leave Miraflores.

Sunday A.M. a big crowd in church; so loud I could not hear myself speak. Much dancing and shouting. In the P.M. we went to visit with Antonio Leiva, who complained that the church had encouraged him to move to Miraflores but failed to give him support. Sunday night we visited with Chief Soria, who asserted that he intends to "safeguard" the *fichero;* anyone who attempts to interfere will be in trouble. Visited Monday A.M. with Hilario Cabrera before leaving for home. Extremely dry; no one can plant crops.

Not only did the presence of both a strong chief and a strong church leader in the same community cause problems, but Leiva's status as an immigrant from Legua 17 with few family members present for support left him vulnerable. His vision, recorded in the

Overture, illustrates the manner in which he looked to the spirits for authority. In this sense his leadership was charismatic in the true Weberian sense. Not surprisingly, he felt abandoned in his struggle to maintain control of the congregation. The problem persisted until Leiva's death, when one of Soria's sons took over the responsibility of *dirigente*.

Sometime after this Mariano Naporichi, a Leiva supporter from Aguará, moved his family to Quinta 8 in Sáenz Peña, where they were located when I visited them in 1988. The extent to which this move represented an escape from the fate that befell Leiva remains undetermined. As occurs with many deaths, there were charges that Leiva was killed by sorcery sponsored by the Soria family. His wife told me during the same visit that Antonio's extraordinary spiritual power could not compete with Soria. The one immigrant family that remained in Miraflores, the Cabreras, never competed with Soria for communal leadership, although they became highly regarded for their agricultural ability. It will be recalled that the Leiva, Naporichi, and Cabrera families were all associated with and educated by the original Mennonite mission headquartered in Aguará.

I am uncertain as to precisely what Soria meant about safeguarding the *fichero*. It was apparently his way of affirming control over community discussion and action in which the *culto* played the central role. Although Miraflores contained a population of approximately one thousand, no other church emerged at that time to successfully compete with the one on his property, despite several attempts.

To Pampa Chica and Campo Medina, August 24–September 1, 1962

Lois and I left Friday noon with Orlando Sánchez, stopping on the way to pray for Antonio Núñez, who lay dying. Arrived in Campo Medina around 5:00 P.M. and had church until midnight! Sat. A.M. I gave my first Bible study class. In the afternoon we went to Cuarta Legua for a service and to Pampa Grande for the evening, including a three-hour healing service for Antonio. A baptismal service Sunday began at 10:00 A.M. and ended at 5:30 P.M.! Aurelio López preached for nearly two hours. Went to bed early, to the annoyance of Aurelio.

One of the rare occasions when the diary mentions anything approaching interpersonal conflict. The lengthy weekend church services had exhausted me, while Aurelio preferred to stay up and talk. Although nothing was specifically said about our early retirement, his absence the next morning without announcement indicated his displeasure.

Orlando Sánchez proved to be the best student in the class. He later became Albert's Bible translator and was elected head of the newly formed Chaco Indian Institute in 1988.

> Next A.M. Aurelio took off early to visit his dad while Francisco Francia and I visited with a neighbor. Monday noon we had our second class with nine present. Later in the afternoon Francisco and I visited with Juan Vera; we discussed the Toba language, about which he is quite articulate. Had another Bible class Monday evening from 8:00 to 10:00 P.M. Ate delicious roasted armadillo before retiring.

Juan Vera was a local Toba school teacher who had been trained in Buenos Aires. We had a sophisticated discussion about Toba phonology and grammar, the most lucid and interesting of any I have had with a Toba speaker. As I recall, he showed little interest in the Toba church.

> Tuesday Aurelio and I visited with Florencio Núñez, whose brother Antonio had died in the morning. He served us some delicious wild pineapple. At noon we had another class. In the late afternoon Aurelio, Francisco, Salustiano, and I went hunting. I shot a *perdíz*, a *paloma,* and two *charata.* Aurelio had stalked a deer for several hours but did not shoot because he could not be certain of a sure hit. Had fifth class in the evening. The women prepared an excellent evening meal for the participants from our catch.
>
> Wednesday morning Aurelio and I went to Pampa Chica to visit Fernando and Ambrosio López. The latter traveled back with us for the noon class. Went to visit Vicente Núñez in the P.M., but he was not home. Thursday we went hunting again. I shot five *charata* and the women picked wild pineapples. The combination made excellent eating the next few meals when the women kept expressing their amusement over our male efforts to help collect and transport the pineapples. Thursday afternoon we went to Lote Cuatro for service. Returned home in the evening for ninth and last class.

Our participation in subsistence activities, particularly male participation in collecting, attracted considerable attention, suggesting that division of labor by gender was still an important cultural consideration. Lois generally spent her time in the country with the women while they cooked. I usually sat with the men or hunted after I had acquired a gun. It was common for men and women to sit together, especially when *maté* was served. However, when Lois did not accompany me, I had very little interaction with Toba women.

> Early Friday A.M. we traveled to 10 de Mayo, stopping at Lote 22 en route. Had delightful visits all day. Ate muskrat for the first (and hopefully last) time. Had service, which lasted until sundown. Returned to Aurelio for a night service that ended at midnight. Saturday A.M. we left, stopping at Pampa Grande and the Núñez home to console the family. We arrived in S.P. early afternoon.
>
> Observation. While Lois cooked several meals in our tent, mostly we shared wild fruits and game with the López family and others. Best trip to date. My dubious success as Bible studies teacher was more than compensated for by the pure pleasure of sustained interaction during hunting and collecting wild fruits. The women were hilarious when describing male efforts to accomplish women's tasks. Hauling the fruit and game in the Jeep was the last straw!

One of our most satisfying visits to a Toba community. It was partly this trip that convinced Lois and me to spend more extended time in a single community rather than to travel so widely on shorter visits. We encountered a wider range of activities than we normally did by traveling to *cultos* all over the place. We also managed to cook some of our own meals and have fun in the process, making us feel more independent yet involved in community life than on previous trips.

My failure to establish a time difference for the Toba between the gospels and the epistles provided one more example of the crucial role that culture plays in biblical interpretation, eventually convincing me that I was in the wrong business. The point was that I saw no need to insist upon my sense of time and history when interpreting biblical texts, yet without some common principles of hermeneutics, how much understanding did we actually share? It was not the lack of authority that bothered me, since I felt no need to be authoritative, but rather the fact that the notion of truth that prompted me to join the mission was one I no longer recognized as valid. This represented another concrete experience that played a significant role in my eventual decision to leave the mission.

A final recollection of this trip was the ease with which we shared meals in the country when there was sufficient food to go around. Our usual procedure was to take staple items from Sáenz Peña and give them to the hostess where we stayed, who in turn took charge of the meals. Here Lois's role was more direct and we even had some meals alone, as did other families who participated in the Bible study session. Other mission organizations that had invited several Toba preachers to Bible study classes had provided full subsistence for the period involved. This was the only one of this sort that was attempted during our missionary stay. The idea of holding it in the country where everyone, male and female, could contribute to subsistence in the normal manner (although provisions would have been more scarce without my gun) was a novel idea that proved more satisfactory than we had anticipated.

To Pampa Argentina, October 12–14, 1962

Lois and I left 6:30 A.M., stopping in Tres Isletas to pick up Pacheco Rodríguez and head for Espinillo. One league beyond Carabajal we met a *gringo* who said the river was too high to cross and the road cut farther along. While deciding what to do, we ate lunch and I shot two *charata,* which we cleaned and took with us to Chief Juan Pablo in Pampa Argentina. He seemed impressed with my hunting skill. After setting up the tent, he and I went hunting before dark. We only found a *copetona,* which I shot. He and daughter were called away in the evening to another daughter who was having a baby.

Saturday I got up early, drank *maté,* and went hunting. Returned with two *charatas* and a *copetona.* Had a delightful visit with Chief Pablo, who spoke for nearly an hour in Toba. Pacheco then spoke for an hour and it was my turn. I managed forty-five minutes, mostly in Toba. By this time the women had cooked the game and we had a big noon meal. Small church service in afternoon and we visited late with the Pablo family.

Sunday up at 6:00 to hunt with Juan Pablo before breakfast. Shot six *charata* and a wild chicken. Returned in time for church. Nice service, big crowd. Afterward a large group stopped off for soup with my morning's catch. In the afternoon we visited with Francisco Rodríguez, where I shot a wild duck for their evening meal. Left for home shortly after 6:00 P.M. I shot a *perdíz* and a *charata* on the way, which I gave to Pacheco for his family in Tres Isletas. Arrived home before midnight.

My reputation as a hunter was enhanced enormously when I once shot two *charata,* a large pigeon-like bird of the forest, with one shot. Word of this feat traveled widely and swiftly. It takes stealth and cunning to bag *charata* because they have great hearing and simply fly deeper into the forest as one approaches them. Pairs often sit with their heads together, which is how I was able to kill two with one shot. The meat is very delicious, preferable to chicken in my opinion.

Although my hunting prowess did not fit any image the Toba had of a missionary, travel to Toba communities became much more enjoyable and I was participating in an activity they valued highly. When in town I could not wait to get back to the country. I could now contribute on their terms to daily subsistence in a way that did not foster dependence. Interestingly enough, the Toba accepted my new status as a hunter with interest and no apparent reservation. Hopefully, it may have helped to prepare them for further image changes to come.

Once I returned to the States, however, I completely lost interest in hunting. Having done it to survive, I could no longer participate in it as sport. Perhaps I had become socialized to Toba reluctance to kill unless absolutely necessary. The lack of enthusiasm for hunting was difficult to understand and accept by my brother and brother-in-law, who were both looking forward to my participation in their annual hunting rituals. Along with the move from mission to anthropology, my disinterest in hunting made me something of an enigma to the family.

To La Reducción, December 2, 1962

What a day! Lois and I left 7:00 A.M., picking up Aurelio López, Luís Primero, and Jacinto Acosta in Quinta 8, arriving at Juan Acosta's home about 9:15. Church started at 9:45 and continued until 5:00 P.M.! Fifteen people preached, Aurelio for well over an hour. It was HOT (43°C) and we ran out of water. After the service Juan sent his kids for water but they only returned with a small amount of muddy surface water. Arrived home around 8:00 P.M. tired, hungry, and THIRSTY. It rained during the night so I was able to feed the spouting into the cistern to replenish our diminishing water supply.

This citation is significant for documenting the most serious problem in the Chaco at that time whether in the city or country—water. While our cistern supply got precariously low on more than one occasion, I do not recall it having dried up completely except when we drained it for cleaning. During the following decade potable water was piped to Sáenz Peña from Resistencia, making cisterns obsolete. The problem in the country where the Toba relied on surface water when wells gave out was much more serious. Much time and energy were spent by the young women in carrying water.

To Legua 17, December 25, 1962

Lois and I took three young men from Quinta 8 on this trip on a hot day. Had church from 10:00 A.M. until 2:30 P.M. Were offered soup and watermelon afterward by the Fermin Notagai family. Later visited Chief Ramón Gómez. In the P.M. we went to visit with Salomón, who now has his own church. We intended to stay for the service, but it started to rain. After a brief meeting we headed home through a tremendous storm of rain, hail, and mud. I had trouble keeping the Jeep running and on the road. When we arrived home we had two visitors from Espinillo waiting for us—Jorge Seferino Castro and Julio García.

By now the routine of trips to the country and return to visiting guests at our home was a rhythm to which we had become accustomed. This last summer (December through March) was the hottest we experienced, thus the diary comments on heat are not surprising. At one point we had thirty successive days of 100° or more temperatures, some days reaching as high as 116°.

Although this entry was on Christmas day, any celebration of Christmas, other than a brief mention of Christ's birth during the church service, was far from our mind. The heat, especially intense on this day, always inhibited a festive mood and there was little public seasonal display in our local city. The relationship between ecology and a cultural sense of ritual is clearly demonstrated here.

We were now conscious of heading into the home stretch where each visit to a community would likely be the last one. Within a few months, as the final entry demonstrates, we began our farewell trips.

To Miraflores, Pozo Toro, and Pampa Argentina, June 22–23, 1963

On this our farewell trip to these areas, Lois and I decided to travel alone. Left at 8:30, stopping for lunch and arrived around noon. Visited with Hilario Cabrera until 1:30 and continued on to Antonio Leiva's, where we visited until 3:30. From there we proceeded to Mariano Naporichi's, who was out looking for an animal. After he returned we all went to Chief Soria's for an evening service. Sat around until late with the chief, who expressed sadness about our leaving and wanted to know when we would return. Could only say we do not know.

Intended to leave at 8:00 A.M., but the Jeep would not start. Eventually it did and we drove to Hilario's, who had prepared *maté* and tortas for us. Juan Acosta and Aurelio López were there and wished to travel with us. The latter preached a small sermon before we got away. Arrived at Pozo El Toro in the midst of heavy dancing and shouting. We all spoke. Large attendance; they agreed to finally fix the church roof. After the service we drank *maté* and visited until 2:30 P.M., when we set out for Pampa Argentina to say good-bye to Juan Pablo and the Rodríguez family. Stayed for evening church service, where a drunk mimicked my speech until Juan Pablo calmed him down. Headed home via Castelli, where we left Juan and Aurelio, arriving home around 9:30 P.M.

The diary records many similar farewell trips around the Chaco. All were bittersweet as we regretfully said good-bye, even while looking forward to renewing family ties in the United States. Deep inside we suspected, but were not certain, that it was unlikely we would return in the same capacity in the future. This uncertainty made it impossible to be as forthright and clear about our future plans as we would have preferred. At any rate, we were convinced we would return by one means or another. The Chaco has a way of wooing back those who settle there for any significant length of time.

Scene 2: Questioning Mission Practice

While I was fully committed to the indigenous mission philosophy that motivated our work with the Toba, the chasm between our standard of living, including health and hygiene, and that of the Toba caused me growing distress throughout our years with the Chaco mission. Our strict involvement in religious life involving the *culto* left subsistence and health concerns unattended. Certainly I did not wish to return to the old compound approach, but already in the first year I developed a growing concern that our missionary activities were too restricted to secularized Western notions of spiritual welfare to be of genuine service to the Toba in major areas of need. The nature of this concern was expressed in correspondence that I initiated less than one year after our arrival in the Chaco.

In a letter dated February 6, 1960, addressed to Field Secretary Nelson Litwiller and to our colleagues the Buckwalters, who were with the Litwillers (Lois Buckwalter's parents) on vacation in Montevideo, I expressed reservations about the Chaco mission program planning that called for adding a third couple to the staff that was trained precisely as we had been. Having recently read W. J. Lederer's *The Ugly*

American (1958), I argued that "paid professional religious leaders have two strikes against them before batting in Argentina (Chaco or elsewhere)" and that we were "unprepared to serve the Toba in major areas of need."

I specifically noted that our training in literacy was inadequate to enable us to mount an effective program, that the Toba were in dire need of instruction in the dangers of contaminated water, the nature of a balanced diet, and the treatment of disease, yet none of us was prepared to contribute significantly to the enhancement of their knowledge in these areas. "In summary, I feel that my training has adequately helped me *understand* the Toba and [their] way of life, yet it has not prepared me to give expert advice in areas of acute need."

In his response of February 19, Buckwalter defended the Chaco mission policy as follows:

> Elmer is evidently going through one of those experiences where one searches through his whole being for *a satisfying answer to his presence in the Chaco* and the responsibility one has before God and the Tobas. And we might as well say it in simple words right away: no one has found a simple answer.

He went on to point out that while the Toba feel that whites are morally bound to help them, those whites who do try find it impossible to live up to Toba expectations.

> The Indians distrust and dislike the individual white man whose assignment has been administration of any program of aid, for though he has worked himself to death, yet he has not been able to supply Toba needs as well as Mother Nature and her primeval forest used to do . . . what *to us* is a *social application of the gospel,* or in other words directly administering of physical aid to a needy people, is understood by the Indians as a moral obligation on our part, and serves to do nothing more than teach them that they are helpless wretches, while concurrently inviting their distrust and dislike.[26]

In a letter dated February 20–23, I commented on Buckwalter's points in the following manner:

> May I be pretentious enough to point out that I do not consider myself unaware of the problems my esteemed colleague is raising. In fact, I would go so far as to claim that the Toba "phenomenal field" itself stimulated the questions I attempted to objectively pose. I do recognize that our programs and plans must be Toba-oriented with a view to how they will be accepted and appreciated. Nor do I harbor these impressions because I want the Toba to "adapt [themselves] to the white

man's world." Admittedly there is a terrific risk involved in attempting to contribute to the physical and intellectual poverty of the Toba, but isn't the same risk present when we attempt to help [them] in spiritual matters? The risk, of course, is that we may make [them] even more hopelessly dependent on the troublesome "white man." It is my conviction, nevertheless, that this risk can no longer be conveniently sidestepped.

What does "making Jesus Christ known" to the Toba imply? Just reading the Bible and translating it into the native lingo? Is it possible (for long) to share Jesus Christ with suffering people while consciously withholding information that could most likely result in their suffering less? Can we long maintain the established "rapport" while sharing with or serving only one part of the individual? Where do spiritual responsibilities end and social ones begin? Is it possible to "apply the Scriptures" in a strictly nonsocial sense? Can the church be "strengthened" by pushing aside "all questions of economics, hygiene, general education"? Isn't Albert himself perhaps too bound by the white man's frame of reference when he indicates that social application of the gospel is in other words "directly administering of physical aid to a needy people?" Couldn't the indigenous principle be applied to the whole of [humanity]? . . .

A closer view of what the governmental agencies are doing by way of administering to Toba health and education needs shows much to be desired. Putting it mildly, this service (when available) is not given in the name of Christ. Recently I witnessed one health official treat a Toba pitifully. Only after I intervened, insisting that the misunderstanding was purely semantic, was our brother treated like a "human." Very few doctors and officials can be counted upon to demonstrate the patience required to help the Toba. . . . Jesus and the New Testament are concerned much about [human] physical and mental health. It is difficult to talk about the gospel and steer clear of these aspects. To tell the truth, I don't know either how one could meaningfully serve the Toba in these areas, but I am willing to give it some consideration and a try.

Shortly after this exchange, the American Bible Society linguist Eugene Nida visited the Chaco and issued a report (1960) that effectively addressed many of these issues, including economic, social, and health needs. Above all, he urged that primary attention be given to language learning in order to improve our proficiency in Toba. He also recommended the development of special training programs for the Toba that concentrate on church leaders, lay leadership, adult members of the churches, and children. In response to these recommendations, the Buckwalters and Lois and I focused intensely on language learning for a period of time, cutting down on our visits to rural Toba communities. We spent more time in Quinta 8 at the edge of town where we were able to practice Toba. Each of us worked at his or her own pace and manner on language learning. In retrospect, apart from my Bible study with church leaders, it is clear that we largely ignored Nida's other recommendations, primarily because they were not priority items for the Toba.

However, the question I originally raised continued to haunt me. In a letter dated August 18, 1961, addressed to the mission board secretary J. D. Graber in Elkhart, Indiana, with copies to Litwiller and Buckwalter, I once again expressed my concern about "our basic philosophy and purpose" for being in the Chaco.

> Our present program is geared to conservatism and the status quo rather than to change and progress. Yet the Tobas themselves are in a tremendous state of change. True, we are likely slowing down the process of disintegration of Toba society, but should this be our primary contribution? Should the process be slowed down? Wouldn't it be wiser to climb aboard and help them make the transition as smoothly as possible?
>
> Toba values today are mostly *criollo* values. There is a great deal of motivation for learning to read and write Spanish, for example, but there is disinterest, even opposition, to reading and writing Toba. We are embarrassed and annoyed when the Tobas indicate too much interest in our wrist watches, electric fans, and Jeeps, but our attitude isn't helping them solve their curiosity. It remains and grows. We may choose to ignore the fact that they spit on our floors and eat from the same unwashed spoon as their brother sick with TB, but this isn't helping them face realistically their health problems. How can we call a drowning man our brother while refusing to throw him our rope? Is he really our brother if we withhold technological information which would be advantageous to his welfare and happiness?

Again Albert responded, August 21, 1961, in his usual cogently thoughtful manner that was considerate yet firm in his convictions. I quote at some length from this letter addressed to Graber, Litwiller, and myself, some of which includes citations from his February 19 letter, cited above, that Graber had not received:

> We get our "Culture for Service" within an American Mennonite environment. Our anthropological orientation plus a few skills, plus theological orientation which helps us understand the non-Mennonite Christian world—this we get from non-Mennonites. We go out from a

nation which not only thinks it has the answers, but also believes these same answers should be handed out as convenience demands.

Now our anthropological orientation warns us that our supposed answers probably aren't answers at all for someone else. And what's more, as we begin work with Tobas, we soon discover to our dismay that what our world calls answers, doesn't seem to fit anywhere into the Toba world. Instead of helping him, it seems to destroy him even more completely than ever. If we give him an implement with which he can work to feed himself and his family, he frequently yields to the temptation to convert it directly into food by selling it to his white neighbors. After he has sold the implement, he sees no reason why we can't give him another one, for we are obviously financially able to do it again. Thus any real friendship between us is ruined by our feeling that he is a good-for-nothing, and his feeling that we are stingy skunks. In a word, this was the Nam Cum [Mennonite mission in Aguará] impasse from which we signed off in 1954.

. . . The world we live in requires that we solve the Tobas' problems. But if the Tobas are incapable of accepting the only answers the white man knows how to give, there is only one conclusion—difficulties.

. . . The Toba is convinced that he needs what the white man has, his transportation, his food, his clothes, and his houses, as well as his language, his written materials, and his accessories. Therefore, not a day goes by that some Toba isn't asking some white man to give him something from this array of features of the "successful" way of life.

The white man, on the other hand, is also convinced that what the Toba needs is this "successful" way of life. This is what's back of missionary work, as well as the government's Indian program, and in addition it motivates the "advice" freely given to individual Indians by the thousands of "successful" people with whom they come into contact every day.

Though the Toba wants these features of "success," yet he has some features in his traditional form of life which he also prizes, such as the tranquil hours of just being together with family and relatives and all that goes with that. The Toba actually prizes these traditional features most, for he will submit to endless suffering in order to carry them out.

. . . In conclusion, I believe that within the general outlines of the Chaco Mission program there is plenty of room for a large variety of individual contributions. I do not want to make any one feel that his particular contribution should be similar to mine. After ten years I've quite definitely concluded what my avenues of service will be. I hope that Elmer will continue to develop his convictions as to what he can do which will be of most value. Once Jim is here he will want plenty of time before he comes to some definite conclusions too. Thus it will be good if we cultivate patience with one another and always keep our hearts and minds open to God's Spirit to whom we all are subject.

In a letter dated September 6, 1961, addressed to Albert (with copies to Graber, Litwiller, and myself), Norman Derstine, an administrative assistant for the mission board in Elkhart, commented on the discussion to date by calling attention to the Reyburn report of 1954 in which Reyburn discussed the future church among the Toba in the following manner (1954b:63–64):

> Since the current orientation of the Toba is aimed at identity with the *criollo* population, the church should aim at spreading to the *criollo* groups. As identification becomes more complete in a non-church direction, the church will become less meaningful. Therefore, the Toba should become aware of this fact and aim to direct the movement of the church in the *criollo* direction where life will find its future setting. In short, a missionary work among the Toba which does not attempt to keep abreast of this drift may find itself without a Toba church and beginning from scratch with the new *criollo* order. The zeal to accomplish the job exists among the Toba today. This may not be so ten years from now.
>
> It was pointed out earlier that the church becomes spiritually meaningless to young people at the approximate age of puberty. This has always been the period when young men became quite independent from their parents. Puberty-age girls are likewise granted considerable freedom but tend to remain in groups near their female siblings, mothers, and aunts. The motivation for the presence of these boys around the outside of the church is primarily sexual. There, staring through the holes in the mud and wattle, these youth are given the best opportunity of the week to inspect as in a showcase the girls of their choice. The Tobas' lack of Christian education which will offer these young people a Toba Christian approach to life has nipped in the bud what could (but may yet) be a flowering church. Coupled with this fact is the commonly expressed desire of adults to get their children educated so that they can go to the cities and work. Many older people feel that the church has been a lifesaver for them, and it has in many respects, but they do not see the church as a heritage to pass on to their children. . . . The failure to achieve an effective communication for the younger Tobas may actually witness a breakdown in the church which will never be reparable. In this connection it should be borne in mind that these young people are the ones who are achieving the highest degree of *criollo* identification. In short, the future of the Toba church is at stake, and the next few years will determine much of its course.

In his response dated November 7, 1961, Albert pointed out that the situation is more complicated than the discussion to date suggested.

> During the seven years since Reyburn made his study, there has been such a kaleidoscopic shifting in the general picture as to make one dizzy. During these years we have observed one church start from scratch and reach a drawing power of a couple hundred on a Sunday morning. During the same time we have observed churches that had their hundreds at the beginning of this period, and now are almost down to zero. This has very little correlation with concern felt by missionaries. It is a direct commentary, however, on a foot-loose people being blown to and fro by such unsubstantial things as visions and dreams. We have observed the churches of Leagues 15 and 17, which Reyburn described as lacking of young people in 1954, impress visiting J. W. Shank in 1958 with the large number of young people who obviously considered the Church vital in their lives. We have seen *criollos,* who had married Indian wives, become converted through Indian preaching and regularly take part in the services. But we have also seen these same *criollos* finally leave never to return.
>
> The Toba Church service with its occasional disorders, and irregularities, doesn't seem to appeal to the *criollo* very long. He soon goes elsewhere. Yet there appear to be continuous accessions to the Church from among the relatives of those Indians who have been the most deeply loyal to the faith.
>
> During this same period we have observed a native revolt in which the Indian preachers of one mission declared themselves independent of all foreigners (meaning missionaries) and called themselves "native missionaries." This movement has pretty well floundered by now.
>
> My honest conclusion, then, is this: As the Toba nation further disintegrates through death, scattering and intermarriage, the Toba Church will also die out. Neither do the Tobas themselves, nor any anthropologist, seem to know how to join Tobas and white people into any kind of a happy and permanent relationship within the Toba Church.
>
> Reyburn seems to imply that it would be a disgrace for the Toba Church to come to an end without there being a *criollo* Church growing out of the ruins, or at least in some way being an obvious continuation of the former. I honestly question this assumption. If experience has shown the impossibility of mixing Tobas and *criollos* in the same congregation, it would seem apparent that two distinct methods of work would be called for in meeting the needs of these obviously disparate peoples.
>
> One Indian asked me whether the new missionaries (meaning Kratz-

es) would learn their language. Another told me he'll be glad when I can converse with him in their language, for then we'll understand each other. There are some men who, though they proudly display their Spanish, yet they betray themselves at every turn as being more at home in the Toba language. Preaching is almost 100 percent in Toba. Moreover, you can still find Toba youngsters with whom it is practically impossible to converse in Spanish. There isn't a Toba colony where they don't talk exclusively Toba among themselves and where they don't enjoy hearing us attempting to use their language.

With regard to the integration of Toba and *criollos,* a letter from the Buckwalters dated September 1990 pointed out that the Toba church at the outskirts of Sáenz Peña, which once had a large Toba audience, increasingly attracted *criollos* owing to the active presence of a Swedish missionary. This has resulted in decreasing Toba attendance as they form smaller church groups in surrounding neighborhoods.

Today it is not uncommon for the Toba to refer to their own leaders who travel around preaching as "missionaries." Foreign missionaries are distinguished as "fraternal missionaries." In the early 1960s, the term *missionary* was reserved for the foreign missionary, which at the time consisted primarily of the three Mennonite families residing in Sáenz Peña. White Argentine preachers who visited and preached among the Toba were generally referred to as *pastors.* The new terminology was apparently introduced by a new generation of church leaders.

In reviewing this literature, I feel sympathy for the headaches my preoccupations must have caused the Buckwalters, who continued until their recent retirement to pursue mission work among the Toba in the manner they saw fit. Nevertheless, the concerns I raised continued to be a factor in the decision I faced as how best to be a brother to the Toba. My growing inclination was to leave the comforts of Sáenz Peña and move to a major Chaco community where we might confront more directly the daily life of the Toba.

In June 1963, shortly before leaving the Chaco, I wrote a letter to the board in Elkhart that attempted to summarize our experiences among the Toba as Lois and I conceptualized them at that juncture.

It may sound trite to begin with the observation that Toba society is in a process of tremendous transition. This fact must nevertheless be kept in mind since it colors all our experiences and planning. All societies are constantly changing, of course, but Toba society seems to be in a particularly extreme process of disintegration and assimilation. Old myths and values no longer satisfy while new ones frequently aren't sufficiently rooted to provide social and spiritual stability.

One example of this conflict is in economics. The "stuff and starve" economy (to borrow Nida's [1960] terminology) of former years is an inadequate basis for understanding and adjusting to the white man's "slave and save" one. In the area of health, it is quite a leap from the conception of disease as spirit originated and controlled, to the use of pills and injections for cure. Yet the Toba have and are making these adjustments. Many more Toba now take advantage of medical facilities, for example, than when we first arrived, and the Kratzes have made the same observation in their even shorter stay here.

Another overall factor that complicates our relationships with the Toba is their spirit-world orientation. We observed that old myths and values are disintegrating. The other side of the coin is that these beliefs still play a major role in the thought patterns of most Toba, and in many ways, the gospel has strengthened rather than weakened these concepts. The New Testament world of evil spirits, healing miracles, dreams, and visions fits in nicely with the Toba understanding and explanation of things. While the missionary with his [or her] scientific *Weltanschauung* needs a satisfactory explanation for the nonoccurrence of these phenomena post–New Testament, the Toba neither need nor seek such explanations since this is part of their experience or worldview. The result is that the missionary and the Toba are frequently thinking in completely different categories.[27]

Differences of opinion arise when it comes to carrying out a constructive program of Christian sharing in this situation, and, of course, most of the time no one viewpoint is entirely right or wrong. In general, however, we Mennonite missionaries have tended to be drawn into a pattern of work quite similar for all, a pattern dictated to a considerable extent by the Toba themselves. This is understandable since our background and training is quite similar and we are here, after all, to serve the Toba. It is fortunate that our training and mission board permit us to seek to serve Toba felt needs and not merely put on a program that the home folks envision. It should be pointed out, however, that the Toba have learned from long years of experience how to handle the white man so that they get maximum benefit from him. . . . Even though we seek to work for the growth of the Toba church in a manner detached from self-interest (i.e., we encourage and help them establish their own organization with no attachment to the Mennonite church; we don't count noses for the registry back home), the Toba have not always thought in these terms. They enthusiastically supported the idea of acquiring their own legal document (*fichero*), not merely to be free from the yoke of denominational bodies, but rather (at least for many) because they at first interpreted it as a handle whereby they might receive more from the white man. Many thought that the Ministry of Cults would now send funds directly to them for running their churches, and when this material aid was not forthcoming, quite a number lost interest.

Our efforts, along with those of our colleagues, have generally fallen into the areas of personal and public-worship visitation, Bible instruction and preaching, language work, and medical aid. There are, of course, the "extras," such as helping them with legal documents, serving as go-between before lawyers, judges, and other government officials, knitting instruction, etc. As already suggested, the Toba themselves determine to a considerable extent what our contributions shall be. They seem to place a premium on personal visits and Bible learning, and this is where we have exerted ourselves most. When Lois and I first arrived in the Chaco it disturbed us a great deal that so much of our time was taken up with simply visiting Indians. After a period of time, however, it dawned on us that this is exactly what the Toba demand and expect of the missionary. The Buckwalters had correctly sensed this and consequently dedicated themselves to this task.

The letter went on to suggest that the board think in terms of turning over the Toba work to the Argentine Mennonite church since North American missionaries work in a tricultural context while the Argentines would work in a bicultural one; the Argentine standard of living is more comparable to that of the Toba and would require less adjustment; the Argentine church is developing a conviction for outreach that the Toba situation may well satisfy; and the day may arrive when North Americans will not be welcomed in the Chaco as they are today.

To my knowledge, this suggestion fell on deaf ears, not only among colleagues in the Chaco, but at the mission board as well. I am unaware that it ever received serious attention or response. My own efforts in this regard went so far as to invite a young man from Buenos Aires, who showed promise of leadership in the church, to spend several weeks traveling with us among the Toba to determine his interests in the Chaco mission. He later traveled to the United States to pursue graduate work in seminary and has not returned to Argentina as far as I am aware. I am informed that there is more communication between the Argentine Mennonite church and the Chaco missionaries today than there was during our stint with the mission, but I am unaware of any significant interaction between Argentine Mennonites and the Toba.

These exchanges on the subject of mission philosophy occurred, it should be noted, at a point in time when the role of the Western missionary was under serious reconsideration in many churches. It was a period of decline in mission personnel and budgets in the United States, a period when indigenous church leadership began to assert itself instead of relying upon North American or European missionaries. These discussions anticipated by more than a decade challenges to the assumption that anthropologists could go anywhere in the world to study whom they wished at will.

My final letter to the board was written from Pittsburgh while in graduate school. Dated January 9, 1965, it explained why we found it necessary to discontinue our relationship with the mission. I affirmed, above all, that we had no complaints about our working arrangement with the board and with fellow missionaries, that we could think of no other board or colleagues with whom we would prefer to work were we to pursue missionary activity. Our differences of opinion about how best to carry out our work were also insignificant in our decision to sever our ties with the mission.

> Our problem is primarily philosophical/ideological. We assume that a missionary is one who is wholeheartedly convinced that [people's] basic need is spiritual—that men and women everywhere must be brought to assert that "Christ is Lord," however that is interpreted. We accepted and sought to execute our assignment in the Chaco with this basic assumption. Particularly during our early years with the board, we never seriously questioned the validity of this dogma. However, it is only fair to the board, in fact, it is our duty, to indicate that we, particularly I, have come to question this position.
>
> I continue to be agitated and concerned—even to some extent involved—in the fundamental moral and ethical questions of our day. I also recognize the key role which Christianity has sought (sometimes effectively) to play in this regard. To put it forthrightly and honestly, I have deep-seated and ever increasing doubts regarding the validity of the Christian mission in today's world—at least as I have conceived it. . . . I am no longer in a position to propagate beliefs which I cannot support vigorously.

Note how the term *doubt* is employed here to communicate a fundamental shift in discourse from Christian affirmation to one that considered Christian claims comparable to others available in the marketplace of ideologies. It was the *uniqueness* of the claim to truth that I could no longer affirm. This letter marked the end point in a doubting process, germinated in college and seminary, that inevitably produced a total rupture with the church community in which we were raised. It represented the public affirmation of a major shift in discourse, one that endangered social bonds that continued to hold strong meaning for us. It was a painful letter to write, just as it must have been painful to read by those with whom we had established close ties.

The responses from Mission Board Secretary Graber, of whom I had grown very fond, as well as from Regional Secretary Litwiller and colleague Buckwalter, were heartfelt, sincere, and sad. My attempt to explain thought processes of a highly personal nature that had taken place in the context of anthropological study was doomed from the start. It was unrealistic to expect former colleagues and friends to comprehend the discursive contexts and experiences that left me no choice but to take the action I did. Anthropological discourse, with its own claims to knowledge and truth, represented an alternative for me, one that eschewed the notion of absolute truth in any exclusive sense. Later I would discover that anthropologists often make their own claims to truth about the nature of the world as they perceive and explain it, although they don't call it truth. Theoretical debates in the discipline can be as dogmatic and tedious as any I encountered in theology.

I have since concluded that some of the distance that my letter created was due in part to my enthusiasm for the new discourse, and that my definition of the problem in specifically affirmational terms made them concerned for my spiritual welfare, which might have been avoided had I explained my position in terms more compatible with their logic. I had begun to operate in a different symbolic world that made communication with past friends and colleagues much more difficult than I had initially anticipated. In an attempt to be forthrightly honest, I closed off channels of communication that need not have been closed. Once closed, however, they proved difficult to reopen. Commitments to any given discourse can be held deeply, impacting upon and disrupting close relationships established over extended periods of time.

Thus ended our association with a mission program that I continue to view as significant for the Toba. It is a program that has encouraged diverse expressions of faith over ideological conformity and Toba self-determination over missionary management. In this sense one could argue that it has been a model for the indigenization of mission programs. It is not the sort of mission activity characterized by mission critiques, such as the novel and film *At Play in the Fields of the Lord*.

Contrary to what many supporters appear to think back home, however, it is not a program in which missionaries have made a serious adaptation to native lifestyle, nor do missionaries pretend to have narrowed dramatically the cultural distance that separate them from the Toba. While this observation may have significance for mission policy and practice, it is only of passing interest here.

What was not addressed in this discussion of mission philosophy was the resolution of my engagement with the notion of revelation, which significantly influenced my decision to leave the mission. Experience with the Toba served to demonstrate the precarious nature of all versions of revelation to which I had been introduced previously. If the Toba religious experience was to be accepted as genuine, and all Christian organizations working among the Toba had come to consider them Christianized, it became obvious to me that an entirely different notion of revelation was required. I reasoned as follows.

The North American religious community needs a theology to explain miracles, dreams, and visions as recorded in biblical texts since miracles and visions are not a normal part of daily North American experience. However, for the Toba, dreams, visions, and miracles constitute the essence of daily experience. Communication with spirit powers calls for no special status in the logic of things. For the Toba, Christian vocabulary is simply incorporated into an ideological structure already in place. No explication, no theology if you will, is required. In fact, the Toba version of Christianity seems to work better with the accounts in the New Testament than do North American theological versions based on Western thinking.[28]

For example, Toba visitors would arrive at our house in Sáenz Peña with the explanation that they had come to see us on the basis of a "heavenly vision." As recounted in the Overture, they often anticipated our visits to them on the basis of dreams as well. Healing services for the sick in regular assemblies were thought to replicate "miraculous" healings of the sort accredited to Jesus in gospel accounts.

Why, then, should North American Mennonites attempt to complicate Toba understandings by introducing their versions of biblical texts when Toba readings appeared to conform more closely to the original? This awareness, along with a developing understanding of Toba cosmology, served to consolidate my anthropological approach to knowledge.[29]

Furthermore, the Toba concept of God was so centrally tied to an understanding of power beings that it was in no way equivalent to the images I had conjured up before. Clearly any notion of revelation that depended upon a fixed image of divinity was untenable given these observations and experiences. From this perspective, images of God could only be socially produced and interpreted. Humans create God in their own image rather than vice versa. It was my involvement with Toba faith and action, then, that finally put to rest my struggle with revelation.

Thus, as our missionary field experience progressed, Lois and I became increasingly uneasy about our role as spiritual experts. We were highly conscious of the fact that while the Toba church certainly generated its own autonomy, our missionary lifestyle was anything but indigenous. When visiting Toba communities we occasionally experienced hunger and thirst, but we could always return to our comfortable house in Sáenz Peña, where there was no shortage of food and water, an option not available to the Toba. Furthermore, although I was called upon to explain the Bible and give advice concerning the application of biblical texts, I was fully conscious of the fact that the Toba reading of what I said often had very little to do with the explanation I thought I had given.

For example, during the ceremony of Holy Communion I was asked repeatedly to explain the text of Jesus with his disciples at the Last Supper. My response always involved a symbolic explanation of the commemoration of Christ's sacrificial love through drinking wine that represented his blood and eating bread that represented his body. Upon completion of my presentation, the local preacher invariably would stand up and say, "As the good brother said, there is healing power in this blood"![30] The diary indicates that the few formal Bible classes I did attempt to teach were not particularly successful as far as I could determine, although I was occasionally surprised to hear some of my sermons and discussions repeated almost verbatim months and even years later by more than one Toba church leader.

Lois, on the other hand, had some success in teaching knitting to Toba women, although her attempt to convince them to dry sweet corn on hot tin roofs was a failure. The problem was that no one would eat the stuff after it had been dried. She did hold some Bible study discussions with women from time to time and frequently spoke in church services. Her most satisfying experiences, however, were simply the interactions she had with women as they went about their domestic tasks, mostly cooking and serving *maté* during the times we visited. The few occasions she had to accompany women in their collection of wild fruit and vegetables represented an interesting diversion from routine.

In retrospect, my primary missionary function as far as the Toba were concerned was to be available to listen while they complained about the whites' failure to treat them fairly, to serve as mediator between the Toba and the white world when disputes and misunderstandings occurred, and to explicate biblical texts upon request. While this role was pleasant and satisfying, although it obviously had frustrating moments, it did not conform to what the majority of those who supported our work back in the States appeared to think we were doing.

The conflict with which I struggled involved representation and notions of authoritative control on the part of the folks back home. In a word, discourse. On the one hand, we were to represent our understanding of the Bible to people who didn't need that understanding since their readings of the text seemed more compatible with the nature of reality described by biblical authors than did ours. On the other, we were to represent the Toba church to supporting congregations who thought we were doing something different than we were. This was further complicated by the fact that these congregations provided the funds that made it possible for us to be in the Chaco in the first place.

While on a trip across the States during the summer of 1964 in which Lois and I visited Mennonite congregations and talked about the Toba church, it became painfully clear that our Chaco experiences had distanced us from those who supported the mission even more than we had imagined. Their main concern seemed to be the extent to which we were "expanding the Kingdom" and making Christ known in the manner that made sense to them. At least that is how we interpreted their responses to our presentations on Chaco mission activity. Clearly it was time to seek a new career.

Thus, during our first field experience with the mission I experienced anthropological doubt of the sort Lévi-Strauss had described. I discovered that doubt can involve a deeply felt and emotional trauma as one comes to sense a distance from everything one has held dear during a major portion of life, while at the same time coming to recognize the extent to which one's sense of personal identity shifts in the context of a different socially produced reality. It seems to me that this is precisely the point that Lévi-Strauss was making in the epigraph to the Preface. Doubt provides the impulse for a shift in discourse of the sort I made from theology to anthropology. The sense of both angst and freedom that the exploration of alternative discourse options provides can only be comprehended fully by those who live through the experience. It also argues for the central role of experience in the production of knowledge.

However, Lévi-Strauss's notion of an "ever-shifting position of the subject" in relation to an object of knowledge is an idea that needs further development. What is the relationship of consciousness to the knowledge produced in ethnographic work? To what extent can this knowledge be considered scientific or valid when it is clear that the subject is more a product than a "prime mover" in the construction of knowledge? Questions of this nature have been extensively debated in French intellectual thought where Foucault, Derrida, Lacan, Kristeva, and others have contributed, along with Lévi-Strauss, to the notion of a decentered subject.

Mennonite ideology traditionally has placed particular value upon group identity. One form of self-denial in Mennonite theology means submitting individual disposition to group will. Another form involves rejecting the material values and attractions of the broader society that detract from spiritual concerns and values. But the stress on community is not upon just any community; rather, it is upon a community called by God to "come out from the world and be separate."[31] The notion of separation served in my youth to produce conformity to the standards of the Mennonite community in individual behavior. Discourse on community also provided a unique background for my interactions with the Toba where an active sense of community was involved in daily lived experience.

While the communal spirit of the Toba fit right in with my Mennonite ideology, the Toba spirit grew out of their cultural identity whereas mine came by choice. Toba values of sharing and communal cooperation appear to have their foundation in a common ecological experience rather than in a conscious ideology. Thus, while both my Mennonite and Toba cultural experiences stressed discourse involving community, the nature of community and its expression in social action was quite different in the two instances. The Mennonite sense of community was ideologically marked in order to distinguish it from a larger society of which it was a part but to which it did not belong. Its expression in local discourse involved kinship structures and a sense of family history. The Toba sense of community was even more strongly tied to kinship structures and family histories, but also to ecological niches. However, rather than rejecting the world, they perceived that world as encroaching upon and rejecting *them*. As the Toba become increasingly self-conscious of their indigenous identity, it remains to be seen how traditional communal values and norms will be articulated.

In terms of my particular experience, then, even as I came to be aware of a distancing from a Mennonite community that had contributed enormously to my own sense of identity, I was also increasingly aware of drawing upon the values of that community without consciously intending to do so. Furthermore, some of those same values were unintentionally reinforced by my experiences with the Toba, again without conscious awareness.

Of course, I recognized much of this in hindsight rather than at the moment when the struggle for a sense of identity and direction was most intense. In the practice of anthropology I have experienced little awareness of community in the sense that I have felt it in Mennonite youth and among the Toba, although this may represent more a reflection of my own particular place and time rather than a statement about the profession.

To what extent does a Toba individual experience an "I" comparable to that of a North American Mennonite? Or a Christian missionary to that of an anthropologist? What are the grounds, if any, for common understanding? Where are the breaks in the socially produced ideological systems that constitute consciousness, and how are they maintained or transformed? How can one conceptualize an Other with coherence and systemic quality without reifying the notion with positive content? Even if considered in French structuralist terms as a semiological process that becomes articulated in objectified thought, how does one conceptualize these processes as one moves from a Mennonite world to a Fundamentalist one to a liberal theological one to an Argentine one to a Toba one or to an anthropological one? Where and how are the "sights" and "oversights" of consciousness produced?[32] Can one live indefinitely with doubt or does one come to depend upon a constantly reconstituted Other for self-awareness and understanding so that the doubting process becomes a way of life? Are such doubts most characteristic of individuals socialized in closed worldviews where religious doctrines play a central role in identity perceptions or are they found among all human beings inquisitive about themselves and the world about them?

Although long since distanced from my early fieldwork experiences, this sort of questioning continues to provide the touchstone for much of my sense of self today. It also defines for me the problems of ethnography involving self and Other that are widely discussed currently in anthropology and other disciplines.

There is irony in the observation that my encounters with Toba spirituality served to resolve my intellectual struggle with religious affirmations, confirming an increasingly secularized sense of self. The Toba with whom I interacted most closely, in contrast, seemed to become more committed to the *culto*, which increasingly constituted the center of their lives. We appear to have nudged each other in our separate directions.[33]

Graduate school in anthropology, a topic I found to be of increasing interest ever since my first classes with Professor Leser at Hartford, provided the opportunity to pursue the option of a new career. My initial interest in anthropology was further strengthened during our years with the mission by contacts with Argentine scholars, as the following scene will demonstrate.

Scene 3: Initial Interest in Scholarly Work

In the pursuit of bibliographic source material on the Toba, initiated at Hartford and expanded during my years with the mission, I developed a growing interest in Chaco history, which put me in touch with Chaco scholars in Argentina who contributed significantly to my research and ultimate career choice. Several of these scholars went out of their way to provide assistance and strong encouragement for my own investigations. Their contributions to my developing interest in scholarly activity was invaluable at a time when I had not yet considered such activity a serious option.

Professor Enrique Palavecino of the University of Buenos Aires introduced me to the collections at El Museo Etnográfico and provided personal information on many Chaco authors, thus expanding my interest in other Gran Chaco people beyond the Toba. His view of ethnography fit the realistic image I had captured in courses with Professor Leser. Ethnographic data were there to be collected. The role of the ethnographer in shaping the data was not considered to any significant degree.

For Palavecino I was a source on the Toba irrespective of my mission identity. He considered my observations particularly valid because I lived and traveled in the region over an extended period of time. On many an occasion we discussed specific cultural practices mentioned in the literature and in his own writings.[34] He invariably asked to what extent the published materials conformed to the cultural scene as I observed it in the early 1960s. The fact that my observations and comments were taken seriously by a scholar of his stature at the time provided invaluable inducement to pursue further my growing interest in Toba traditions and activities with a view toward writing about them. His encouragement made me begin to believe that I could perform solid anthropological work.

Father Guillermo Furlong made available the wonderful Jesuit Collection at the Colegio del Salvador in Buenos Aires, opening up a world of scholarship that I found exciting.[35] The rich source materials produced by Jesuit scholars prior and subsequent to their expulsion from South America in 1767 began to absorb my attention. Furlong suggested that I pursue the study of Jesuit writings at Seville, Spain, where the partial collections I encountered would be complete. It was an idea I found intriguing, but unrealistic. My only disappointment was that Furlong knew little about the Toba except that they had killed the Jesuits who sought to "pacify" them. Thus, he loved the Abipón, long deceased, but considered the Toba a belligerent and treacherous people. Nevertheless, he was keenly interested in my knowledge and experiences, and he convinced me that I had the capacity to do serious bibliographic research.

Professor Hernando Balmori opened up the collection of Chaco files at the University of La Plata and provided helpful clues to the etymologies of the terms *Toba* and *Chaco*. He called my attention to the early work of Bárcena on the Toba language and encouraged me to study the Toba language.

Carlos Reyes of the University of Tucumán assisted my research into Chaco materials at the library there and continued to search out rare and obscure source materials for me throughout my mission years. He was a genuine friend who cared deeply about what he viewed as the "inevitable" destruction of Toba culture.

Dr. Antonio Tovar discussed with me at length on various occasions the status of Toba language study and translated several German works for me.[36]

Each of these distinguished scholars contributed in his own particular way to the budding image of myself as a possible scholar. When I initiated the bibliographic study at Hartford I did not imagine myself a serious scholar, but by the end of my mission assignment in the Chaco I certainly fancied the potential of such a prospect. The encouragement and persistent support from each of these scholars provided the self-confidence that made scholarly pursuit a reasonable alternative.

Discussions with Argentine scholars also encouraged me to write about my experiences. My first publication on the Toba, "Seeing Christ through Toba Eyes," appeared in a church magazine (1961). The following selections from that article provide a perspective on my thinking at that time and illustrate my writing style. The article was accompanied by four photographs showing Lois with Toba women while they cooked and me standing by the Jeep with several Toba men. The setting for this piece was the precarious trip taken to Bartolomé de las Casas during our first year.

All day long the rain came in successive downpours. The flat earth, saturated with water, refused to take more. From the protection of three mud walls we could see the area outside the hut take on the shape of a miniature lake. Inside, we huddled with our Toba hosts around a fire, strategically located where the grass roof leaked least and where the creeping lake delayed longest in overtaking its dying embers.

The fire had served us well throughout the day, counter checking the chilly dampness while heating water for *maté*, a tea which appeases to a surprising degree one's inner urge for food. About 5:00 P.M. the rain withdrew and we were free to stretch aching bones by sloshing our way to the Jeep where there were some oranges, bread, and drinking water.

Presently our Toba host, the local preacher, appeared. He wished to know if we had bread or anything to eat. The can of drinking water reminded him that their jug was nearly empty. Could the women fill it from our can since the well was quite a distance away and it was already getting dark? Swallowing hard, we responded in the affirmative.

The latter request was a trifle irritating since we were 250 miles of dirt road (mud now!) from home and we had hoped to avoid drinking untested country water. But this was no time for a discourse on amoebas or white man's preference for cistern water carried from the city. We slowly filled the jug, glancing ruefully at the diminishing water level in the ten-gallon can.

We returned to the fire. Someone had found wood not too damp to burn with coaxing and the teakettle was boiling. Once more we sucked on the familiar *maté* straw, this time with our bread and oranges contributing additional flavor. No one seemed impressed with our generosity; each person sipped *maté* and chewed bread in silence. When conversation did resume, we heard again about the government's failure to fulfill its obligation toward the poor.

Later in the evening a cold, damp breeze found its way through the cracks in the hut. I offered to share my blanket with the preacher sitting beside me on the bench. He pulled part of it around his shoulders with no comment. Before retiring to our cots, which we placed in the mud and water under the grass roof, our host asked if we had any blankets to share since there were not enough ponchos to keep everyone warm. Thinking of our nice warm sleeping bags, we ungrudgingly shared two spare blankets. We dozed off wondering how the family keeps warm when the missionary doesn't visit.

The Toba are not mere beggars, however, they are also extremely generous givers, as the missionary has sometimes learned to his chagrin. Take, for example, a visit we made to the home of a chief last July. Cotton harvest had been over for several weeks and the income it provided completely dissipated. Cotton hoeing, the next source of income, was still several months away. We arrived on a Saturday afternoon. In honor of our visit he killed the fatted goat. It seemed to matter little that this was the last of the flock, that there would be no more goat meat (a Toba specialty) for hungry weeks ahead. Also, this was a mother goat so that next year's flock must come from another source. The weekend roasts and soups consumed all the goat except one front quarter which the chief's wife managed to reserve. When we were ready to leave on Monday morning, the chief insisted that we take this meat home with us. The preacher's family also wished to send along a chicken before the flock disappeared. Knowing how short the food supply would become in succeeding months, we accepted the gifts with considerable reluctance. We resolved to bring more staples for distribution on our next visit.

As though these lessons in economic thought were insufficient to baffle the missionary, he encounters many other perplexing experiences that contradict his training in money management. Frequently he gets visitors at his home in town who have no funds for the return trip. After visiting for several days when meals and lodging are supplied by the missionary, the guests ask to borrow money in order to return home. Sometimes they wish to borrow enough to pay off the loan they received in order to arrive! Eager to travel, they constantly ask to accompany the missionary on his weekly visits to various parts of the Chaco. The latter soon discovers that he is often responsible for food and blankets on these trips. The Toba travel lightly and can be ready at a moment's notice. If the missionary eats nothing, they willingly suffer with him. If he has food, they take their share for granted and may even offer some to others who obviously "don't have anything."

But the missionary isn't the only one who finds Toba economics disconcerting. The government agency responsible for Indians finds the going tougher. What to do when the Toba sell implements, loaned to them on a credit basis, because they are hungry. Where to begin when implements provided for one colony appear in another fifty miles distant. How to punish one who "borrows" a neighbor's horse since it obviously isn't being used.

By now it must be obvious that Toba economy functions differently from our own. Ours is an *acquisitive* society. An ideal person is one who *acquires* the most in the shortest time (honestly, of course!). From poverty to riches makes headline news. Wealth is determined by the amount one *possesses*. The more one can accumulate, frequently of something he will never *use,* the richer he is and the more prestige he obtains among his peers.

The Toba see things differently. Although contact with the dominant "white" society is producing drastic changes, Toba society remains basically *consumptive*. He who *contributes* most toward group consumption gains the admiration and envy of others. Products are evaluated in terms of their *use* value. Food is for eating, clothes for wearing, and horses for riding. The acquisition of an item is insignificant, its use is what matters. Thus, personal ownership is of only secondary importance. If a blanket is available and you are cold, you ask to use it. You will return it when the owner needs or asks for it.

The article goes on to demonstrate that it was in this context that the missionary message arrived, and that the message could certainly be interpreted as strengthening the giving-consuming values of traditional society rather than weakening them. As I argued, "One who refuses his brother in need is certainly a 'bad' Christian, if a Christian at all." However, I also pointed out that the Toba live and interact increasingly in an Argentine society where these values are in conflict with others more nearly approximating our own. The boss who hires the Toba to hoe and pick cotton may have many bags of flour stored and accumulating bugs. Unless one can pay for them, however, they sit and rot while the Toba go hungry.

> As a result of this culture contact, the Toba tends to adopt the *methods* of an acquisitive society while maintaining the *ideals* of a consumptive one. The result finds him continually frustrated and confused in his relations with the broader society.

I concluded the article by arguing that the missionary is cast inadvertently into the role of a cultural broker in this context because he or she is best able to interpret the misunderstandings that occur between the Toba and their white neighbors. "This is a difficult and thankless task that gives one little to write home about. Rather, one's reward is inner contentment, a sense of fulfilled responsibility."

It is difficult to reconstruct all the motivations that prompted this article, but a major intent was obviously to describe Lois's and my experiences to Mennonite readers throughout North America who had some knowledge about or interest in the Chaco work. I wanted to demonstrate that one does not simply share the gospel as one does a cup of coffee, that sharing means mutual understanding, and that Toba understandings were sometimes baffling to the missionary, even one trained in language, anthropology, and fieldwork. The sociological analysis of an acquisitive versus a consumptive society appears simplistic and underdeveloped in retrospect. However, the point about Toba adherence to the *ideals* of a consumptive economy even while adopting the *methods* of an acquisitive one was well taken, although poorly developed. The idea was that the Toba adopted waged labor and a money economy but continued to value sharing over production.

Of all my ethnographic writing, it is the one piece that describes best the contextual experience in which my cultural understanding took place. It depicts the dilemma of the fieldworker (in this case the missionary, but equally true of the anthropologist) in knowing how to share meaningfully and what role to play in facilitating understanding with the broader Argentine society. Written approximately a year after our arrival, this piece contains more insights into ethnographic experience than do my later anthropological writings.

The editor attached a blurb to this article above the title which states, "When a people's religion changes, so does their way of life. Both may get a little mixed up in the process." Apparently that is what the editor thought the article was about or what he imagined his readers would think it was about. Perhaps the statement was intended to clarify a metamessage about problems in missionary communication that I had left deliberately ambiguous. If the latter was his intent, the editor articulated the message in an opposite direction from what I intended because the article is not about how Christianity changed the Toba but rather about how the Toba adapt Christian teaching and principles to their own cultural understandings. This experience with the editor made me conscious of the problems I could expect to face when returning to the States to explain our Chaco activities.

I learned subsequently, however, that the central problem is not simply one of an editor imposing a particular theological slant on what one writes for a church magazine. Rather, it goes to the very heart of how one goes about *representing* ethnographic experiences to those who have not lived in radically different cultural settings. The misreading of the editor was simply a portent of problems to come in anthropology. How does an ethnographer go about transcribing field experiences into texts that make sense to folks who have little or no cultural basis for comprehending what the experiences were all about? The problem I initially saw as theological thus became broadened to this larger question lying at the very heart of what this book is all about. How does one present ethnographic experience to those who have not lived in a radically different culture? Can one ever fully communicate deeply felt personal experiences to others who have no comparable basis for interpreting them? Such questions constitute a fundamental subtext, the raison d'être, for this work.

It does not take a great deal of reading between the lines to recognize that the above article, written early in our mission experience, contains Lévi-Straussian "seeds of doubt" about the task to which we had been assigned. Despite satisfying rewards, the contradictions of faith and practice simply became too great throughout the assignment to continue. The break came reluctantly and with some regret, however, as a significant chapter in our personal lives approached closure.

The following act describes how my ethnographer role changed upon leaving the mission to one that allowed a greater sense of intellectual freedom but jeopardized the relationships firmly established with the Toba during this first extended stay in the Chaco.

Act 3 | Professional Discourses and the Doubting Process

Scene 1: Graduate Training in Anthropology

Theologians speak about a "leap of faith" in which an individual affirms certain Christian premises and acts upon them as if they were true, despite lingering doubts. Sometimes this involves abandoning job security in order to act upon a sense of divine calling. My father-in-law, for example, abandoned his painting and carpentry business at considerable financial and physical risk in order to provide a halfway house for men released from prison because he felt called to do so. It was a career change he never regretted despite difficulty and discouragement. A less dramatic example involved my own decision to enter college in June 1950.

In retrospect, the move away from the security of the mission and its support system (including family and friends) to the insecurities of graduate school constituted a similar type of leap. The broad jump to a new profession with no guarantee of successful transition involved risk taking and insecurity. At the time, Lois was pregnant with our first child and we had no funds nor financial support apart from my teaching assistant stipend of $2,100 per year. Nor did we have medical insurance for our two daughters born while I was in graduate school. We remain grateful to the obstetrician who volunteered his services in a special program designed to assist graduate students at the University of Pittsburgh and to Magee Women's Hospital for the reasonable charges that made it possible for us to leave Pittsburgh in 1966 penniless but without debt. Lois was a young girl when her father lost the farm in the depression; she learned from her mother how to manage the household with frugality. That knowledge came in handy in Pittsburgh.

But the leap involved much more than mere concern about financial or career security. It entailed acting upon personal doubt concerning truth affirmations expressed in contemporary Western Christianity, the culmination of a process begun on a Sunday afternoon in June 1950 at the Elizabethtown Mennonite Church. Intellectually, the break with the mission came while still in the Chaco. The final decision to act upon that break in the form of a letter of resignation, however, was a year and one-half in the making.

Before leaving the Chaco in August 1963, Lois and I had decided to return to the Kennedy School of Missions in Hartford. I decided to seek a master's degree in either linguistics or anthropology with a view toward possible further study. This allowed me to pursue my intellectual quest in a familiar setting while leaving open the question of our attachment to the mission. Lois took courses both at Hartford and at the University of Hartford.

During that academic year two experiences contributed crucially to my decision to pursue a career in anthropology. The first involved Professor Peter Berger, whose courses and public presentations on the sociology of religion nudged me in that direction. I had never studied with anyone before whose lectures came across like paragraphs in a book. After the first week of classes I went to the library to find and read everything he had written. At one point during the fall semester I was in the local coffee shop with several other students when Professor Berger arrived. The excitement of having him all to ourselves was overwhelming and none of us knew quite where to begin. Finally, I blurted out the question burning within.

"Professor Berger, why are you a Christian"?

Berger: "Ah, but I don't know that I am."

Miller: "Oh, but you are, you wrote *The Noise of Solemn Assemblies*."

Berger: "Yes, but that was three years ago."

The simplicity of that response left me flabbergasted. Was I overcomplicating the decision for myself? Could I arrive at such a simple conclusion without the world coming to an end? Needless to say I took every class I could that Berger offered that year and I also attended all of his public lectures and debates. It was my initiation into the social construction of reality perspective.

Meanwhile I also took all of Paul Leser's classes in anthropology, which I found more intellectually satisfying than linguistics. The decision to compose my Toba bibliographic study into a master's essay under the supervision of Professors Leser and Battles was the second experience that strengthened my interest in pursuing anthropology. As my intent matured, I spoke with these two mentors at Hartford and with Professor Sydney Mintz at Yale about prospects for doctoral studies in anthropology. It was Mintz who recommended, among other departments, the University of Pittsburgh, which had recently expanded its program with the hiring of Professor George P. Murdock. He suggested that my experiences in Latin America would be enhanced and supported by Professors John Gillin and Hugo Nutini.

The recommendation was a wise one as my choice of Pitt, and vice versa, was fortuitous. Not only did I proceed through the program rapidly, owing to prior training and field experience, I also had the good fortune of working with an outstanding cohort of graduate students who contributed immensely to my developing identity as anthropologist.

The mood with which I entered Pitt in September 1964 can best be inferred from the first paragraph of my career statement required in the application: "My interest in anthropology has grown in proportion to my disenchantment with theology. This does not mean that anthropology has become merely a reactionary flirtation. The fact is that I find anthropology to be more relevant, intellectually stimulating, and practical."

Now that I have been practicing the profession for twenty-eight years I would place less emphasis on the relevant and practical. Relevance was even then a tired term that failed to capture the mixture of intellectual excitement and apprehension with which I approached further graduate study in anthropology. As for practicality, I have suggested already that theoretical debates in anthropology can be as tedious, dogmatic, and inconsequential as any I encountered in theology. Apart from applied anthropology, a subfield viewed skeptically in the broader discipline, practical implications of anthropological research tend to be inferred rather than directly applied. Like theologians, anthropologists apply their knowledge with mixed results.

I recount this decision-making process because it underscores the extent to which my apprehension about succeeding in graduate school was mixed with personal concerns, a point to which most graduate students can relate. In my own case, apprehension influenced the way I responded to advice from major professors at the University of Pittsburgh with regard to ethnographic approaches to fieldwork. I was inclined to take their advice seriously even though it would at times contradict my better judgment. Unlike the vast majority of my student colleagues, I already had extensive field experience and could relate these experiences to theoretical discussions in the classroom. However, the fact that my fieldwork was with a Christian mission seemed to taint its value. In retrospect this may have reflected more my imagination than reality, although of this I am uncertain. Clearly my graduate training, particularly in linguistics, was valued by professors. However, it was made clear to me, both overtly and implicitly, that as an anthropologist my primary interest in the Toba must be in the quality of "data" produced. The impact of this awareness will become apparent in the diaries and field notes I wrote upon my return to the Chaco.

The midsixties was an interesting time to be a graduate student in anthropology, particularly at a place like Pitt where Professor Murdock had recently brought his Human Relations Area Files cross-cultural approach to cultural study. He established the journal *Ethnology* with its ethnographic atlas and taught the basic required seminar in the history of anthropological theory. At the same time, a younger group of professors was confronting the "new ethnography" that challenged such predetermined categorization. Intrigued with the more symbolic approaches to cultural study beginning to appear in the literature, I felt caught in the emerging debate between established theorists and younger scholars who spoke a language much more in keeping with my previous experience and graduate training. At issue was not only what constituted data, but how to collect and analyze them. Little did I realize at the time that I was witnessing the first steps in the decline of the modern period in anthropology when fieldwork in the style of Malinowski in nonindustrialized cultures served as the sine qua non for professional identity.

The debate concerning the nature of data came home to me personally during my second year of graduate study when Professor Murdock bestowed upon me the honor of requesting an interview to document the Toba for his ethnographic atlas. I recall vividly the uneasiness and discomfort with which I responded to his attempts to reduce house types, for example, to a statistic. The scenario went something like the following:

Murdock: "Are Toba house roofs gabled or shed?"

Miller: "Well, actually, both occur."

Murdock: "Which occurs more frequently?"

Miller: "It depends upon time and region, but I suppose gabled."

The atlas file on the Toba reads "gabled." A note was to be added indicating that shed also occurs, although it did not appear in the final publication (Murdock and Spoehr 1965).

But it was not only the ethnographic atlas approach to cultural study that was being questioned by younger faculty and graduate students. The whole ethnographic enterprise, while accepted as necessary and important, was generally devalued in comparison to the more "scholarly" work of theory building.

At the same time, the emerging "new ethnography" associated with cognitive anthropology and ethnoscience attempted to minimize the limitations of predetermined categories, and thus revitalize ethnography, by establishing procedures for *eliciting* cultural categories rather than *imposing* them with predetermined ones, such as those in Murdock's *Outline of Cultural Materials* (1961) or *Notes and Queries on Anthropology* (see Royal Anthropological Institute of Great Britain and Ireland 1951). It may be of interest to point out that this more indigenous approach to cultural knowledge came on the heels of indigenous approaches to missions a decade earlier.

My other major experience with Professor Murdock during that second year of graduate study was his decision to publish in *Ethnology* an article I had prepared on Toba kin terms (1966). On the one hand, it was a confidence builder because Murdock made a point of emphasizing that this was the first article written by a graduate student he would publish. However, I was disappointed that he was interested only in the kin terms per se while I had written an elaborate statement about generational interaction and social context that was meant to provide a conceptual model for the terminological descriptions. It was devastating to learn that my theoretical and contextual material ended up on the cutting floor, and I seriously considered withdrawing the piece. However, the notions of being the first graduate student to publish in *Ethnology* and of getting a professional publication under my belt were too inviting.

Much later I came to acknowledge that Murdock's decision to cut the elaborations was probably wise in that my speculations about generational interactions and local settings were somewhat redundant to the terminological descriptions. However, I suspect that my failure to write much about Toba kinship in subsequent publications may have been due partially to the devastation I felt over having my first conceptual efforts on the topic discarded.

The transition from missionary to anthropologist entailed apprehension and hypersensitivity to criticism of my initial steps in the discipline. Furthermore, my most respected peers were highly critical of data production for its own sake. To simply *describe* kinship terms without *explaining* their contextual significance was no longer considered acceptable practice. I wanted to pursue the more innovative approaches emerging in the discipline rather than become identified with tired established practices, which is why I chose to study religious syncretism and social change for my dissertation. I remain grateful to my dissertation advisors Professors Gillin and Nutini for their solid support in this endeavor. Gillin played a crucial role in my decision to remain in the program at a critical point when I was tempted to abandon it. His support was consistently solid and meaningful until he became ill during the final stages. Nutini assumed supervision at that juncture.

Having completed course work, preliminary exams, and a dissertation proposal at the University of Pittsburgh by the spring of 1966, I returned alone to the Chaco one month after the birth of our younger daughter, Lisa, who chose to arrive on the day of exams. My dissertation proposal called for an analytic study of the evangelical movement among the Toba from the perspective of the developing literature on revitalization and millenarian movements around the world. One of my doctoral examination topics was socio-religious movements in the context of culture change, for which I had prepared an extensive bibliography on the social movement literature. Two questions framed the background for my dissertation research: why did Pentecostalism provide the creative synthesis that sparked the movement while Catholic and other Protestant missions failed to do so despite more intensive efforts? and why did the movement emerge and flourish at this particular time in Toba history?

Upon return to the Chaco I considered it important to establish a new role that might enable me to learn about aspects of Toba culture that may have been reluctantly shared, if at all, during my previous role as brother and spiritual advisor. This concern may have been based partly on my recollections of how difficult it was to convince many Toba elders to recount traditional lore during the early years of mission activity. They frequently objected that those were *"cosas de antes"* (things from the past), that they now had the Bible, which replaced such stories.[1] Only after it became apparent that my interest was genuine did storytellers appear at our house in Sáenz Peña to volunteer tales, which I recorded. Once word got around that I had recorded the excellent storyteller Carlos Temai, for example, subsequent visitors often asked if they could listen to his "tales of old times." I was surprised to discover how knowledgeable even most church leaders were of these stories, especially since most of them had initially demonstrated little or no interest in them.[2]

Furthermore, I felt that it was important for the Toba to learn that I was no longer the person they knew during my years with the mission. In retrospect it is apparent that I was still too emotionally involved with the separation of professional roles to simply let the chips fall where they might. On at least one occasion I recall smoking a cigar to convince fellow Toba that I was no longer the same guy.

The task of acquiring a new identity, however, proved much more difficult than I had imagined. It soon became obvious that the Toba would decide what my role among them would be. While I had chosen a new discourse as the basis for our interaction, old friends responded to me much as they had done previously. When called upon to participate in *culto* services, I did not preach. Instead, I conveyed greetings and news of my family, explaining why I had returned alone without Lois and our two young daughters. I also described the purpose of my visit and the nature of my current study, including why I felt it important that others have the opportunity to learn about

Toba struggles to pursue their own cultural identity in a rapidly changing environment.

My low-key participation in the *culto* did not appear to disturb people. With but one exception, they never complained about it to me.[3] However, they showed little interest in my new role for the most part. Inevitably they asked if Lois and the girls would come to visit sometime and I assured them that I would make every effort to return with them in the future when the girls were older and better able to travel. I soon learned to simply travel about and visit with friends without worrying a great deal about how I was defined. At the same time, I sought to establish rapport with individuals whom I had not known well, or at all, previously. Several proved to be highly articulate about traditional customs, but even those inactive and uninterested in the church acknowledged the central role played by the *culto* in community life. This observation supported my impression that contemporary Toba life was fundamentally tied to *culto* activities.

What changed dramatically during this first return trip to the Chaco was the lack of convenient transportation, making it impossible to visit all of the communities I had intended. I felt it desirable to reach as many Toba communities as possible in order to carry personal greetings from my family and show pictures of Lois and our daughters. The broad-based social network we established during our first stay required nurture and maintenance. To restrict my time to a single community would have been like returning to visit one's family after a long absence without greeting a favorite relative. Furthermore, it was important to visit as many communities as possible in order to determine the nature and extent of the revitalization process I aimed to investigate.

It was impossible to rent cars commercially in the Chaco at that time. As a diary entry will indicate, however, a friend in Sáenz Peña with whom I had hunted duck on occasion during mission years loaned me his Jeep for my first excursion into the Chaco interior. I was required to rely on public transportation and the goodwill of fellow missionaries Buckwalter and Kratz, together with the missionary doctor Cicchetti in Castelli, for further sojourns to Toba communities. My experience with the inconvenience of public transportation made me appreciate in a new way efforts made by the Toba to travel from one settlement to another in the maintenance of social networks.

During the summer of 1966 and on later visits I came to perceive my role as ethnographer vis-à-vis that of missionary in much more problematic terms than I had originally imagined. While associated with the Mennonite mission from 1959 to 1963, the Toba determined a role for me as religious savant and instructor that was gratifying, although not always easy to fill. It was a role they clearly valued high-ly. My knowledge of the Bible and biblical texts, of singing and evan-gelical music, of other religious organizations and the legalities of legal permits (*ficheros*) for *culto* activity were in strong demand ow-ing to the need for the newly formed indigenous churches to become established and legitimate.

Yet I certainly did not consistently live up to Toba expectations. I recall vividly one dialogue with the popular *culto* leader Aurelio Ló-pez toward the end of our first stay in the Chaco. We were in the Jeep traveling with three other Toba male companions when I used a Toba idiomatic expression that impressed them. Upon their com-ments of admiration that I had managed to learn the Toba language so well, Aurelio López stated, "Yes, you are *ŷoqta qom* [genuinely Toba], but since you are, you must know that it is important to teach us to perfect our Spanish, just as we taught you to speak fluent Toba. Even more importantly, you must teach me to drive a Jeep because my work depends on travel and I cannot always rely on your avail-ability to chauffeur me around!"

It is doubtful that I ever quite got over the shock of that request, particularly as it came at a crucial time when I was seriously ques-tioning my missionary role with the Toba. I say shock because it never occurred to me that Aurelio had any intention or urge to drive a ve-hicle. The shock was learning how out of touch I had been with his thinking and desires. I did fail López in that I never taught him to drive (maintaining a Jeep seemed much more out of the question in 1962 than it did in 1988 when his nephew served as primary driver for the Sáenz Peña settlement), just as I suspect I never quite man-aged to convey all the knowledge of spiritual insight expected of me.[4]

However, those failures clearly paled in comparison to my limita-tions as ethnographer. The point is that the Toba simply saw no cen-tral purpose or value in anthropology; it fit no cultural category. No logical role for ethnographic research had been established that made sense. On the contrary, it carried negative tones since the investiga-tor "took away" thoughts, ideas, knowledge, photographs, recordings, but gave nothing of significant value in return. Not only was anthro-pology irrelevant, it was distrusted. I found this to be particularly true during this first return trip and the following one in 1972, a time when few Argentine anthropologists had yet established sustained relationships in the community. Fortunately this situation has changed considerably owing to a new generation of anthropologists who have formed enduring social bonds with the Toba that reflect genuine concern for their welfare.

While I found rapport with old acquaintances easy to reestablish and our time together pleasant and informative, the limited amount of quality time we had to interact placed a constraint on our relationship that was not present during my original mission assignment. My initial idea upon my return to the Chaco in 1966 was that I would gain greater ethnographic insight because of my advanced training. Alas, I was soon to discover that I had better rapport and probably gained more genuine ethnographic insights while a missionary, despite the fact that the new role allowed me to gain some perspectives I had missed previously. This observation was difficult to share with professional colleagues who found it incredible given their impressions of missionaries. Such awareness only reinforced my image as pilgrim that I had hoped to shed when joining the profession.

The other major change in personal relationships in the field during this time was the establishment of closer ties with the scholarly community in Resistencia and Buenos Aires. These ties had a significant influence upon my new professional activity, contributing not only to my professional sense of identity but to my scholarly productions as well by introducing entirely new perspectives that I had not considered previously. Their presence in the diaries that follow indicate the nature of the relationships we established.

Scene 2: From an Ethnographer's Diaries and Fieldnotes

The following diary and fieldnote journal excerpts describe the nature of my sentiments and activities during several return trips to the Chaco as ethnographer. Although my missionary diary was kept for the simple purpose of recording my activities in the Chaco interior, the following ones have a more motivated objective. On my first return trip I needed to acquire information that would enable me to write a dissertation. Thus, the diary took on a professional tone and objective that was not characteristic of my missionary musings. In addition to the diary, I kept separate fieldnote journals on topics related to my research interests. I will occasionally cite pages from these notes in order to give the reader a sense of the relationship between the two documents and the kind of information recorded in each. The latter contains specific documentation relative to the dissertation and related research while the former depicts the contexts in which my activities took place. As I became farther removed from the Murdockian positivistic influence at Pitt, which placed priority on the notion of "raw data" in contrast to interactive experience, the two documents became combined and the diary took on decreasing significance. At that stage I kept the diary more as a matter of custom than for purposes of research.

The first diary is cited in greatest detail because it documents most clearly my changing role among the Toba as I moved from the intensive interactions of missionary days to increased contacts with professional colleagues and non-Toba friends. The change in diary form and content is most apparent in extensive and complete citations.

Resistencia, June 2–3, 1966

Met Prof. José Miranda in the museum at 9:30 to review Chaco collections. He later took me to the Land Office to order a large, detailed map of the Chaco. From there I went to Rev. Sarli's house [a Disciples of Christ minister], who accompanied me to the Office of Indian Affairs. The director (friend of Sarli) was in Lavalle; we made arrangements to meet him at 10:00 tomorrow morning. Spoke with Sarli on the street about his church's work with the Toba. Went downtown to buy airmail envelopes and paper. Returned to pick up map after buying 200 pesos stamped paper and writing a note addressed to the señor director. Ate *bife* [steak] for lunch that did not sit well.

After a short siesta, met José in the university; he introduced me to Professor Eldo Morresi, in charge of the indigenous census getting under way, who sought my direct participation. I declined, but offered to cooperate in any other way I could. If done well, it could be of enormous value to my study. Morresi also gave me a copy of the report of the First National Anthropological Convention held last May in Resistencia. Only a few copies remain. Met a school teacher assigned to Barrio Toba who said the Toba population has grown to nearly 1,500 as a result of the development of handicraft work. Later met Rev. Peiró [another Protestant minister] on the street, who agreed to meet me after dinner. He picked me up in his Jeep and we had a good conversation about the Toba. He promised to get data on the initial work of Lagar in Resistencia and brought me up to date on the current churches in the barrio. Took me back to the hotel around midnight.[5]

The different tone of this diary from the previous one is immediately apparent. Although unaware of it at the time, I was writing about *data* and I searched for documents that might help me understand historical events that had contributed to the current Toba situation. While I also compiled bibliographic materials during my original stay, my interest then was more in collecting than analyzing.

The excitement was in the chase, more in unearthing source materials than in their content per se, although I did read them. From this point on my approach to documents became analytical rather than merely acquisitive.

Writing the master's essay had forced me to examine the sources in an entirely new light. Now the need to write a dissertation would change not only my approach to documentary materials, but also the manner in which I interacted with the Toba in their various rural and urban settings. Now it was information I was seeking, not mere social interaction to promote Christian growth. My career as an anthropologist had been launched. An interest, the pursuit of information for the clear purpose of text production, now motivated all my actions. At the time I was oblivious to this change in diary style, although highly sensitive to potential changes in interpersonal relationships, which proved to be less dramatic than I had anticipated.

Clearly, contacts with anthropologists and other non-Toba personnel in communication with the Toba were becoming central to my recorded activities.

> Met J. Miranda at the museum at 9:00, where we went over more prehistoric material on the Chaco. At 10:00 sharp I was in the señor director's office at Indian Affairs. He arrived at 10:45 and shortly after that Sarli appeared. A number of Toba came by for shoes; we recognized one another and the greetings began. Highly emotional scene. Director Calvo was very helpful and explained the program as best he could in the short time available. He offered to continue at 7:00 P.M. I went to Señora Marquez's house, the Catholic woman working with the Red Cross in the barrio, who explained her work. She was also forty-five minutes late for our appointment.

The experience of greeting old Toba friends in the office of Indian Affairs was one that is still clearly etched in my mind. These were the first Toba I encountered in my new role as ethnographer. They had no idea I had returned, much less that I would be there, and I had no thought of meeting them. Our mutual excitement was clearly evident to all as they began speaking to me in Toba and I responded in kind. What a way to mark our new relationship. Both of us in the Office of Indian Affairs where neither of us had been during my mission stay. The high emotions I refer to also concerned my uncertainty about how this bond of friendship might be interpreted by governing officials who observed us but could not understand what was being said. They expressed astonishment at the emotional intensity of our interaction.

The complaints about late appointments indicate the extent to which my temporal clock was already rewound according to North American standards. How quickly one reverts to the tyranny of firmly formed internalized culture.

> After lunch I tried to contact Mrs. Duddi, who taught the Toba their basketry, but could not locate her. I checked the bus schedule and found one leaving for Sáenz Peña at 5:00 P.M., stopped by Aerolineas to learn that my airmail package would not arrive before Saturday and the office would not be open until Monday, so I made a quick decision to leave for Sáenz Peña. Called Sarli and asked him to give my regrets to the señor director, paid my hotel bill, and rushed to the bus station, arriving just as the bus was leaving. Bought ticket on board. A lovely new bus ride of two and one-half hours over paved road deposited me at the new bus depot across from Derka Brothers Garage, where my Jeep had been bought and serviced. Paid a boy twenty-five pesos to help carry my bags to the Buckwalter house, where I was met with open arms. They had already eaten, but Lois Buckwalter insisted on preparing fried potatoes and Spam with a big tomato salad that I could not finish. Showed my pictures of the family and we talked.
>
> Later Albert and son Tim accompanied me to our old house now occupied by the Kratz family. We only stayed a few minutes since the kids were getting ready for bed. Returned to the Buckwalters', where we put my stuff in the Jeep and headed for Hotel Chaco. I wanted to stay at Residencial but they are no longer in business as of Tuesday! The room was filled with mosquitoes and the bath was a mile away. I doubt that I will stay here long. The Kratzes invited me for breakfast and to a picnic tomorrow, along with the Buckwalters. After Albert brought me to the hotel we sat and talked for two hours until midnight. Will meet Juan Acosta, who is visiting with the Kratzes, tomorrow morning.
>
> Note. The paved road to S.P. has changed the Chaco a lot, although the town looks exactly as it did before. Can't wait to see Perríns and other old friends tomorrow after the picnic. I underestimated the nostalgia and sense of excitement that would be generated upon returning to S.P.

This entry fails to communicate the profound emotions I felt upon returning to Sáenz Peña, accounting for my need to get there as quickly as possible once it became apparent that my baggage would be delayed. Nor does it communicate the thrill I felt when riding a modern bus over paved road to get there. A trip that took over four hours when the roads were in decent shape, an unpredictable amount of time when they were cut with mud holes, was now accomplished in a comfortable two and one-half hour ride. The transformation was sensational, yet I recall the overwhelming impression that the city and people remained the same. It was truly a homecoming.

Sáenz Peña, June 4–9, 1966

Mosquitos, burning spiral mosquito chaser, poor night. As I descended the steps, Jim Kratz was on his way up. He felt "ashamed" that I had spent my first night in a hotel, calling it "a cold reception" and inviting me to get my stuff and sleep in the front room with their son Jimmy. I consented. Had an emotional visit with Juan Acosta at our old house in the Toba room. Picnic celebrating the Kratz wedding anniversary was nice. A nurse from Castelli also participated. Had my second emotional encounter of the day with Edgardo and Olga Perrín at Español Theater; they invited me to dinner and asked me to stay with them. They seemed awfully pleased to see me. Edgardo took me to Kratzes after midnight in his new Valliant. Also saw many old friends in the theater and on the street. If Lois were here it would be like old times.

The excitement of seeing Toba friend and preacher Juan Acosta was clearly on the same order as that of seeing our very close friends the Perríns. During our first stay it had been difficult at first for our friends in town to understand the close relationships we developed with the Toba, but over time they not only came to accept it but to respect and appreciate it. No such relationship, however, developed between any of them and the Toba, which is a commentary on the social distance that continues to separate whites from Indians in the Chaco.

I had looked forward to seeing Edgardo and Olga but underestimated their exceptionally warm reception. The movie was already in action when I was ushered up to their seats. The hugs and greetings interrupted everything for those in the immediate area but no one voiced an objection since we were known by all and they understood the excitement of the moment.

The diary report of an open-arms reception at the Buckwalters stands in contrast to Kratz's comment about a cold reception. Apparently I was unaware of the contradiction between the two comments at the time. My recollection is that the reception was warmer than I had anticipated. I was somewhat anxious about how our former missionary colleagues would receive me since I had not only left the mission but challenged the basic philosophy that sponsored it. Perhaps it was this uncertainty that motivated the comment about an open-arms reception. The fact that I was not invited to stay with the Buckwalters came as no surprise; it was a symbolic act framing my new status. Nevertheless, I was delighted to accept the Kratzes' invitation, especially following my bout with mosquitoes, despite the fact that they had less available space. On later visits I did stay with the Buckwalters and we became increasingly comfortable with our separate relationships and roles with the Toba.

> To Legua 15 with the Kratz family.[6] José Durán is his old self. Kids have really grown. Carlos and Casimiro Temai were in church for the first time in years. Carlos claimed he was there because he had a dream in which he was told that "someone special" would arrive to visit! José also dreamed last night about our daughters, but didn't know they were ours until I arrived to show their photos. Got good kinship update on the José Durán and Celestino Pereira families. Everyone seemed delighted to see me and sent greetings to Lois. The photos were fondled by all. Stopped at Aguará on the way back. Miitaqte was her usual enthusiastic self. Talked with Jim and Dorothy Kratz until late.

Several families in Legua 15 had sought to maintain ties with us after we had returned to the United States. While I knew most everyone and their links to one another, this was my first attempt to construct a kinship chart that allowed me to fill in the names of the newly born and newly wed since we left the Chaco. No doubt this reflected Murdock's influence and my Pitt training. The kinship update became a routine throughout the summer as I traveled from one community to another.

At this point I continued to pursue personal relationships and ties developed during my missionary days in much the same way I had previously. My interest in kinship took on a data-oriented focus, however, as I searched for structure and order that might provide the basis for a better understanding of migrations and intercommunity communication.

Toba discourse about dreams anticipating my return to the Chaco is nicely documented here. It is of interest that the local preacher had even met our daughters in a dream, but did not know who they were until I supplied the photographs.

> Spent A.M. with the Buckwalter family packing books I had left behind and shipping the first four packages. Talked with Juan Chifa, my old friend and hunting companion, about renting Buckwalter's old Jeep that he now owns; he agreed since he is not us-

ing it at the moment. Made plans to leave for Colonia Chaco [La Reducción] tomorrow. Lunch with Kratz family. Empanadas with the Lesa family in P.M.; also saw more friends and acquaintances on the street. Dorothy Kratz fixed me a medicine kit and suggested some food items to buy. Good talk with the Kratzes about Toba acculturation conflicts; to bed by 10:00 P.M.

Although the original diary did not report the manner in which I went about preparing for a trip to the country during missionary days, in retrospect I am amazed how similar it was to the activities described here and on the following morning. Clearly I was repeating old habits. The one major difference was that I packed less provisions and did not arrange for Toba traveling companions.

My strong recollection is that I was highly pleased with the warm welcome of friends in town but impatient to travel to a Toba community where I could interact on my own. All of my communications with the Toba thus far had been in contexts associated with prior mission activity. It was time to get down to serious ethnographic research on my dissertation.

To La Reducción, June 10–17, 1966

Spent A.M. in S.P. buying matches, cheese, cookies, crackers, oranges, bread, dried fruit, sugar, canned meat, and Off for mosquitoes. Gassed up Jeep and filled water can. Lunched with Buckwalters and a son of José Carmelo, who had arrived to visit. Stopped by to wish Laura Perrín a happy birthday and left her my last pack of Hershey bars. Traveled to Quitilipi to visit René Sotelo and learn about the Friends of Indígenes Society. He provided good statistical data on La Reducción. Drove to Naño Mendoza's house and set up tent before he returned from work at the Administration Carpenter Shop. Visited until 7:00 P.M., when we all went to school at the Central Administration, where he and his wife are taking night classes. Returned to Naño's for *maté* and to bed by 11:00.

The ambivalent sentiments I felt on this first foray into the interior on my own are well disguised here. While it was exciting to visit former friends and acquaintances, Lois had always been there on prior trips to take charge of meals and provide companionship. When she did not travel with me, I was either with Buckwalter, Kratz, or Toba companions, usually preachers. Here I played it safe by going to the home of an acquaintance who knew the white world well and who would be able to comprehend my needs and interests.

La Reducción, which most non-Toba refer to as Colonia Chaco, is a large area, and Sotelo's data on the number of Toba and Mocoví households were an important addition to my knowledge about an aboriginal settlement that I had visited frequently but not extensively. Our visits had been confined primarily to the homes of four or five church leaders.

My tiny tent served as a good spot to review notes (by flashlight) and reflect on the day's activity during the summer of 1966. It also provided a touch of privacy that my revived cultural sense of proxemics demanded.

> Spent the A.M. at the administration buildings of the colony and visiting with Naño. In the P.M. I helped cut firewood in the forest, as it was turning cold. He provided good information on his family relationships and on a powerful spirit (*'oiquiaxai*) healing of his wife. I contributed bread, oranges, and cookies for the evening meal. Planned trip to Bailón Domingo the following day.

Note the statement about good information rather than my mission diary's frequent comments on people's moods or the comforts and discomforts associated with food, dust, mud, and mosquitoes. While I had known some of Naño's family members previously, I did not know all of them; most still lived in Espinillo, where I seldom visited. The initial diary made numerous references to Carlos Rodríguez, the father of his first wife. His current wife was of the Gómez family, whom Lois and I had known quite well, and also a relative of Osvaldo Gómez in Buenos Aires, whom I would learn to know on subsequent trips. The construction of a kinship chart enabled me to see connections between family members and their various Chaco locations in clearer perspective.

> During the night a big storm came up. I took down the tent at 2:00 A.M. since it was in a low spot, called Naño, and told him I would drive to Quitilipi until the storm was over. Found a hotel but not the owner. Slept in front seat of Jeep. It didn't rain! At 5:30 A.M. I explained to the owner what I was doing there and returned to Naño's place just as they were getting up. An old uncle had arrived: he provided a lot of information on the 1924 uprising south of Machagai in which he had participated. Later visited a highly acculturated neighbor who explained why he does not attend church. Said what he reads in the Bible and sees in the churches are two different things.
> Left midmorning with Naño, wife, and daughter Matilda.

> Stopped by the Olivera family's (her folks) and left wife and daughter. Continued on to Antonio Domingo's with Naño. Arrived just as Bailón Domingo was leaving for church at Alberto Flores's (Antonio and his wife were in S.P.). Took two daughters, Naño, and Bailón on the running board. Could not get Jeep to church due to water. Walked through the lagoon. Took good notes on the service, which lasted from 10:30 until 3:00 P.M., including a healing ceremony. Returned to Antonio's and set up tent. Naño walked home. Drank *maté* and talked. At dusk, Antonio and his wife arrived. To bed early. Lightning flashed most of the night, but no rain.

It will be recalled that the 1924 uprising was mentioned on my first extended journey among the Toba. However, this was the first time I realized the significance of those stories I had heard repeatedly all over the Chaco. Here I was near the spot where the encounter with whites had occurred, and I was speaking with people who had personal memories that were obviously deeply ingrained. The significance of this event for my dissertation became apparent to me on this day. I determined to investigate it further in subsequent interviews and in historical records when I returned to Resistencia and Buenos Aires.

Once again I found myself sitting in on church services. Walking through the muddy lagoon to get there was no fun, either. As the journal entry will demonstrate, I documented every action of the *culto* in order to catch something I might have missed previously due to familiarity.

> Up at dawn before others. Washed and made tea with sugar. Had a good session with Bailón in which he told about olden days and his experience with the church. Antonio also contributed his perspective. Walked with Antonio to where he wants to put a road. Took pictures of Antonio's wife washing clothes in the lagoon. Studied the Sotelo report. About 4:00 P.M. Aurelio Villalba arrived and I got family data from him. Got some information on his escape during the 1924 battle. Had evening service with fifteen to twenty present. Mosquitos were terrible. Thunder and lightning during the night again, but no rain.

My days were beginning to settle into a routine. I was surprised at my own independence and enjoying it immensely. Wasting no time collecting data, I found myself constantly with pen in hand.

> Good session in A.M. with Bailón on his knowledge of shamanism and conversion to Christianity. Ate *tortas* and left with him for

Martillo. On road we passed Ciriaco Gómez, changed our plans, and went to Jertrudio's, whose wife is a sister of Clemente Gómez. Got life history material and completed family tree (from previous materials). Went to pick up Jertrudio's mother and agreed with Bailón to meet him at Ciriaco's church later on. Intense conversation with his brother Fernando, who wants nothing to do with the church.

Drove his mother home and went to meet Bailón. Took down testimony of Jertrudio's wife, who was once a *curandera* (healer). Still gets strange visions even though she attempts to reject the "old power." It began to storm and lightning in the evening and I reluctantly set up my tent inside the house in an unoccupied room. Kept knocking some animal (frog?) off of tent during the night. It rained heavily; fortunately I was inside.

A "good session" involved life histories, family trees, and data collection about the *culto* and shamanism. Nothing about the length or quality of a *culto*, however, as in the missionary diary. The references to data, clear examples of my Pitt training, disappear on later field trips.

It should be noted that Bailón was another one of my favorite persons from missionary days. Not only had he been a shaman who reoriented his practice upon conversion to Christianity on a visit to the old Mennonite mission at Aguará, but he was also *dirigente* of a *culto* in his home community. It was rare for a former active shaman to become leader of a *culto*. His leadership qualities were not as overtly apparent as those of Agusto Soria or Juan Pablo, for example, but he was highly respected for the quiet yet steady direction he gave to the local congregation. Truly he was a saint in the Catholic sense of the term, a person most highly respected by those who knew him intimately. As a subsequent entry from my notebook will record, however, I became annoyed with him at one point on this trip.

Up early and took down tent. Made tea, ate *tortas,* and visited. Later went to Ciriaco's place and visited there, getting good family tree material. Was supposed to meet Juan Acosta but he was in the forest cutting trees. Went to look him up. While on break, got his story of visions and conversion to Christianity. Explained that I am also a salaried worker, and no longer supported by the church. Everyone seemed impressed, but perplexed. All concurred that a good believer who preaches should not be obliged to work for a living! Left logging spot and visited with Juan Garay briefly. Visited a *mesti-*

zo farmer near Bailón who explained the history of the reservation from his perspective; he also volunteered why he is not, and has no intention of being, a church member. Returned to Bailón and said good-byes. Drove to the Central Administration to meet the administrator, but he had gone to Resistencia. Said good-byes to Naño and wife and proceeded to Quitilipi, registering in a cheap hotel.

Parked Jeep off street and walked to see René Sotelo and Dr. Burlli, who explained the Friends of Indígenes movement. The doctor provided good data on Toba diseases and their use of the clinic. Agreed to meet and discuss more tomorrow.

The choice of community for this first visit certainly influenced the direction of my research and eventual dissertation due to the emphasis placed in the community upon the 1924 uprising. I was also delighted to obtain more objective data on regional health and family resources provided by Sotelo and Burlli, which my Pitt mentors would be expecting. We developed a good relationship since they provided statistical data I lacked and I offered knowledge about Toba understandings and practices that they desired. They also contributed significantly to my understanding of how white people in the Chaco viewed governmental policies and practices in the territory reserved for Indians. Their research supplied significant information on the number of Toba, Mocoví, and whites living in the colony, together with their implement and animal resources, which I had no access to previously.

Went to school where Sotelo is director and got good information on land tenure practices in the province as it affects aborigines. Dr. Burlli also arrived. Talked until noon, when I was interviewed by a correspondent for El Territorio. Late lunch in hotel. To Sotelo's home in P.M. for more conversation with him and Burlli. Explained Toba kin terms and extended family practices. Got good perspective on their views of Toba experience with evangelicalism. Not all positive. Returned to hotel and planned to travel to Bajo Hondo, but the weather threatened. Decided to write notes and travel tomorrow.

Left early for Bajo Hondo. Could not arrive at the church for water. Walked through water only to discover that everyone was out harvesting! The road was completely cut; impossible to continue on to Camilo Sánchez's. Returned to S.P. Had good reception and lunch with Buckwalters. Asado in my honor in the evening with Julio Lesa family.

On this first trip to the country on my own, it is clear that I panicked initially when I escaped to Quitilipi at the threat of rain. However, had I not promised to return the Jeep, I would certainly have stayed longer once I got the hang of the daily routine. The week had slipped by more quickly and easily than I had anticipated. Clearly I was enjoying myself and getting much valuable information at the same time.

It will be observed, however, that I now had categories of information to acquire. Conversations were determined primarily by my research topics rather than by the Toba, as occurred during missionary days. This obviously constrained the type of ethnographic information I would acquire. In time this observation would flame doubts about the ethnographic exercise in which I engaged initially with enthusiasm.

My previous experience proved advantageous in that I didn't have to spend time establishing rapport and figuring out daily patterns of interaction. On the other hand, that experience shaped the nature of my interaction and determined to a considerable extent the information I was able to acquire. The dissertation proposal also narrowed the focus of my discussions, which in turn revised and redirected the scope of my study. In order to illustrate further the nature of information collected, I will include a few pages from my fieldnote journal.

Fieldnotes, Resistencia, June 11–18, 1966

In a discussion with Naño this P.M. he mentioned that the churches dance very little in La Reducción because the people want to hear the preaching. I asked him what churches were active at the present time and he named the following:

1. Luís Salteño, composed of both Mocoví and *criollos*—Beams of Light.
2. Camilo Sánchez, Toba—Church of God Pentecostal.
3. Luciano Ramírez, Toba—IEU (no services at present time).
4. A new one in the administration of mixed participation, but he was not certain who was *dirigente*.
5. Victoriano Leguisa, Toba—Beams of Light.
6. Marcelino Olivera, Toba—Church of God Pentecostal.
7. Bailón Domingo, Toba—IEU.
8. Alberto Flores, Toba—IEU.
9. Juan Acosta, Toba—IEU.
10. Ciriaco Ascencio, Toba—affiliation unknown.
11. Luís Canteros/Armando Garay, Toba—IEU. (Former quit after wife died)

12. Eleuterio López, Toba—Independent (no services at the present time).

This account of churches and leadership in La Reducción gives an overview of the extensive nature of church formation in an aboriginal colony with a population according to Sotelo and Burlli (1963) of 2,258. They also reported 268 *mestizos* (first generation offspring of Indians and whites) and 332 *criollos*. The latter, with the exception of administrative personnel, were not supposed to occupy colony land, but in practice did. One way a *criollo* could acquire entree to the colony was to marry a Toba woman with access to land.[7] Once in the colony, he could bring in other members of his family and eventually take the land out of Indian control.

> Early this A.M. shortly after we had gotten up, Naño's wife's uncle Toledo Gómez (first cousin of Ramón Gómez in Legua 17 and brother to Olivera whose real name is Gómez but he changed it due to the fact that a murderer had the same name) arrived on horseback. After greetings and a long wait I asked him if he remembered the killing at Matanza (La Reducción) in 1924.
>
> He said he did, that he was there when it happened. The Toba and Mocoví had grouped together under the direction of Cacique Macha' who proved to be a "deceiver." He performed miracles to keep the bullets from killing the people, but he could not be trusted. He had the power, but he used it for his own purposes rather than for the people. "For this reason people follow the gospel because it does not deceive." There was a lot of dissension between aborigines and whites about selling their cotton. "To equalize things," the aborigines killed a number of *criollo* cattle. Later on they killed twelve whites with bows and arrows, lances, and clubs. It was after that when the army came and killed about three hundred men, women, and children.[8] After that Toledo escaped with others to the north, only coming out of the forest weeks later in the area of Legua 17. The cacique fled to Resistencia and died much later. He was an *'oiquiaxai* and spoke with voices from below the earth. Toledo's final words on the topic were, "for this reason we are all evangelicals, which teaches good things." However, this man does not go to church nor take any part in it. In fact, he demonstrated very little knowledge about the church.

The discussion with Toledo Gómez served to orient my dissertation problem in a particular manner. As such, it played an essential role in my research. The contrast between deceptive shamanic leadership that resulted in death/destruction and the gospel that does not deceive was a comparison I had heard repeatedly during missionary travels. When it showed up here in my discussions with a person who was not active in the church, as it did later with other nonchurch respondents, the comparison seemed ethnographically significant.

In my dissertation I called upon this indigenous comparison to document the nature of the new beliefs that "mobilized participants for action" (Smelser 1962).[9] I argued that "structural conduciveness" in which "the nature of the Toba world view (magico-religious), the structural arrangement of the colonial situation (exploitation with no mechanism for redress), and traditional channels of communication (open and constant exchange between communities) contributed to the emergence and spread of Pentecostalism among the Toba" (1967:176–77).

A careful reading of my analysis will show that the loss of faith in shamanism that I documented was not in the nature of power nor in the position, but rather in the way that power was put into practice and legitimated. Shamanism is still very much alive among the Toba, it simply takes on new forms as *dirigentes* (the new shamans) legitimate their position through identification with foreign mission organizations and, more importantly, the new "Companion Spirit" (the Holy Spirit) associated with the gospel. The contrast I understood the Toba to postulate was one between a deceptive exercise of power for personal ends as opposed to its genuine utilization for the benefit of the community. In other words, the contrast was in the ends toward which power was directed.

> Naño spoke of Victoriano Leguisa, who was the first to preach the gospel here in La Reducción. He claims that Juan Lagar [North American Pentecostal preacher] arrived here as well. He said that Victoriano had been a troublemaker, always fighting and getting in trouble with the authorities, who often took him prisoner. "But he accepted the gospel that Lagar announced and quit fighting." Nevertheless, the police continued to pursue him for the gospel that he accepted because they did not want him to be an evangelical. But he told them that he would never leave the gospel even if they killed him and he asked if they would prefer that he return to the life he had previously. "The police did not want the people to convert to the gospel."

From the time I first arrived in the Chaco I did not find this latter assertion to be generally true. Most police affirmed that the Toba were easier to "manage" since they had become Christians. Nevertheless, there were still some communities that encountered opposition to local assemblies from regional police, which was one of the reasons the official *fichero* was received by the Toba with such enthusiasm. It gave their meetings legitimacy, protecting them from the harassment they sometimes experienced from local officials.

Church service at Albert Flores's. Service opened at 10:45 with eleven songs and two prayers which lasted for one hour. One lady limped into church, barely able to walk, with a sick baby. She sat up front and nursed her baby face to face with the song leaders who were standing before her. Everyone had arrived on horseback except those of us who came in the Jeep and walked through water when the Jeep could not make it all the way. The building is in pieces, with a roof on one side only. The benches have no backs. When the service began there were thirty-five inside and six to eight young boys outside. Later there were forty-eight inside and ten to twelve outside. The young boys outside, and some people inside, talked aloud during the service.

At 11:45 the speeches began. First I spoke, then a song, then Naño spoke, followed with another song. A young man then spoke about sound doctrine and spoke mostly of healing from Titus 2 and 2 Timothy 4. Two young girls were then called up front to lead a chorus. Flores then called on a man to speak, but a woman stood up and started talking, giving her "testimony"; she rubbed herself all over the front part of her body as she spoke. Then Luís Arce spoke without an intervening song. Afterward, Naño led a new song. Next Sibrano Chico (in necktie) spoke about healing, led a chorus, and spoke some more. He led four more choruses, calling up the girls to help. Bailón then explained Holy Communion. Prayer. A hymn was sung during the distribution of bread, then Bailón spoke further and everyone ate their piece of bread. Prayer. Reading of Scripture. Singing of "The Blood Can Cleanse You" while wine was distributed in one small glass. The person taking it around often spoke before offering it. The young boys outside who appeared to be making fun of the singing and preaching thus far all drew near to take communion, laughing to each other as they took the wine. Everyone took bread and wine, including the children. The power is in the stuff itself. After they partook, the young men withdrew to talk and laugh again. After all had drunk but before he did, Bailón spoke about the healing power of the wine. Prayer. Chorus. Bailón turned service over to Alberto Flores, who spoke a while and then called the congregation to their feet as he announced the final song. At this juncture a man spoke up and asked that his daughter and granddaughter be healed. He said they were at a place they should not have been and on the way home the cart upset and spilled them all. A snake scared them but did not bite anyone. He said they wanted to be reinstated. Everyone affirmed approval. A young white boy [the only other white person present] gave a testimony of healing. A healing song followed. The leaders laid hands on the sick woman who sat up front and offered a long prayer of healing. The service ended with a final farewell healing song.

The above description of a church service is one example of more than a dozen I recorded in 1966. Having participated in hundreds of these meetings during missionary days, I was concerned not to overlook crucial features of the *culto* that might help me identify its basic structure; therefore the detailed account. At the time I was toying with the notion of contrastive sets and immediate constituents with an eye toward an ethnoscience analysis. As it turned out, I used these descriptions in a 1971 article on the *culto* and left it at that.

Little manipulations. When I arrived at Bailón D's on Sunday A.M. with Naño, Bailón was about to leave for Holy Communion at Alberto Flores's place. I wanted to go on foot or horseback since I remembered the mud from before. They insisted that the road was dry and Bailón begged me to take his daughter, who had just returned from Buenos Aires, in the Jeep because she was "sick." I drove. There was mud! We had to leave the Jeep and finish the trip on foot through mud and water. After church was over the girls apparently could not wait for us so they took off on foot without advising us, including the sick one who seemed perfectly okay. I learned later she had a pimple or something on her foot which apparently was now okay, although no one made much of it.

On Sunday night Antonio (Bailón's brother) and wife arrived on foot from Machagai. They had been to Sáenz Peña and told how Brother Jertrudio had hurried to return home because Lois and I might be there for Sunday evening service. They all thought we *must* go there right away because they would be expecting us and holding services. It didn't suit my plans and I did not go. I later learned that there had been no Sunday evening service, although there might have been had we arrived. The next morning Antonio sent his two daughters with the wagon to bring back oranges from Ascencio's. This was the apparent real reason for his hurry to get to Martillo! I later learned from Lois Buckwalter that they claimed to have made the trip to S.P. to see me, whereas I learned in La

Reducción that they had the trip planned for a long time before they knew I was anywhere in the territory.

This journal comment about deceptions is significant because it demonstrates some annoyances that I experienced on the trip that do not appear in the diary. Comments critical of the Toba do not appear in my diaries, although slight frustrations can sometimes be detected beneath the surface. I would have totally forgotten this incident had it not been recorded here. My current recollection of interactions with the Toba, both as missionary and anthropologist, are strongly positive, although Lois and I were obviously aware of having been manipulated at times, as the diaries indicate.

Lois and I sometimes found Toba visits to our home in town overwhelming during our first fieldwork, particularly when we had other activities scheduled that had to be interrupted and rescheduled or when the groups were large and the scheduled stay indefinite. However, this statement of frustration is clearer than any I recall feeling or making during our mission assignment. Perhaps I was more free to examine and express my frustrations in my new role than I was during the years with the mission.

To Legua 7 and Riacho de Oro, June 25–27, 1966

Jim Kratz invited Carlos Moreno and me on this trip. The road was terrible and when we arrived the preacher was absent. Returned to Luís Estrada's in Lavalle, but he was also away. Spent the night by the river. Sitting around campfire before retiring, Carlos told how the preacher Luís Escalante had been killed by a shaman in L. 17.

Missionary trips to Toba communities continued to be focused on church leaders. If the preacher was not present the visit was called off, limiting the range of social interaction in the community.

Escalante had been an active church leader in Quinta 8, Sáenz Peña, and Legua 17; he appears frequently in my first diary due to his travels with us. I had known he was accused of not returning borrowed items, but I had no idea his reputation had reached the point it apparently did. Such accusations were not uncommon among a people who have a tradition of use and consumption based on sharing. It is interesting to note that Moreno made no reference to Escalante's role as church leader, despite having participated regularly in services under his direction in the growing community at the edge of Sáenz Peña.

Crossed Bermejo at 6:00 A.M. on ferry and drove to Bailón Suárez's at Riacho de Oro, an old-timer who had a lot of memories to tell.[10] Attended three-hour church service in the A.M. and visited until evening, returning to Lavalle for a night service at Nolasco Rodríguez's. Spent the night under a tree on his patio.

Up at 6:30 for discussion about how the gospel had spread among the Toba. Juan Tomás Palmer was the first missionary these people knew. But the big factor in mass conversion from their point of view was Chief Pedro Martínez, who had urged his people to join. Definite correlation between material goods and religion in their minds. Left midmorning for S.P. but had Jeep trouble on the way. Big dinner with Kratz family in evening. Read *Time* magazine and prepared for next day's trip by bus to Miraflores.

Kratz demonstrated an interest in ethnographic observation on this trip and I discovered that he had useful ethnographic notes, which he generously shared with me later. For example, he observed the value placed on the male provider role in selection of a mate; in sharing, voluntary gifts involve no obligation to give something in return while requests do require return favors; on the behavior of chiefs, he quoted José Durán as saying, "I am not a chief, I am a listener." These and other insights were helpful to confirm and elaborate upon my own observations on a broad range of topics.

It was exciting to travel again with Carlos Moreno, who had accompanied Lois and me on various excursions in the early 1960s. The following journal entry provides more texture concerning the nature of data obtained on this trip.

Fieldnotes, Lavalle, June 25–27, 1966

On the road to Lavalle with Kratz and Moreno (*Soxonaic*) the latter told about how the ancient people would call upon powerful gods to help them. They would pray at any time of the day when they needed help. He recalled his father calling out, *"Huapogoxoyi, aŷim 'autauan"* (Huapogoxoyi, help me). He spoke of another shaman, Tapchi, who had received ten sick persons, curing six of them immediately and putting the others on the road to health in a few weeks. Sitting around the fire that night he said that Luís Escalante was killed by the shaman Malchin in Legua 17. First the shaman made Luís crazy by working over a pine needle and throwing it away with the command to go cause him harm. Luís managed to save himself on this first attempt but the shaman later worked over a piece of meat eaten by Luís and this time he died. Moreno said the shaman did it because Luís appropriated a wagon and sold it in S.P.

I sensed no doubts about the continual presence and power of the shaman among those who participated in this discussion. Not only was the killing act reported, but also the means by which it was accomplished, information that was not readily shared during my previous stay. While I had heard such stories often, the fact that sorcery was practiced on a close personal friend who also had been a preacher was disconcerting. The crucial role of sorcery in the maintenance of social control is nicely documented here.

Nolasco Rodríguez spoke a lot about the early days when only the Toba lived in this area. He recalled that in 1933 Juan Tomás Palmer arrived from Espinillo in a cart to announce that he came to preach the Word of God because the people had not heard of the gospel. Old Cacique Bachorí did not agree because he thought it was a lie; he did not trust the message. Palmer gave the people seeds of corn, cotton, peanuts, sweet potato, manioc, and beans. There were those who worked and those who didn't. He taught the people to be responsible, to work. Now the people are thinking that they must wait for major help. "We work but we don't earn anything. That is why we are awaiting help." Palmer conducted the services; the people did not take part.

Nolasco also stated that Cacique Pedro Martínez rode around on horseback and started churches in many places. He would pick out a young man and say, "This one will be your *dirigente*," one that understood Spanish. He had a secretary by the name of Victorio López that helped him. Nolasco also accompanied Cacique Martínez in his travels throughout the Chaco and Formosa provinces. They took Bibles and song books to people to help them start churches. Nolasco said that Pedro Martínez learned from Juan Lagar. He also stated that President Perón named Martínez general chief and put him in charge of the region. Nolasco stated that he is planning to travel around the Chaco and ask the people if they would like to choose him. If they don't, he will pray more. He says they are waiting to see what will come of the IEU. They think a center is important, but they fear that the money will be stolen. He claimed that all his people accuse Aurelio López [IEU President and general representative of the organization] of being a thief.

These were communities that I had visited infrequently during missionary days, thus I gained a perspective on church history and activity in the region that I did not have previously. The fact that the discussions demonstrated a clear connection between material goods and church formation is of interest in that the association was stronger than I expected. At least on this occasion the connection between cargo and church life was clear-cut.

Once again, ambivalent sentiments about a center were expressed. Aurelio López, the super communicator of the IEU, had a stroke several years later that terminated his ability to speak. In light of the accusation cited above, it is not surprising that the symbolic nature of his illness prompted speculation about sorcery as the cause of this affliction. It should be noted, nevertheless, that Nolasco's accusation of the IEU president was not entirely uninterested in that he expressed an ambition to occupy the position held by Aurelio.

To Castelli and Pampa Argentina, June 28–30, 1966

Bus to Castelli. Left things in dingy room at Hotel Santafesino and proceeded to Dr. Cicchetti's, where I received a warm welcome, an invitation for dinner, and offer of their guest room. Got things and spent the night. It was very cold.

Up at 6:30, breakfast with the doctor, and on to Pampa Argentina in his truck. Visited with Juan Fernández and Gregorio Díaz; Juan Pablo was not home. Went to Francisco Rodríguez's later, carrying my big duffle bag and tent. Good information on diets and early church formation. Froze around the fire. Set up tent and went to bed early.

Cold A.M., but beautiful day. Francisco took my things by horse while his wife and I walked to the administration. Juan Pablo still had not returned so I talked with the administrator, Fernández, and Díaz. Dr. Cicchetti came for me at 4:00 P.M. Got information on cotton production and literacy from Mrs. Cicchetti. Spoke with nurse about the TB situation. Bought galleta and oranges for trip next day.

This unannounced surprise visit to Pampa Argentina was enlightening in that I managed to speak with the regional white administrator and with local family heads with whom I had had little contact during previous missionary visits, given that we always stayed with Chief Juan Pablo or the Rodríguez family. Apparently the chief was losing strength and influence, although they said his wit was as sharp and biting as ever. I saw how my perception of the community had been shaped previously through our close association with the Pablo and Rodríguez families, which limited contact with other members of the community. Perhaps the chief's influence was never as strong as I had assumed. This observation highlights the limitations in perceptions of community life based strictly upon my missionary years. In this instance anthropological field experience broadened the missionary perspective.

Most Toba communities were held together by a family head or chief during our early years with the mission. The provincial Office of Indian Affairs did support a small contingent of white administrators throughout the Chaco who responded to a central office in Colonia Chaco (La Reducción). This particular community had an administrative officer whom I had not met previously. His major responsibility was to encourage agricultural development and provide loans for seeds and equipment. The idea was to collect the loans during harvest time, but they never quite got paid. He seemed congenial enough, although his expectations for community development seemed low, based no doubt on experience. I did detect an attitude of authoritarianism, which seems to go with the territory among regional whites who have administrative responsibilities over Indians.

To Miraflores, July 1–6, 1966

Left with Dr. Cicchetti, who stopped to give injections en route. He dropped me off at Hilario Cabrera's, where I unloaded my things. Hilario was sick so the doctor took him back to the hospital in Castelli. Mariano and Manuel Naporichi and José Benítez are all camped here with their families. I spent the day visiting, getting family tree updates and data on diet and sexual practices. Antonia cooked a fabulous meal. Slept in tent; heavy frost.

Spent A.M. getting more information. Taken by cart at noon to storekeeper Veleff's, where I met Dr. Griva and an anthropologist named Edgardo Cordeu from Buenos Aires. In the P.M. I helped them work with Cayetano Burgos, who was describing sex habits, a topic about which I know very little, although some of the information seemed dubious. They shared their barbecue with me. Got a point of view from Veleff and Reyes, another storekeeper, about dealings with Toba that provided another perspective. They claimed the Toba attempt to cheat them, such as when they dip arrow quills in mud to make them weigh more. I explained some of the complaints the Toba have with them and why *they* frequently feel cheated. At 11:00 P.M. Reyes took me back to Hilario's place in his car.

Weather warmed during the night. Eggs and onion for breakfast! Walked to church with Mariano and Manuel while Antonia took my sleeping bag and mosquito netting in the cart. Singing was already in progress when we arrived. Dr. Cicchetti, a nurse, and the two scholars from Buenos Aires arrived later. I was given a tremendous welcome and asked to speak first. Under some inspiration, I spoke for more than thirty minutes almost exclusively in Toba! Words tumbled out that I had not thought about in years. There was communion but no dancing on orders of the doctor. Spent afternoon with Chief Agusto Soria and Antonio Leiva until evening service. Talked late into the night with Agusto. Slept in church on ground with netting. The tent was back at Hilario's. Warm night; nearly fell asleep talking.

It will be recalled that Lois and I had a special attachment to Miraflores. Most frustrating was having to wait until the third day to get to see my old friend Agusto Soria. The overwhelming excitement I felt upon seeing him and the others all together in the *culto* came bursting out in my speech. Its length appears to contradict an earlier statement that I only spoke briefly about personal greetings and my research in *culto* ceremonies. This represented an exception. I honestly cannot recall what I talked about, but I do remember being inspired. It seemed strange to be in a Miraflores service with no dancing, which I was told was due to an order from Dr. Cicchetti, who disapproved of it. I was impressed by his influence over the *culto*, which is more than either Albert or I ever had or wanted. His health work with the Toba was highly influential and respected by all people in the region.

Spent all day with Agusto getting information on how he and his people were pushed out of Castelli and given land in Miraflores in early 1930s. Recorded extremely lucid and valuable material on shamanic healing practices, witchcraft, etc. The Cabreras sent a cart for me in the late afternoon, stopping en route at Klosters's (another store owner), who gave a more sympathetic, but still paternalistic, view of the Toba. Ate at Mariano's with José Benítez and Facundo Ramos. Sat around talking and listening to Mariano's radio! Agusto had also asked me how the war (Vietnam) was going when I first arrived. What a shock! Transcribed notes from my visit with Chief Agusto by flashlight in the tent before retiring.

Much of the material in a 1975 article on shamanism was collected this day. Soria seemed highly pleased with my interest, as he had always wanted to share his insights and knowledge with me on this subject. The description of the relocation process forty years earlier was also lucid, detailed, and emotional. Clearly his shamanic call and supervision of the migration to Miraflores represented highly significant events in his life. He obviously viewed his role in the Miraflores community with pride.

The transition from an emotional church service one day to an intense discussion of shamanism the next was perfectly natural in context given the nature of power relations at work in both instances. The spiritual power exhibited in the *culto* was conceptualized as of the same order as the Companion Spirit power that enabled him to heal and lead his people.

> Up at 6:30 as usual. Coffee with milk and *torta* for breakfast. Walked to Antonio Leiva's, who gave me a lucid view of his experiences with the church. Was intrigued with the notion of memory, given his, Agusto's, and Mariano's accounts of events, some of which I had witnessed. Since Antonio's wife was out harvesting, we also discussed sexual practices more openly than would otherwise have been possible. She returned to make *tortas* for our lunch. In the afternoon I visited Cabral Naporichi; asked why he left the church and drinks so much. Interesting response which demonstrated his disillusionment with the difference between church theory and practice. Stopped by Facundo Ramos's and visited before he accompanied me back to the Cabreras'. All the women were gathered around Antonia visiting. A huge *yarará* snake came into the patio around dusk that was killed by the men. Visited with Mariano and Manuel and listened to radio. Antonia spoke frankly and critically with me before I retired about why we had abandoned our Chaco work.

The statement about memory is of interest given that my comments here are based primarily on my own recollections refreshed by a reading of the diaries. In this instance, it wasn't the conflict in memory that struck my attention, although there were conflicts, but rather the unique spin on events expressed by each person in comparison to my own.

I have called attention above to Antonia's inquiry as to why Lois and I left the mission. She expressed it in terms of personal loss but also wondered why we had chosen to leave the church. I responded as best I could without getting into philosophical questions about doubt, which seemed irrelevant to her concerns.

> Up early for coffee with Mariano and Antonia. Packed things. Large gathering, conversation, and prayer before leaving. Iginio Cabrera took me to the administration on his wagon. Talked with the

school director and got Toba attendance records. Had lunch with Cordeu. Visited with Robustiano Cabrera during siesta and got information on Toba cotton production. Spoke to Director Calvo and rode back to Castelli with him and Cordeu. Talked until 1:00 A.M. with Cordeu about my thesis and tried to help comprehend his tapes of Toba myths.

This was a special trip for several reasons. It put me in touch with my favorite community and enabled me to systematize the notes on shamanism that Chief Soria had provided during my missionary days. It also introduced me to the Argentine research scholars Edelmi Griva and Edgardo Cordeu, both of whom demonstrated considerable interest in my study. We agreed to maintain ties and I had further contacts and exchanges with both researchers.

Several changes in the community caught my attention. I was surprised to observe, for example, how much the presence of radios had changed the topics of conversation in the community. The fact that Chief Soria would ask immediately how the Vietnam War was going and if my family was safe astounded me since there had been little awareness of events in the national life of Argentina on previous visits, let alone conversation about world events. The number of bicycles and other commercial products also caught my eye. The Toba world seemed to be undergoing transformation in fundamental ways.

A few selections from my journal will provide additional insight into the nature of my research activity on this trip.

Fieldnotes, Miraflores, July 2–4, 1966

On diet with Antonia Cabrera. When a child is born, the woman must not eat anything sweet, such as sweet *maté*, watermelon, melon, meat (except cold tripe), honey, fish, oranges. She can eat hardtack, sweet potato, squash, *algarroba*. The old-timers only ate small deer. This diet lasts for about two months. The man can eat anything.

When a woman's menstrual period occurs, she follows the same diet. It is very dangerous for a man to enter the forest when his wife is giving birth or menstruating because there are many *lampalagua* (water snake?) who will smell the scent and pursue the woman's husband or the woman herself.

There were old-timers who didn't have a nose because if a man had sexual relations with a woman he did not know, or if the father wasn't known when a woman gave birth, then the child was killed and pig's hair was placed in the nostrils of the dead child and the father caught a disease that ate away his nose. They don't do this anymore and the people aren't as careful about sexual relations as they once were.

At the time of death, it is customary to eat goat, sheep, tatu, wild pig, and wild fruit. The same is true for births and menstruations.

On diet with Agusto Soria. During menstruation and childbirth, the woman should not eat fat of any kind. No meat, least of all fish and honey. Soup without fat is okay. No oranges nor watermelon. After the blood is gone she must take a complete bath and then she can eat something. Flour, salt, bread without grease, *algarroba,* and other wild fruit can be eaten. One should not eat meat and honey because they will get mixed up with the blood. The diet must be practiced for one to two months after childbirth to guarantee the good health of mother and child.

The man cannot hunt nor fish nor ride horse during this time, but he can eat anything. Soria's family never eats fish.

A menstruating woman does not go to church nor does she go to the country to work because a snake might smell her blood and try to enter her. Also, if a new mother does not take care of herself—stay in bed for two weeks and follow the diet—she will get skinny. If she eats meat, or even worse, honey, she will get sick in the stomach.

Mariano Naporichi later assured me that no woman while menstruating goes to church anywhere in the Chaco, citing as reason the woman water hole snake destruction story that is widely recounted among the Toba.

Conversations with store owners Veleff and Reyes. These men gave me another perspective on the Toba. They claim they can see no difference between Christians and non-Christians when dealing with them, with the exception of Hilario Cabrera. In fact, they claimed that Facundo Ramos and Mariano Naporichi are the most shameless of all in their dealings. They sell white colonist's cotton to the Aboriginal Administration at a higher price for a fee, which is forbidden. They bring cotton bags to them for sale at a lower price just to get even with the administration. They also claim that 90 percent of the Toba in the colony get drunk at one time or another throughout the year. They appear to be more suspicious of the church attenders than others.

I collected the material on diet with the intention of incorporating it into my dissertation. A great deal of similar material was in my notes from missionary days and I solicited additional accounts in other communities. However, the dissertation took a different turn, and I never published the article I considered writing on food practices and taboos.

My discussions with the local store owners were significant because their critical comments about active *culto* participants had not been made to me previously. I am uncertain to what extent this may have been due to my disassociation with the mission and involvement with Argentine anthropologists or simply to changes taking place in the community. I had often stopped to chat in previous years with both men, who tended to be critical of the Toba, but never in terms of their church affiliation. It did provide confirmation for some of Mariano Naporichi's charges in my initial diary, although it also indicated that his own behavior was not above reproach.

To Laishí and Formosa, July 8–11, 1966

Left early with Albert Buckwalter for Misión Laishí, picking up three Toba men at Makallé. Stayed with José Francia at Laishí. They were emotionally touched to see me; did not know I was in the Chaco. Had a fit over the girls' pictures. Did some work on animal and people classification. Big, long church service. To bed around midnight. My air mattress attracted considerable attention. Decided to give it to them when I return to the States next month.

The Francia family lived in Campo Medina before José's son Francisco had been killed by a hired hand on the ranch where he had worked. After his death the family, including Francisco's wife and twelve children, moved back to Laishí, where José had grown up.

Big holiday; church until 1:30 P.M. after which a huge meal awaited us. In P.M. Buckwalter took me to the town of Laishí, where I went to the Catholic parish and spoke with a friendly priest about their Indian program. He said they do not have one, and the one they had previously was completely mistaken. Spent over three hours going through records attempting to understand their work and influence on the Toba. At 7:30 P.M. I took a bus to Formosa City, arriving at 9:00. Selected a hotel, showered, and went to see John Dring, who agreed to see me the following day. Continued on to John Church's, who was not home, but his daughter gave me a book on the Emmanuel mission that contained valuable information. Returned to hotel and went out to eat with some teachers I had met on the bus. Talked until 1:30 A.M. about aboriginal peoples around the world and about philosophy. Delightful people.

Up at 6:30 to read Church's material on the Toba mission so I could return it by 10:00 A.M. From there to John Dring's for an intense conversation that continued until 2:00 P.M. His view of the Toba work is quite different from that of both John Church and the Toba. They served me lunch. He took me to the edge of town, where I visited various Toba families until dusk. Walked back the nearly three miles. Had dinner and talked again with the teachers until late.

Spent the A.M. getting a map of Formosa from the proper authorities, talked with the director of Indian Affairs, met a local Catholic priest who had valuable information on Laishí, and interviewed Clemente Rojas, who had been active in the Toba church but is now in indigenous politics. Had soup and took 1:00 P.M. bus to Germandería, where Buckwalter and companions were waiting for me.

The constitution of my anthropologist self is clearly at work in these reports. Note the discourse that now gets incorporated into both diary and journal. Almost every entry contains comments about data and anthropological themes. I had learned my lessons well in graduate school so that my interactions with the Toba became strongly focused toward the goal of acquiring "good information" to write a dissertation. At the time I had not yet thought much about articles or books.

This trip proved particularly useful for my dissertation. I remain grateful to the Catholic priests at Laishí and Formosa City, as well as to John Church and John Dring, for their forthright discussions and open-door policy of making available records and accounts of their respective missionary activities. The latter two were involved with some of the earliest Protestant missions to the Chaco in this century. In these few days my understanding of the formative years of missionary impact on the Toba, both Catholic and Protestant, was enhanced enormously.

Upon my return to the United States in August 1966, we moved to Philadelphia, where I had acquired a job in the Department of Anthropology at Temple University. During that first academic year and the following summer I wrote a dissertation on the Toba while preparing and teaching four sections of introduction to cultural anthropology each term. Having completed my dissertation in the fall of 1967, I began teaching upper-level courses and graduate seminars. The following spring I was named chair of the undergraduate committee and became actively engaged in curriculum revision and planning.

In June 1970 I was appointed chair of the department with the encouragement of the dean of Arts and Sciences to develop a doctoral program. The proposal was written in consultation with departmental faculty and acted upon positively by the graduate board the following academic year, so that I became deeply involved in hiring senior faculty, acquiring graduate assistantships, developing a graduate curriculum, and improving library resources. This activity constituted a milestone in my professional career because I began to develop an administrator self-image that was to impact upon, sometimes by conflicting with, the maturation of my scholarly self-image. While time for research and writing was reduced to a minimum, during the first two years in administrative office I did manage to rework my dissertation with a view toward publishing the new version in Spanish. Sensitive to the complaint of Argentine colleagues that North American researchers do not make their materials available in Spanish, I prepared a manuscript for presentation to an Argentine publisher.

In 1972 I was awarded a study leave at Temple, which allowed me to return with my family to Argentina in order to reestablish ties and pursue research on the changing conditions confronted by the Toba. Following good scientific tradition, I had developed a hypothesis in my grant proposal: *"given major economic changes within a society, fundamental adaptations are necessary in the cognitive world of that society in order to prevent cognitive dissonance."* I proposed to make contributions to knowledge in the following four areas: "(a) an understanding of Toba cognitive systems and their range of variation, (b) the effects of economic change on these systems, (c) an increased knowledge of the animal ecology of the region, and (d) a more dynamic approach to the study of cognitive systems." The intention was to study these processes in the urban environs of Buenos Aires and the Chaco, where attempts to resolve cognitive dissonance could be expected to be most conspicuous. Given that cognitive anthropology played a dominant role in the discipline during that period, it is not surprising that the buzz word here was *cognition.* My particular interest in the concept grew out of the hope that the new cognitive approach to ethnography might allow me to identify indigenous categories and thus enhance my understanding of Toba praxis.

As frequently happens with research proposals, field circumstances led in unanticipated directions. My efforts to identify cognitive processes appeared to distract rather than facilitate insight into Toba interests and concerns. Instead, I found myself revising the manuscript I had prepared for publication in Spanish around the theme of harmony and dissonance. The following diary excerpts describe what I actually did, as opposed to what I set out to do, during this third excursion to the Chaco, showing that my anthropological field experiences were not strictly governed by considerations of research design.

Since 1966 Lois and I had exchanged correspondence with only a few Toba families, as they had to rely on mission personnel or schoolteachers to send airmail. The church leader Guillermo Flores once mailed us a letter with local postage that arrived by boat over four months later. We did stay in touch with missionaries, particularly the Buckwalters (the Kratzes resigned their Chaco assignment), who managed to forward occasional correspondence to us and through whom we sent greetings and news about our family in return. Thus, when we arrived in Buenos Aires shortly after the end of the spring semester of 1972, not only were we entering new settlements where we had no prior knowledge or experience, we also had lost touch with some of the families with whom we had maintained close ties during our first fieldwork.

Buenos Aires, May 23–June 8, 1972

Met Osvaldo Gómez at his job on Uruguay Street and traveled with him to his home near Quilmes. Met his wife and kids, his brother Clemente and family, Alberto Cabrera (son of Hilario) and family, a brother-in-law of Hilario, and a Roberto Rojas family. Sixto Ramírez is also here, but I did not see him, since he works late. About two hundred Toba in barrio according to Osvaldo. Most are from La Reducción and Resistencia. He says there are another forty or so in Ezpeleta who came from Las Palmas, twenty-five to thirty in Ocalito from Resistencia, another forty or so in Las Tunas from Resistencia, and twenty or more in Monte Chingolo from Resistencia. There are others in Avellaneda and Adrogué. On the trip down Osvaldo was recounting Toba tales, which he seemed to know quite well. Long trip back on the bus after dark. Had call from Edelmi Griva and plan to see him tomorrow.

This first trip to an urban Toba settlement in Buenos Aires came as a shock since I had no idea of the substantial migration to Buenos Aires subsequent to our leave in 1963. By the end of the trip I estimated approximately five hundred Toba in the city's suburbs. Most impressive were the varying forms the urban settlements took. This particular barrio (squatter plot) contained better housing and a cleaner environment that those I had known in Sáenz Peña and Resistencia, but this was not true of others. The small Toba nucleus amidst *criollo* squatters was also characteristic of other Buenos Aires settle-

ments, where the Toba kept to themselves rather than develop social bonds with white neighbors.

Osvaldo Gómez had been living in this barrio for a number of years
and he continued to hold the same job in a restaurant. His familiarity with folktales surprised me since I had only been successful in
getting old-timers to recount them previously and since he is one of
the most urbane Toba I know. I contacted Gómez on the advice of
Harriet Klein, whom I had introduced to Toba culture and language
materials in anticipation of her dissertation research. She had selected him as an informant for her language work. Although we did not
know him personally, Lois and I were close friends of his siblings.

> Met with Edelmi Griva in the A.M. to talk about our mutual in-
> terest in the Toba. Had lunch with the painter Luís Micheluzzi, who
> invited me to Las Carritas, where the food was excellent. Returned
> to the hotel at 3:30 to find Edgardo Cordeu waiting at the hotel
> and accompanied him to the Museum at Moreno 350. Spoke with
> him and Alejandra Siffredi for a while. They presented me to Pro-
> fessor Bórmida and we talked for several hours. Returned late after
> Cordeu and I had a sandwich and coffee.[11]

> Went to Fernández Blanco Bookstore, where I found some real
> gems. Spent the entire A.M. there. In the P.M. I changed some mon-
> ey and returned once again to the museum, where I had another
> long talk with Prof. Bórmida and his team. Met a Mataco scholar
> by the name of Califano who had participated in the Chaco cen-
> sus of *indígenas*. He gave good advice on my anticipated trip to
> Cuzco. Discussed the construction of a curriculum in social anthro-
> pology with Cordeu and Siffredi.[12] Had a call from Griva, who had
> traveled to Santa Fé; he invited us to travel with him to Corrientes
> next week. Highly unlikely. Read Cordeu and Siffredi book until 2:30
> A.M. Got very angry! Will write a rebuttal.

My anger was based on a deep sense of what I considered betrayal
of trust and friendship on the part of Cordeu. We had corresponded
since our first encounter at Miraflores in 1966 and I had sent him a
copy of my dissertation. While subsequent correspondence mentioned in passing that he and Siffredi were working on a manuscript
dealing with millenarian movements in the Chaco, I had no idea that
they had published a book (Cordeu and Siffredi 1971) on the theme
of my dissertation. To make matters worse, I felt that my dissertation had been appropriated without proper documentation, misrepresented, and unfairly criticized. My response (1972), discussed in
scene 3, was highly critical, not only of what I clearly saw as misap-

propriation of my materials, but also of the overall scheme of the book. Perhaps my biggest disappointment was the rupture of a personal and professional relationship that I had high hopes of developing. It was an inauspicious beginning for a new field trip in which I had high expectations.

> Our family accompanied Osvaldo to his home at noon. Girls got bored, but visit was good. Saw Sixto Ramírez, wife Celestina, and two children; also his brother Roberto and family and another brother Juan. Had *maté,* shared cookies we had brought, and got reactions to life in B.A. In general, they like it. Visited Osvaldo's kin and wrote down all their names (twenty-two). Drank more *maté* and visited seven other families involving sixty-four people, all of whose names and relationships I recorded. Houses are clean and decently furnished. Returned before dusk.

The decision to drink *maté* was a difficult one, as it had not been easy to break our dependency on it after returning to the States in 1963. Its significant role in social interaction led us to imbibe lest we be left out of the loop. By the end of the trip we had become accustomed once again to the lure of *maté* and upon our return to the United States we missed not only the flavor, but the social interaction it occasioned as well. Despite our daughters' boredom, the Toba demonstrated genuine interest in them, providing immediate rapport and a topic of conversation.

My comment about clean housing refers to the fact that most urban houses where the Toba lived had mud brick or temporary walls with dirt floors. When I returned in 1974 the walls of Osvaldo's house were redone in brick. My recollection at the time was that comparable housing in the Chaco urban settlements tended to be less well-kept and more temporarily occupied.

> Daily afternoon taping sessions with Osvaldo Gómez on themes in Toba culture. Mornings spent transcribing tapes and identifying topics for further discussion and visiting local bookstores. Found some fantastic buys at Pardo [bookstore with ethnological materials].

This report of the period's activities summarizes the essence of my daily diary entries. In addition to life history material, we spent a great deal of time discussing Chaco flora and fauna as seen from a Toba cultural perspective. We also worked on folktales.

My first experience working with a paid "informant" was initially discomfiting. Since Gómez had already worked for wages with Klein, he appeared to have no difficulty dealing with the pecuniary relationship involved. However, I found it strange and artificial, particularly since the recordings took place in our hotel room on Florida Street, where the hotel staff found our daily interviews perplexing. They were at first reluctant to let him into the hotel, much less into our room. Once the nature of our work was understood, the staff was courteous and accommodating. Gómez himself consistently arrived in an upbeat mood and left reluctantly despite the long ride home. While I sweated over the new relationship, he seemed to thrive on it.

Extended trip, June 16–29, 1972

Trip to Tucumán, Salta, Jujuy, La Paz, Tiahuanaco, Lake Titicaca, Puno, Cuzco, Machu Pichu, Lima with my cousin Lee Swartz. Fantastic!

Unquestionably the best tourist trip I have ever taken in South America. The time away from Buenos Aires was good in that it took my mind off of the disappointment and tension I was feeling about an inevitable confrontation with Cordeu. It also introduced me to highland Bolivia and Peru with their living remnants of high civilization that stood so much in contrast to the lowland peoples of the Chaco. I wondered about Inca incursions into the Chaco region and speculated about their legacy there in more than name (the term *Chaco,* which the Spaniards encountered when they first arrived, appears to have been of Quechua origin).

Buenos Aires, July 4–14, 1972

Worked at Di Tella Institute transcribing Gómez tapes and recording more. Intensive discussions with Esther Hermitte and Leopoldo Bartolomé about Gran Chaco history and culture. Had Cordeu, Siffredi, and husband Pepe over for dinner Sat. the 8th and rode around with them Sun. the 9th in Martínez and La Lucila.

Hermitte was able to acquire a private space for me to work at Di Tella, which was convenient for Gómez to reach after work at the restaurant. The library resources were also useful, as were conversations with scholars connected with the institute.

In retrospect I suspect that I missed a good opportunity to broach the subject of my reaction to Cordeu and Siffredi's book on this occasion. However, I had not yet sorted out all of my thoughts on the subject nor reread the book carefully to determine whether my initial response constituted an overreaction. Upon rereading the book on the way to the Chaco the following week, I became even more angry and frustrated than at the first reading. I regretted not having confronted Edgardo and Alejandra personally.

Sáenz Peña, July 16–25, 1972

Stayed at the Residencial Sáenz Peña Hotel. Visits to Quinta 8 for interviews with Pacheco Rodríguez, Mariano Naporichi, Carlos Moreno, José Sánchez, and others. Observed the growth and changing nature of the Toba barrio at the edge of S.P. People are more settled on a permanent basis. Invited for meals to the families Buckwalter, Perrín, Romeu, Díaz, Lesa, Horst [Kratz replacement], Pokorney, and the Catholic brothers. Trip to Río Bermejito with Perríns and the brothers; also to Confluencia where we met some Toba families. Driven to Resistencia by Perríns.

By this time my diary entries had become increasingly abbreviated as I gave greater attention to the journal, now my most significant documentation. What does not appear in the diaries is the pride and excitement both Lois and I felt at showing off our daughters to friends in Sáenz Peña and to the Toba. By now Rosina and Lisa, ages eight and six, had learned to communicate fairly well in Spanish and their phonetics were impeccable, much to the satisfaction of their parents. Everywhere we went the girls were the major attraction. We were no longer childless and our new status was appreciated by everyone. Our biggest disappointment, together with that of the Toba, was that we were unable to travel to as many communities as we would have liked.

Furthermore, rather than bunk with the missionaries, where the Toba arrived on their visits to town, we stayed in a hotel, where they often had difficulty finding us. We needed to rent a vehicle, but in 1972 that was still impossible in Sáenz Peña. The result is that we spent more time on this excursion renewing old friendships in town than we did visiting Toba communities.

Resistencia, July 26–31, 1972

Extensive discussions about Chaco history and Toba culture at Northeastern University with Professors Maeder, Morresi, and Miranda. Searched in archives for old issues of *Heraldo del Norte* and other papers. Discussions with López Piacentini, Marcos Altamirano, and Ramón Tissera about Chaco history and aboriginal populations. Dis-

cussions also with Cerruti and Sotelo about Toba crafts and provincial indigenous policy. Traveled to Toba barrio for extended interviews with local leaders.

The expanding contacts with Chaco scholars, helping to solidify
my new professional status, is well documented here. The Toba settlement in Resistencia became the focal point for my Toba interactions over the next several months. I had only visited there occasionally during our stay with the mission, thus I was not as well
acquainted with these urban Toba as with those living inland. Consequently, it was easier to exercise my new role of ethnographer in
this less familiar context.

Furthermore, many of these people had lived in the urban setting
for long periods of time. Young people in their teens knew only this
place as home. Here was a new kind of Toba person that I had not
known previously. During this time we rented two rooms at the Cel-
ta Hotel and searched for more suitable accommodations upon our
return in September.

Buenos Aires, August 1–30, 1972

Worked with Osvaldo Gómez at Di Tella Institute in afternoons
and transcribed tapes in the mornings. Talked a lot with Hermitte
between times. Visited national institutions and bookstores to collect information for Toba bibliography. Made a trip to Santa Fé to
see Edelmi Griva and work with a Toba informant on animal classi-
fications. Traveled with Sr. Lange to visit slum villages in search of
Toba. Visited Barrio Pan Americano, Barrio Victorio, Barrio San
Fernando, and Barrio 48. Found no Toba in the latter after lengthy
walk and search, following false leads. Impressed with the variety
of slum situations found in Buenos Aires. Returned home with Clemente and Valentín Gómez and visited Ezpeleta as well. Met many
longtime friends from the Chaco. Saw Cordeu and Siffredi briefly,
but did not discuss book.

This period represented my most intensive efforts to identify Toba
settlements in the greater Buenos Aires area and learn about their
composition. I was surprised to discover the variety of crowded urban housing areas where the Toba had managed to establish semi-
permanent roots. All returned continually to the Chaco in order to
maintain contact with their families, taking commercial products and
returning with indigenous foods. Although frequently encountering

former acquaintances, I also met Toba families whom I had not known previously. This provided a broader perspective on the impact of Pentecostal symbolism and the extent to which it played a significant social role in urban adaptations. I could ask new questions and receive fresh responses from people without concern about sustaining former relationships based on different expectations.

Except for a brief weekend family trip to Santa Rosa to visit friends from our missionary days, my time was spent with the urban Toba while Lois supervised the girls' studies and served as homemaker.

Resistencia, September 14–October 10, 1972

Beautiful trip to Resistencia on Austral. Met at airport by Clemente and María Bonaire, who took us to the Covadonga Hotel. Rented house at Pellegrini 575 and moved in the 16th. Spent numerous mornings working in the historical archives, records of the municipality, the Herrera Library, and in the public library on old editions of *La Voz del Chaco*. Bought bike for daily rides to Toba barrio in the afternoons. Had intensive discussions with Marcelo González, originally from Campo Medina, Juan Vera, and Ramón Corvalán, who proved to be highly articulate about Toba history and culture. Frequent discussions also with José Miranda and López-Piacentini. Social excursions with the Miranda family, who got along well with our girls.

We had become friends with the Bonaires in Philadelphia, where they had lived for a period of time. This was an important period in my research because I developed some ideas for revising my dissertation for publication in Spanish. The Toba informants I worked with spoke freely and coherently of their cultural knowledge, perhaps because more extensive contact with whites enabled them to see their traditions in clearer perspective than did the Toba from the interior, whom I knew more intimately. The greater interpersonal distance also enabled me to broach subjects that would have been considered insensitive among close acquaintances. It was during this period that I began to write a critique of Cordeu and Siffredi's book.

Miraflores, October 11–12, 1972

The Bonaires took our family to visit in Miraflores. Agusto Soria was ecstatic to see us, especially our girls, whom he named before we left. *Culto* meeting was conducted by Carlos Soria, but enthusiasm was low. We all slept in a tent. Had delicious goat dinner with Hilario Cabrera family before leaving Miraflores. Visited Dr. Cicchetti in Castelli on return to Resistencia.

This brief entry fails to convey the excitement of returning to Miraflores with Rosina and Lisa. The emotion of that reunion, of witnessing Soria's obvious profound pleasure and satisfaction upon seeing us and the girls, is not communicated here. The girls remain proud of their Toba names. During our first stay Soria had been sufficiently concerned about our inability to have children that he had offered his curing powers. Despite our failure to pursue the offer, he seemed to take some credit for our progeny, of whom he seemed quite proud. It was my last good visit with Chief Soria. In 1979 Albert and Lois Buckwalter took me to see him briefly when he was clearly losing strength and approaching death, although he survived for several more years.

This first trip to our most favorite rural Toba community with white friends who had no connection with church life went very well. The Bonaires had a wonderful time and often spoke of the experience on subsequent occasions. This constituted the highlight of our family time with the Toba during the 1972 trip. It produced little by way of research notes, but enormous satisfaction in terms of personal interaction.

Buenos Aires, October 16–20, 1972

Spent the A.M. in the university library archives. Beautiful one-hour flight to B.A. To Transocean Hotel and later to the journal La Opinión to submit article. Called Esther Hermitte and arranged to see her tomorrow.

Met with Hermitte and the Di Tella Institute people. Set up meeting with Jaime Bernstein of Paidós to discuss publication of my manuscript. Spoke with Frank Johnston [acting department chair at Temple], with Ramón Tissera who was in town, and with the Micheluzzis.

To museum library in the A.M. Lunch in Belgrano with the Micheluzzi family. To Paidós for interview with Bernstein at 3:00 P.M. Got agreement to publish my revised dissertation. To Opinión for interview with Miss Walsh at 5:00 P.M. To Hermitte's for dinner.

To La Plata and the museum library. Returned by car with Rex González [noted Argentine anthropologist] in the P.M.[13]

Lunch with Leopoldo Bartolomé. Met with translator at 2:00 P.M. To hotel for siesta with head cold and fever. Dinner with the Bartolomé family.

This was a business trip I made to publish an article and a book while Lois remained with the girls in Resistencia. Little did I imagine that it would be seven more years before the book would appear in print, not with Paidós, but with Siglo XXI, not in Buenos Aires, but in Mexico City. By the time it appeared I had developed other interests and had forgotten what it was about.

Note the social engagements now routine during visits to Buenos Aires. Lois and I cherish the friendships we have established in the capital city. The death of Esther Hermitte in 1990 represented a personal and professional loss that I still feel.

Rosario, October 21, 1972

Up at 6:00 A.M. to catch 7:15 flight to Rosario. Edelmi Griva arrived late. Spent the remainder of the day with him and Maricel Stroppa discussing life history and the Toba. Also visited Victoriano Arce.

Little did I imagine at the time the extent to which Rosario would become a major attraction for the Toba. By the time I returned in 1988, Rosario was home to several thousand. The life history work of Edelmi Griva and Maricel Stroppa (1983) inspired me to do something with my Aurelio López materials, but the inspiration was short-lived after my return to Philadelphia, where administrative obligations soon commanded my full attention.

Resistencia, October 23–November 8, 1972

Spent time writing critique of Cordeu and Siffredi with help from José Miranda, Carlos López Piacentini, and Edgardo Perrín, who had arrived to visit November 1–2. Also worked on Paidós manuscript. Visited extensively with Miranda owing to his brother's sudden death.[14] Reviewed books at Herrera Library and took notes. Traveled to Barrio Toba to speak with the school director Amancio Sánchez and with Marcelo González. Also met with the botanist Agusto Schultz, who provided valuable information on Chaco plants.

My intention had been to write a long essay, or possibly a book, on Toba interactions with their Chaco environment. For this reason I sought to clarify my technical knowledge of Chaco flora and fauna, together with Toba knowledge and appropriation of their ecological niche. It is a subject that continues to attract my interest and attention.

To Asunción, Paraguay, November 9–12, 1972

Left at noon with Miranda for Formosa City. Met Rex González from La Plata at Bellas Artes who was there for a lecture series.

Up at 3:45 A.M. to get 4:00 bus for Puerto Pilcomayo. Took 7:30 ferry to Asunción, arriving at museum to meet Dr. Susnik at 8:45. Went from the museum to search for Miguel Chase-Sardi, who put me on a 2:30 P.M. bus for San Francisco de Asís. Old bus with wooden benches and aisle filled with bags of tubers. Had to wait at the Paraguay River for three hours owing to possible bad roads on other side. Finally crossed and arrived at Franciscan mission at 8:30 P.M. after dark. The brothers made supper for me, gave me a beer, and put me to sleep in the music room.

Up at 5:30 A.M. and walked out to meet the Emok Toba only three blocks away. All recognized my Toba speech and were flabbergasted. Fantastic experience with people crowding all around and wanting to touch me. They had thought it impossible for a white person to speak their language. Had completely lost touch with the Argentine Toba, although they knew some of the old-timer names I mentioned. Fascinating interaction. Although their Spanish was fairly good, they insisted on my speaking in Toba. It rained hard and I got soaked. Returned to mission for cup of tea. Got bus at noon and arrived midafternoon in Asunción. Returned to Formosa late afternoon.

Up early and out to Formosa barrio by 7:00. Had unusually fruitful session with Clemente Rojas on Toba shamanism, folk medicine, and general lore. Invited to lunch by Rex González and friends from Bellas Artes. Returned by bus in P.M. to Resistencia.

This excursion represented another highlight of the 1972 field trip. Although my contact with the scholar Branislava Susnik was disappointing in that she provided little information on the nature of contemporary Toba settlements in Paraguay, the travel to encounter Paraguayan Toba was an experience I shall never forget. For that I can only thank Miguel Chase-Sardi, who did the right thing by depositing me on the bus and leaving me with little choice but to go.[15]

While I was at the Paraguay River waiting for the rain to stop and standing at the mission cutoff in darkness with no idea how to proceed, however, my feelings were anything but grateful. Gratitude came the next morning when I saw all those Toba faces that were astonished to hear me speak Toba. As the crowds gathered around, clutching for a chance to touch me, I got carried away with excitement and began to call upon every Toba phrase I could retrieve from the recesses of my mind. Who knows what came out? Whatever it was, the crowd was in awe and I didn't know what to do, except escape. The few old-timer names I mentioned, such as Jesús Bachorí, prompted tears of joy and excitement.

I did not want to wear out my welcome with the mission brothers, who were no doubt perplexed about what I was doing there speaking to the Toba in their own language, so I caught the only bus available that day back to Asunción. I have often regretted missing an opportunity to learn more about this group of people who apparently had escaped Argentina during the early decades of this century, losing all ties with their Argentine compatriots.[16]

Branka Susnik also deserves credit for this encounter because she published the vocabulary (1962) that made me aware that there were Toba in Paraguay who spoke eastern dialect Toba, or at least something very akin to it. The story of their isolation from Argentine compatriots is one remaining to be told by an ethnohistorian. Historical linguists would also find the dialect differentiation an interesting problem for research.

Resistencia, November 27–30, 1972

Worked each day with Bernardino López, who has excellent insights into Toba culture.[17] On the last day he brought José Echeverría to record music from his tin-can violin. The varieties of sounds and animal communications he produced are fantastic!

At this point I was writing freely about *working* with the Toba, whereas during mission days I never thought of my interactions with them in these terms. Here is as good an example as any of a fundamental change in relationship. At this point I was paying wages with little personal compunction to specific individuals I asked to interview. It was my only means of reciprocity.

The tape of violin music was an unanticipated bonus because I had not been aware of the sounds of animals and natural forces that could be produced. While I was familiar with Toba flutes and drums, this was the first violin I encountered. I prize the tape recording and photographs as among my most valuable acquisitions during our stay in Resistencia.

Resistencia, December 1–10, 1972

Last days in the Chaco. Time of good-byes and packing, including a quick trip to Sáenz Peña to say farewell to our friends there, a number of whom had visited us during our stay in Resistencia. Lots of dinners and exchanges. Mixed emotions. Not wanting to leave, but looking forward to our return to Philadelphia.

Upon my return to Temple in January 1973 I again chaired the department until resigning in December 1977. During this period we consolidated our doctoral program and hired new faculty. I mainly taught graduate seminars, although I taught an occasional introductory class for variation. I also prepared invited papers for conferences in Buenos Aires and Quito and published several articles based on my most recent fieldwork.

One of my activities during the 1972 field trip was to participate in the formation of a working group of Latin and North American anthropologists. It all began with conversations that I had with the late Esther Hermitte at the Di Tella Institute, where we discussed the desirability of establishing a kind of center where Argentine and North American anthropologists might gather to work on projects of mutual interest and concern. Esther soon incorporated Leopoldo Bartolomé into the discussions and the two of them took it from there. I do not recall who came up with the name Working Group in Social Articulation but I believe it was Esther. She was also responsible for establishing the relationship with Consejo Latinoamericano de Ciencias Sociales (CLACSO) that funded our first meeting held in Buenos Aires in 1974. At that session I presented a paper on Toba shamanism, which was published in English the following year. Papers from that first conference were also published in Spanish, edited by Hermitte and Bartolomé (1977).

Two additional conferences with presented papers, also sponsored by CLACSO, were held in Quito in 1975 and 1976. There was serious talk of further publication, including a translation project involving production of works in both Spanish and English, English translation of Spanish works, and vice versa, but it never materialized. The 1976 meeting was expanded to include anthropologists from Peru and Mexico. Dissention over the group's composition, theoretical orientation, and future direction resulted in its demise subsequent to the 1976 meeting. It was a disappointing end to a promising beginning. The papers I prepared for these sessions were an important means of maintaining contact with Argentine colleagues and research activity in the midst of administrative tasks.

In 1975 I also traveled with my family to Brasília for an extended semester to teach in the university's new graduate program and contribute to program development. The invitation was made by Roberto Cardoso Oliveira, who had attended the first session of the Social

Articulation Group in Buenos Aires. Working with Brazilian colleagues and graduate students in seminars and on theses, one involving the Brazilian Yanomamo, was an essential component of my professional socialization. The Brazilians were deeply attentive to ethnographic concerns about the plight of Amazonian Indians, and they brought an intensely urgent perspective to ethnographic endeavors.

After the 1974 conference in Buenos Aires and the stint in Brasília in 1975, I made brief trips to the Chaco to greet friends and renew acquaintances with as many individuals as possible.

In January 1978 I resigned from my administrative position to take a semester's study leave in order to pursue research and writing that had been placed on a back burner. Rather than return to Argentina, I decided to work on materials at hand that might be made available to colleagues. These appeared several years later (1979a, 1979b, 1980b, 1980c). During the summer of 1979 I also made a brief trip to the Chaco in order to check on some of the information I planned to publish and to touch base with friends and colleagues.

I returned to chair the department in January 1981, where I served until appointed to a three-year term as director of Temple's Program Abroad in Rome in July 1982. In June 1985 I returned from Rome and was named associate dean of Arts and Sciences the following year, a position I held until resigning in 1989. It was from that position that I acquired a study leave during the fall of 1988 to return to the Chaco, where a new generation of Argentine anthropologists had begun to produce interesting analyses of developments among the Toba.

Precisely what effect the years in Rome, together with travels in Europe and the Middle East, had on my formation as an anthropologist is difficult to assess. It did establish distance in time and space, which obliged me to place my Chaco experiences in broader perspective. On a few occasions I gave lectures in Italy or engaged in discussions about lowland peoples of South America with particular attention to the Chaco, but apart from these I gave little or no attention to events and circumstances involving the Toba.

Of significant influence was the intellectual climate of Italy with its connections to French thought that shaped my understanding of current debate in the discipline. Certainly my readings of Lévi-Strauss, Lacan, and Foucault, originally stimulated and influenced by my late friend and colleague Abdul Hamid el-Zein, together with graduate students in the department, were modified and reshaped by my encounters with the works of Pirandello, Calvino, and Eco in Rome. Perhaps most significant of all was a new perspective on history, which daily travels among Roman ruins pushed back by millennia, only to be pushed back even further by travels to Greece, Turkey, Israel, Jordan, Syria, and Egypt.

While the latter travels and encounters contributed to an expanded intellectual horizon and served to further internationalize my perspective of anthropology, distance from the Chaco experiences that shaped so fundamentally my professional sense of self appears to have been the key factor nudging me toward greater attention to reflexivity at this crucial point in my career. Distance causes one to forget, to place prior experiences in new perspectives that require rethinking about self-images. Upon my return from Rome, the Chaco was far from my mind as I considered new topics and areas of research. It quickly returned to center stage.

The first reminder that the Chaco was still an essential component of my professional self was a letter I received shortly after arriving in the States from Pablo Wright describing his research interest in the Toba and asking about some of my writings. This jolted me back into wondering what was happening with the Toba, prompting a desire to return. Shortly after this I was invited by the Latin American Scholarship Program (LASPAU) in Cambridge, Massachusetts, to travel to Argentina and Chile in 1986 to help select Fulbright scholars for graduate training in American universities. On this trip I met with Wright in Buenos Aires to discuss his activities and that of several other young scholars working with the Toba, further stimulating my desire to return.

Finally, in the summer of 1988 Lois and I returned to Argentina both to visit friends and to investigate reported Toba migrations to and from the major cities of Buenos Aires and Rosario. Having just completed a major project for the college involving the implementation of a new core curriculum, I wanted to pursue once again my own research interests. When the Inter-American Foundation (IAF) learned of my plans to return to the Chaco, they contacted me and asked if I would spend two weeks investigating their four projects among the Toba and Mocoví. This I agreed to do.

When we arrived in the Chaco the time gap since 1972, except for the brief revisits already mentioned, had created a distance in our ties with the Toba that we had not experienced previously. New leaders had emerged with whom we were not well acquainted because they were still youngsters when we knew them, and a number of elders with whom we had been particularly close, such as Chief Soria, Carlos Temai, and Juan Acosta, had passed away. Having felt their loss from a distance, it was even more painful to return to the Chaco knowing that they were no longer there to greet us and to revive the bonds of friendship. They had been essential components of both my missionary and ethnographer selves.

Mrs. Domingo washes clothing in a lagoon at La Reducción.

Antonio Leiva's home in Miraflores.

Lois with Toba children near Barrio Nam Qom.

The preacher Victorino Arce and his wife at home in Rosario.

Barrio Empalme in downtown Rosario.

Durán daughters fetch water in Legua 15.

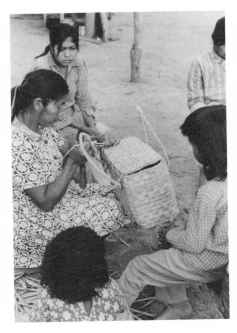

The daughters of Alberto Gómez watch their mother weave a basket in Legua 17. (Courtesy of Albert Buckwalter)

Counting the offering for music in a *culto* at Legua 17. (Courtesy of Albert Buckwalter)

My Spanish ethnography of the Toba (1979b) was not widely distributed in Argentina until the military government was replaced by a democratic one in the early 1980s. No Toba with whom I conversed in 1988 appeared to have read it, although many obviously knew about its content because they were eager to have me recount experiences with several well-known shamans and storytellers depicted there, persons still regarded highly and sometimes remembered as larger-than-life individuals. I discussed plans for a new book with several young leaders, exchanging ideas about what might be important to record. All expressed nostalgia for the past and thought I ought to write about my interactions with old-timers. Such nostalgia generated some of my own for the intense interactions of the early 1960s when elders spoke of a more glorious foretime.

The diary notations for this period tend to be short and to the point because my writing energies were directed once again to the journals. Nevertheless, the diary does depict the nature of my activity during this latest trip to the Chaco and it provides the basis once again for commentary. An unpublished report to the IAF (1988a) describes my observations on their projects.

Buenos Aires, August 2–5, 1988

Had lunch in Córdoba St. bar with Pablo Wright, Marcela Mendoza, and Cristina Messineo, young Argentine anthropologists carrying out research on the Toba, to discuss research and writing about the Toba. Spent P.M. at Fulbright. Lectured at the YMCA in the evening. Dinner with Ricardo Lange in the hotel.

Pablo Wright's ongoing contact was a significant factor in redirecting my attention to the Toba. He arranged this meeting. While I had not met Mendoza, I had known about her work and looked forward to meeting her. Messineo, who works on the Toba language, I had not known about previously. The discussion here centered around the value of sharing our research interests on the Toba with a view toward coordinating efforts rather than working at cross-purposes. Pablo was subsequently admitted to the doctoral program in anthropology at Temple, where we both profited from a sharing of mutual experiences with the Toba.

Spent A.M. with Hilario Wynarczyk, who accompanied me to the office of the Argentine representative of Siglo XXI. Spoke to Belgrano Colombia High School students at noon, presented by Ricardo Lange, who also took me to see a lawyer in P.M. to help arrange a visit by a U.S. lawyer group in which my cousin Lee Swartz is active.[18]

Wynarczyk, a sociologist who published a two-volume study on Toba settlements in the area of Castelli, continues to be interested in the sociology of Toba religious action. Now that Siglo XXI was again open for business in Argentina, I was interested in knowing what was happening with the sale of my book.

To Chaco, August 8–10, 1988

Trip by train to Chaco via Corrientes. Tracks in bad shape; arrived late. Bus to Resistencia and on to Sáenz Peña, where Edgardo Perrín picked us up at the station. I arrived with fever and grippe. Spent several days recuperating.

Lois and I decided to take the train for old time's sake as we had on our first journey north. Travel via the western entrance to Sáenz Peña from Añatuya was no longer possible so we took the train to Corrientes and a ferry and bus to Resistencia and eventually Sáenz Peña instead. Our train was nearly as late as it had been the first time and for the same reason. Heavy rains had undermined the stability of the track. Although this was no narrow gauge track with wood-burning engine, the cabins were much the same, as were the fabulous six-course meals.

Once again there was the excitement of reuniting with our friends, the always faithful Perríns. Unfortunately, I arrived a physical wreck, but recovered quickly under their doctor's care. They took us north to spend a few days in Río Bermejito, where we also met Virginia Cicchetti, wife of the doctor who had passed away. Upon return to Sáenz Peña we visited with Albert and Lois Buckwalter, who had returned meanwhile from their trip in the country. They brought us up to date on events among the Toba in the Chaco interior.

Sáenz Peña, August 18–24, 1988

Lois and I spent entire day in Barrio Nam Qom with Silvestre Durán, José Sánchez, Mariano Naporichi, and Juan Medina. Also visited Barrio Nala' and spoke with the curer Juana. Visited the Indigenous Research Center and spoke with the directors; also addressed Toba and Mocoví participants.

Spent A.M. xeroxing articles collected by Lois Buckwalter and visiting with Kenth Johannson, Swedish missionary working with the Toba. Met Salustiano López there as well. Time was limited and we agreed to meet later. Went to the municipality to get maps of what we knew as Quinta 8, now called Barrio Nam Qom. Had lengthy discussion with Mayor Ducca about the Toba and municipal hiring policies.

In addition to encounters with Toba friends from the past, I contacted municipal authorities, researchers, teachers, and new mission personnel with extensive activities among the Toba. Rather than focusing primarily on the Toba in their rural and urban settings, at this time I explored the broader societal context in which actions external to the Toba shaped their lives. While this was true to some extent of my previous two trips as ethnographer, the death of close Toba friends and the limited time available for establishing new friendships on this brief travel to Sáenz Peña prompted me to direct greater attention to the broader sociopolitical context, which I had come to recognize increasingly as much more determinant of Toba experience than I had previously considered.

Mayor Ducca wanted me to know that the city regularly hired Toba on municipality jobs. Upon inquiry, he confirmed that they were generally considered good workers. When I asked whether the jobs were full-time with benefits, it turned out that, with but one exception, they were part-time with no benefits.

Worked on Buenos Aires lectures in the A.M. and also acquired copy of *Barrio Nam Qom Plan* at the Land Office with authorization from the mayor's office. In the P.M. Edgardo Perrín helped to translate my lectures into Spanish. Interviewed by Hugo Alberto Mathot for television interview in the evening.

The lectures referred to are described below. Edgardo did a yeoman's job with my Spanish, which had become rusty owing in part to the intrusion of Italian during our years in Rome. As for the TV interview, it was shown while I was traveling by bus to Resistencia.

Although it seemed important to acquire a copy of the Toba barrio blueprint, documenting which family occupied each plot, I have not since made use of it. The evolution of this settlement is a story that deserves telling. At one point when the Toba first squatted there they were carted off in a truck to an abandoned forest area several miles out of town. When the Toba came to our house to complain, I contacted a lawyer who eventually helped them to return legally. It will be recalled that the owner eventually willed the plot to the Toba.

To the municipality to get names of the plot owners in the Barrio Plan acquired yesterday. Had a long talk with Mr. and Mrs. Johannson about their work with the Toba.

> Worked with Perrín on lectures all day, except for trip to Juan
> XXIII School and lunch with the brothers who manage it. Got bus
> tickets in the P.M. and had a big farewell dinner with guests at the
> Perríns, always the gracious hosts, in the evening.

Clearly the Johannsons had a different image of mission work
among the Toba than that of the Buckwalters and the Mennonite
mission. Their commitment was to strengthen Toba ties to the broader evangelical community and to help them become more fully incorporated into national life. In the process they invested considerable amounts of money in various projects, including running water
for Barrio Nam Qom and a vehicle for Toba use.

By now it is apparent that the Perríns' had become our home away
from home. Their friendship and support has been a bulwark of
strength through the years.

Resistencia, August 25–29, 1988

> Visits with old friends who invited us to lunch and dinner every
> day. Spoke with Miguel Brunswig about Chaco aborigines and IAF
> projects; visited Toba in barrio. Clemente Bonaire took us to his house
> in Corrientes for lunch and put us on the train for Buenos Aires.

Buenos Aires, September 1–4, 1988

> Lunch with Pablo Wright family, where Laura Perrín picked us
> up by car and drove us to her brother Edgardo Jr. and family's in
> Mercedes for dinner and the night. Stopped at the Luján Cathe-
> dral on the way. Impressive.

Our first trip to Pablo's home to meet his family. Little did we realize then that they would be with us in Philadelphia two years later. Seeing Laura Perrín, a nun, and Edgar Jr., whom we had always
called Edgardito (but no longer), was a special treat as well.

> Lunch with Mirta Lange. Taxi to airport where Lois took return
> flight to the U.S. Returned by bus to the hotel.
> Spent most of the time with Ricardo and Mirta Lange who
> helped polish my lectures for the institute.

Those lectures certainly required extensive help. Our visits with
the Langes on this trip brought back nostalgia for the times we had
spent there with our young daughters in 1972.

Rosario, September 6–12, 1988

Met with anthropology professors Garbulsky and Vázquez at the University of Rosario. Garbulsky took me to the Public Housing section of the Rosario Municipality to review plans for a new Toba barrio. Lectured to Vázquez and Bigot class at the university. Introduced to dean of the school by Professor Vázquez to discuss possible faculty and student exchanges with Temple University. Met with faculty and student groups working with the Toba.

Made several trips with Maricel Stroppa to Empalme, where we visited Toba families I had known in the Chaco. Saw Francisco Soria and family, Mrs. Clemente Gómez, Florencio Núnez of La Pampa, and the elder Martín García of Las Palmas. Lunched with Stroppa group working on health problems and demography in the Toba settlements. Visited Cerrito, where we found the Marcelo Cabrera family from Miraflores (she an Avalos of L. 17) and Montiel Romero, whose autobiography Edelmi Griva and Maricel Stroppa had produced. Also visited Victorino Arce and family in a *criollo* barrio, where the Jimmy Swaggart Choir sang songs in English on television inside the house while we spoke in Spanish and Toba outside. Weird!

The visit to Rosario enabled me to reestablish ties with colleagues working with the Toba and to meet some young scholars at the university who were also carrying out research in urban Toba settlements. How the world has changed since the 1960s when so few Argentine scholars had contact with the Toba. The trip also permitted me to see firsthand the large number of Toba in various urban settlements, including a major one in the center of town. It was an exciting experience to interact with colleagues and encounter old friends from all over the Chaco.

Buenos Aires, September 15, 1988

To José Braunstein's for visit and exchange of ideas about his work in Formosa province with the Pilagá. Discussed power centers in Argentina: military (army), church (Catholic), labor (CGT), and business. Valentín Moreno arrived because he dreamed Braunstein would have a visitor! Returned to hotel for late night coffee and discussion with Wynarczyk.

José Braunstein is one of the few Argentine ethnographers who spends extended periods of time in the heart of the Chaco. The discussion was intense and lucid. The appearance of Moreno was a pleasant surprise. Although not well acquainted, we had met previously. Because he was an urbane and informed Toba who served as an informant for Pablo Wright, I was impressed that anticipatory dreams continued to provide rationale and affirmed motivation for his travel and social interaction.

Extended trip, September 21–October 1, 1988

Travel with LASPAU to Comodoro de Rivadavia, Río Grande, Ushuaia, Neuquén, Mendoza, and Santiago, Chile, in order to help select Fulbright/LASPAU candidates.

The trip to Tierra del Fuego was a special treat amidst a highly demanding schedule of interviews. Not only did we touch base with research scholars there, but we also saw some of the most spectacular scenery I have ever witnessed in my life. Our takeoff from Ushuaia in a heavy crosswind on the short runway was scary. One week later a plane crashed into the water when it was unable to stop on the runway. The trip by car across the Andes from Mendoza was equally breathtaking.

Posadas, October 5, 1988

Meeting in the A.M. with Miguel Brunswig and the Ana María Gorosito Kramer team regarding Toba project. Lunch with Brunswig. To afternoon lecture at university after which Leopoldo Bartolomé gave us a tour of his impressive resettlement project. I gave a lecture at the university in the evening on the Toba.

This represented the initiation of my work for Inter-American Foundation on their Toba projects in the Chaco. Brunswig's idea was to link the projects to the university in Posadas. I was not enthusiastic about this prospect given that none of the scholars there, with the exception of Leopoldo Bartolomé, had any experience with the Toba and he was not projected to be involved. It was a pleasure seeing Leo again after so many years. We spoke with fond memories and regret about the defunct Social Articulation Group. The resettlement project he managed resulted from the enormous binational dam project Yaciretá at Posadas.

Resistencia, October 7, 1988

Left early in rented car for Colonia Chaco, arriving at 10:00 A.M. A big crowd was waiting for Orlando Sánchez and authorities from Resistencia to inaugurate IDACH, the new organization of aboriginal affairs to be directed by Orlando. Spoke with Eugenio Martín and Adán Medina of Legua 17 and with Antonia Cabrera of Miraflores. When it became apparent that the group from Resistencia would not arrive, I left for Machagai to visit with Antonio Domingo, who had moved to the edge of town. Traveled to Quitilipi for visit with René Sotelo's daughter and got room in a hotel.

IDACH (Instituto del Aborigen Chaqueño) is the indigenous institute that was then forming to replace the provincial agency in charge of aboriginal affairs. The atmosphere was charged with expectation given that the decision had been taken to hand the agency over to aboriginal people themselves. Failure to initiate the project on the day intended was due to a political conflict between two rival Toba factions over the results of elections to the new positions. Argentina had come a long way from the early days of authoritarianism when Indian reservations were formed and administered in far-off Buenos Aires and when the politics of managing Toba affairs was restricted to whites.

Quitilipi and Legua 17, October 8–10, 1988

Daily trips to L. 17 in order to investigate the Inter-American Foundation project there. Had lengthy discussions with old friends and with members of the new Communal Commission concerning the project. Met with opposition members who had called a meeting intended to replace the present commission in the next election. Key visits with Cipriano Notagai, Eugenio Martín, Santiago Matías, and a number of promising new young leaders. Met on final day in Quitilipi with Nicasio Gómez, the provincial director of indigenous affairs until the new organization is established.

It felt strange to be associated with the IAF project at a time when local politics had heated up over new elections. The division followed traditional lines to a large extent, but not completely. An entirely new leadership had emerged in the community that I had not known previously, but it was not yet well established, as my IAF Report (1988a) indicated. The newly established elected Communal Commission has introduced an entirely new element of politics into the community formerly managed by Chief Gómez.

The interview with Nicasio Gómez was enlightening. It became obvious that the transition to indigenous leadership would not be as simple as the news media projected.

Sáenz Peña, October 13–19, 1988

Up at 6:00 A.M. for trip to Raíz Chaqueña. Visited with commission members until noon. Saw school of thirty-five students in operation. Made tour around the settlement with Florenciano Lorenzo, commission vice-president, and the provincial delegate Segovia, including a visit to the ruins of Guacará. Terribly dry and dusty. Serious water problem. Visited with Antonio Monzón family, who carry water for three miles. Saw nicely worked land by Eugenio Cortéz and Vicente Matías families. Returned to S.P. having driven nearly two hundred miles, one-half in dust and bumpy roads, for an enjoyable dinner with Perríns at the Rotary Club in celebration of Mother's Day.

This entirely new Toba settlement was in an area I had never visited, although most of the people who moved there were acquaintances. The big problem was water as this is a dry area and the region was undergoing a serious drought. It was fascinating to see an entirely new community in the process of formation, throwing light on how some of the older, more established ones may have been formed. Owing to the serious drought, the community was surviving mainly on hunting and gathering. *Not* what the planners had in mind. I strongly recommended that full attention be given to a more permanent water supply.

When I asked directions from a neighboring Russian farmer on the way in, he complained that had the government given him half the support the Indians are getting, he would have this desert blossoming like a rose. Resentment over provincial support for Indian settlements is a sore point with many white neighbors, making already poor relationships even more problematic.

Left early for Dirección del Aborigen, Colonia Chaco, and the official establishment of IDACH by the governor of the province. After flag ceremony and official speeches, the governor commissioned Orlando Sánchez, plus two Toba, two Mocoví, and two Mataco commission members. A group performed traditional Toba music. Saw many old friends from all over the Chaco. Impressive ceremony. Returned late to S.P. for dinner with the Buckwalters.

Perhaps my most unforgettable experience of the 1988 trip. To see Toba men whom I had known as children and young men assume leadership of the new indigenous institution was an emotion that is hard to describe. I kept thinking about the enormous obstacles to mutual understanding and how difficult it would be to satisfy inflated expectations among the Toba, Mocoví, and Mataco groups represented.

The ceremony was, indeed, impressive and included a choral group that sang aboriginal folk songs. While I had heard individual Toba sing and play traditional music, this was the first time I heard a choir that was not strictly religious and evangelical. It was an entirely new experience, yet one anticipated in my *Harmony and Dissonance* volume, as one white visitor from Cordoba who had read the book graciously pointed out. I overheard him say it is too bad that Miller cannot be here to witness this event. At that point I introduced myself.

> Visits to L. 15, Raíz Chaqueña, the two Toba barrios of Castelli, Pozo Toro, Miraflores, and Colchón. Long talks in Castelli with Carlos Benedetto, with Orlando Sánchez, Jorge Collet, and Virginia Cicchetti. The visit to Colchón for dialogue between whites and Toba was very interesting. Big problem was getting whites to listen to what the Toba participants were trying to say. Miraflores visit was not the same with Chief Agusto Soria now deceased. The Cabrera family gave a warm welcome. Saw members who had recently arrived from Rosario.

Once again I encountered new experiences at El Colchón where the Junta Unida de Misiones (JUM) with headquarters in Buenos Aires had sponsored a dialogue that was unique in its attempt at cross-cultural understanding. It was a pleasure to be a part of it, but instructive as to the difficulties involved. Clearly we whites wanted to talk too much rather than listen. When we spoke too soon, or initially misrepresented what the Toba members were trying to say, they tended to clam up rather than speak further.

The quick trip to Miraflores was too brief, but I did manage to visit what remained of the Soria family now that Chief Agusto had died and his son Lorenzo and family were in Rosario. I also visited the large Cabrera family who, at their initiation, all collected their respective nuclear units with children and grandchildren for photographs. They wanted me to take back remembrances for Lois and the girls, exhibiting nostalgia for the times we had shared in the past.

Perhaps it was a superficial impression, but I felt that the spirit in the community was gone. Discussions concerned travels to Rosario and Buenos Aires. There was little talk or interest in local events, of which there appeared to be few, particularly since Soria's son, who was attempting to fill his father's shoes, was in Rosario. Could the loss of Chief Soria make such a difference, or was this merely a superficial temporal impression?

Buenos Aires, October 31–November 1, 1988

Gave three lectures at the National Institute of Anthropology; the first two to graduate students on anthropological theory. The final one was an evening public lecture on the Toba.

Spent day with Marcela Mendoza and Pablo Wright in barrios. Saw Toba family that was highly acculturated. Talked about the urban plight of the Toba.

While I had lectured to scholarly communities at various provincial universities in Argentina, this was my first invitation to speak at the prestigious private institute. The public lecture was well attended and the questions were interesting.

It is apparent that on each successive ethnographic field trip I paid increasingly less attention to the diary and more to fieldnote journals. This shift is not surprising given my developing preoccupation with ethnographic concerns that might be turned into professional texts. The initial ethnographer diary tended to follow the form established during my missionary days. The people I contacted tended to be the same as well. On later trips, however, as I moved out of more familiar habitats to new settings among people with whom I was less well acquainted, the focus became less on interpersonal relationships and more on the knowledge produced. Interpersonal relationships with Argentine colleagues and friends also took on increased significance.

As reported in act 2, my initial visits during missionary days to university and museum libraries throughout Argentina put me in touch with Argentine colleagues interested in the Toba. With the exception of Professors Palavecino of Buenos Aires and Balmori of La Plata, however, their interests were based on curiosity rather than field experience. Obviously this situation has changed dramatically. Thus the frequent mention of non-Toba Argentine colleagues is not only a reflection of my own developing ties with the scholarly community, but also of its ties to the Toba. There is, furthermore, much more awareness of the Toba among the general populace as the former settle in urban neighborhoods throughout the country and become more officially involved in their own administration. Since the democracy movement of 1983, the central government in Buenos Aires has become increasingly attentive to indigenous organizations that lobby for their own concerns. A national Indian policy is currently under discussion in the legislature, but yet to be implemented.

Now that a number of young scholars travel regularly to the Chaco or carry out research among the Toba in Buenos Aires and Rosario, the reports of their field experience have changed the way I think and write. No longer do I write without the added insight of colleagues who bring their own unique perspectives to bear on what is known about the Toba. Furthermore, the Toba themselves have taken an interest in recording their own tribal lore and cultural history (Sánchez 1987). These voices not only expand our knowledge and understanding of the lived worlds experienced by contemporary Toba, dating my own writings and making them less conspicuous than when initially produced, they also point to the variety of Toba interactions with the broader society.

This last trip raised significant questions about the image of my ethnographer self tied to the Toba. First, some of the Toba who meant the most to the construction of that self were no longer alive. Second, those who were had experienced dramatic changes in their world much as I had experienced during our long absence from the Chaco. Consequently, we spent much of the time talking nostalgically about past events. The bonds of friendship were still there, but they did not carry the weight of former years. Finally, young Argentine scholars are opening up new discourses about the Toba that impact upon my self-image. They write about a new generation of Toba, for example, that has increasingly remote connections to the forest culture that I had experienced in the 1960s. Such awareness contributed to the reevaluation of my ethnographer self that led to the production of this volume.

The ethnographer diaries document but do not discuss this growing distance between myself and the Toba. Not only is my knowledge of a new generation of Toba limited owing to contacts that are too brief and narrow in scope, but the forest culture I knew thirty years ago is being reproduced in significantly transformed mode. My developing attention to reflexivity and problems of ethnographic production in teaching and writing can be understood best in this context. Persistent doubt about my ethnographer self-image was at work here. I had become something of a pilgrim in a land where I once felt fully at home, reactivating once again my pilgrim sense of identity.

During my missionary days my doubt was about theology and the role of religious savant that I was being asked to play, both by the mission board and by the Toba. At no time, however, did I have any doubt about the interpersonal relationships established, which revealed keen insight into Toba ways of thinking and acting. Throughout my ethnographic field trips, on the other hand, it was the quality of interpersonal relationships that I found myself increasingly calling into question, which in turn has led me to question the role of the ethnographer as well. From doubt about my role and trust in my relationships, I moved to initial trust in my new role and doubt about my relationships, leading eventually as this book progressed to doubt about the ethnographer role itself.

Earlier I wrote about the distance from my Toba experiences while in Europe in positive terms, arguing that it enabled me to see them in clearer perspective. It must be acknowledged, however, that distance in time and space also weakened the personal relationships established with Toba individuals and families that constituted the essence of those experiences, potentially jeopardizing the basis for solid ethnographic endeavors in the future. The point is that my role as anthropologist does not permit the extended interaction over time that would allow the rebuilding of relationships established during that initial five-year period. Furthermore, the Toba have found no redeeming value in my new ethnographer role as they claimed for themselves in the missionary one. Until such interpersonal relationships are reaffirmed and new ones established, my contemporary ethnographic insights will be running on a near empty tank. The implications of this observation for ethnographic production, as well as for anthropology more generally, will be confronted in the final scene.

Scene 3: Practicing the Profession

In act 2 my missionary diary served as a *text* for analyzing the cultural representations revealed through my personal interactions with the Toba. The experiences recounted there disclose significant insights that continue to provide substance for much of my cultural knowledge about the Toba today. In the act of reproducing the diary here for public readership, I came to recognize an emergent professional self-image. My comments about the *text* constitute an essential component of that self-recognition. While looking over the diary, I recognized crucial ethnographic insights, such as leadership conflicts, that have been underdeveloped in my professional writing.

We turn now to a more standardized form of cultural representation, the formal texts consciously produced for disciplinary consumption. The reexamination and analysis of texts directed to colleagues more directly apprehend a professional self-image at work since such texts constitute its very essence. The idea here is to explore what appear to have been the fundamental contextual factors that motivated and shaped, sometimes without conscious awareness, my professional writings. An exercise in textual self-recognition, this scene represents an examination of the determining factors that influenced the decision to produce a text in its form at a given point in time. Here we are exploring new ground since biographical considerations are normally separated from scientific productions rather than interfaced with them. The argument being made, of course, is that such interfacing is essential to a clearer understanding of how disciplinary knowledge gets produced.

In recent years anthropologists have paid considerable attention to the manner in which their ethnographic texts are constructed. The problem is not primarily a matter of style, although forms of writing are a consideration, but rather of questioned authority. Literary forms and techniques utilized by authors to establish authority over their texts lie at the heart of the debate. This debate has raised broader questions, in turn, about how anthropologists currently exercise their profession more generally, whether at home or in the field.[19]

Not surprisingly, the most crucial factor determining both the form and content of ethnographic productions involves shifting discourse in the discipline itself. These shifts reflect doubts among colleagues about the nature of truth in anthropology, about what constitutes the essence of the discipline. In this instance doubts experienced by individuals are stimulated and encouraged by colleagues.

Although some ethnographers experience greater transformations than others in their intellectual growth and maturation, every ethnographic account is textured by personal history. The more aware and communicative the writer is of this history, the easier it is for readers to decipher the author's intention. Few anthropologists have been trained, however, to think in such reflective terms. On the contrary, those of us educated in the 1950s and early 1960s were trained to write ourselves out of the text. Consequently, my generation has struggled with the notion of reflexivity. The right balance between ignoring self and self-indulgence in the text has been difficult to strike.

I will attempt to provide precisely such a reflexive stance retrospectively by examining the contexts in which my publications were produced, together with some of the factors that contributed to their tone and character. In this analysis I am also learning a great deal about the self in the context of contemporary disciplinary history, because my persona was in a continual process of reconstitution in these works. They represent, so to speak, my written self. By reexamining the creation and recreation of self in textual productions, I aim to throw light on the significance of personal experience (qua the doubting pilgrim) in shaping them. Personal experience, shaped by ongoing debates among professional colleagues, lies at the heart of any ethnographic endeavor. Both *must* be taken into consideration when examining how professional writings get produced. The idea here is to provide insight into the nature of disciplinary debate by contextualizing it in terms of personal experience.

The groundwork for this exercise has been laid in the preceding scenes. An examination of my change in role from missionary to anthropologist is an obvious point of departure. It establishes a reference point. Nevertheless, it would be misleading to overevaluate this career move since my developing awareness of anthropological doubt throughout both mission and subsequent ethnographic field experience demonstrates more continuity than transformation. In fact, the most fundamental confrontation with doubts about theological affirmations occurred prior to and throughout my field experience with the mission. My change in profession simply made it a fait accompli. Additional shifts in epistemology occurred after I came to recognize myself fully as an anthropologist. These shifts, representative of transformations both within anthropology and in Western thought more generally, are reflected in my writings and will be discussed in this scene.

My experience appears comparable to changing perceptions of professional selves that colleagues demonstrate without having undergone such an abrupt change in career. Developing theory in anthropology, including conflicting postures in the discipline toward ethnographic endeavor, framed the nature of my unfolding productions about Toba life in Argentina. Certainly my involvement with colleagues in Argentina and the United States interested in indigenous peoples of lowland South America, as well as with the department and university where I worked, played a significant role as well not only in the content but in the form of what was written.

By reconstructing the particular contexts and circumstances in which my writings took shape, establishing a dialogue with myself, as it were, I aim to illustrate how ethnographic reporting must be understood as an ongoing process rather than a definitive pronouncement. The very nature of field experience involving doubt and self-reflection at the heart of any serious ethnographic endeavor is inevitably ongoing, changing, and endless. To be faithful to experience, ethnographic reports should reflect this dynamic process.

Looking at my professional publications it is possible to recognize a periodization in the development of my professional textual self. The periods are marked by transformations of my ethnographer self. Not surprisingly, these reflect epistemological shifts in the discipline itself that textured the nature of discourse. The theme of social change and identity transformation runs as a thread throughout all of my writings, yet always speaks to the systemic logic driving the change as articulated among the people concerned. This emic approach to cultural understanding was certainly energized by my extensive field experience with the mission.[20]

During the late 1950s and throughout most of the 1960s my concept of ethnography was informed by a classic "realist" tradition rooted in both American cultural and British functionalist legacies formulated during the early decades of this century.[21] Having been introduced to anthropology for the first time in graduate school, my training at Hartford and Pittsburgh was strong on tradition at a time when the field was beginning to move away from its realist roots. The fundamental idea behind the realist approach to cultural study was a natural view of society that called essentially for observation and description.

Throughout the sixties and seventies the realist tradition came to be increasingly undermined by several alternative approaches that called attention to the limitations of observation and description. One school of thought (cognitive anthropology/ethnoscience) continued to value description but sought to elicit cultural knowledge through the analysis of native language categories. These studies demonstrated problems of an emic versus etic nature that raised serious questions about observation in and of itself. At the same time a symbolic or interpretative approach to the study of culture stressed the meanings shared by members of a society as expressed and reaffirmed through public ritual performances. Geertz's call for a "thick[er] description" (1973) of such meanings demonstrated admirably the limitations of mere description. Together these two North American approaches, while maintaining attachments to naturalism, nudged anthropology away from classic realism. We will observe the influence of both approaches on my writings throughout the seventies.

Two alternative approaches, formulated primarily in France and England, constituted a more radical attack on traditional realism. One involved the French structuralist school articulated most prominently by Claude Lévi-Strauss, who demonstrated that cultural description at the level of behavior depicts ideological affirmations but reveals little by way of analytic insight. He called for the analysis of a structuring process that differentiates and mediates reality as signs. The symbolic function assigns meaning systemically so that the very notion of natural society itself is constituted only in relation to other signs that consign its meaning. The implications of this school of thought for ethnography were enormous since they obliged the researcher to construct infrastructural models to explain cultural activity rather than rely on description at the level of behavior. It will become apparent how this approach impacted most heavily upon my writing throughout the seventies and early eighties.

The other radical alternative, neo-marxism, also involved infrastructural modeling. Here, however, the analysis focused on the dynamic nature of the forces and relations of production, which in capitalism were shown to generate class structure and conflict. Again classic cultural realism was shown to be incapable of depicting differing bourgeois and proletarian perceptions of social reality. It will become evident that my tentative attempts to engage this perspective were never fully developed.

Throughout the eighties alternative approaches to ethnography took a more reflexive turn in the United States. Largely unaware of this development while in Rome, I returned in the mideighties with a more reflexive stance of my own, which prompted me to focus on personal experience as a major factor in shaping ethnographic production. This shift away from the decentered approach of structuralism, which had motivated much of my research and writing throughout the seventies, was prompted by the encounter with philosophical trends in Europe.

Upon discovering the attention to reflexivity in U.S. critiques of ethnography during the mideighties, I joined the call for dialogue through which the voices of people being written about are to be given fuller expression. In both my research and teaching, postmodern critiques of our discipline, together with critiques of the critiques, have captured my attention. The impact of these trends upon my scholarly work will become clear as the scene progresses.

With this general schema in mind, we turn now to an examination of my professional written self with the aim of shedding light on shifting discourse in the practice of anthropology.

Ironically, my very first ethnographic production written for a church magazine (1961), discussed in act 2, scene 3, demonstrates best the contextual experience in which my understanding of Toba culture took place. It depicts the dilemma of the fieldworker in knowing how to share meaningfully with the people with whom one is engaged and what role to play in facilitating understanding with the broader nation-state as well as among the folks back home. Written one year after having arrived in the Chaco, this piece contains more insights into ethnographic experience than do my later writings in anthropology. Seeds of anthropological doubt are more clearly expressed here than in my later writings.

When I began to publish in professional journals I was unaware that my writing style had changed. Presumably my notion of what professional writing was all about, learned primarily at the University of Pittsburgh, inhibited my ability to create the ethnographic scenario as well for anthropological journals as I had for a religious one. Growing awareness of this problem contributed later to my questioning of the professional practice of ethnography.

It has been established previously that the editor played a determinant role in my initial professional publication on Toba kin terms (1966), just as my advisors did in the master's thesis (1964) and doctoral dissertation (1967). Together with publications on the Toba *culto* (1971) and social categories (1973), these constitute my contributions to cultural study under the more strictly realist rubric. It is no accident that two of the three articles were published by *Ethnology*, where description in and of itself has been awarded priority.

The critically annotated Toba bibliography initiated at Hartford in 1956 and presented as my master's thesis in 1964 contains a great deal of ethnographic information, although this was not its primary objective. Particularly in the annotations, but also in the introduction, I inserted ethnographic insights not available elsewhere in print. Throughout subsequent field trips to the Chaco I continued to update the bibliography with a view toward publishing it. When it became apparent that the job of rewriting annotations compiled over more than twenty years was too formidable a task for the time allotted, I decided instead to partially update the study (1980b). I added new materials that had come to my attention, but I made no attempt to cover the field systematically as I had in my thesis. More time and effort went into this research of Chaco source materials than on any other writing project I have undertaken.

The introduction to the update, essentially identical to the one in my thesis, contains a description of the historical shape of cultural information available on the Toba throughout the centuries of contact and the aspects of Toba culture disclosed over time. It demonstrates the enormous wealth of information available on a people when one is willing to search widely. More importantly, it depicts the limited nature of European knowledge about the Toba throughout more than four and one-half centuries of superficial contact.

When I recall the long hours spent in poorly lit and sometimes damp museum libraries, I wonder what drove me to the chase for sources. I suspect it was the inspiration of Professor Leser, who proposed that I would find much more material than I had imagined and in places I would not have originally suspected. Furthermore, his insistence upon a clear distinction between sources and secondary writings provided much of the impetus for my searches.

No only did the long hours spent in compiling bibliographic materials shape significantly my sense of Chaco ethnography, but it also put me in touch with Argentine scholars interested in Chaco ethnography. Above all, it provided a historical sense of context that has influenced my interpretation of cultural expressions encountered over more than three decades. Furthermore, it made me consciously aware that much more documentation is available on the societies anthropologists study than ethnographies tend to indicate. My mentors at Hartford merit credit and recognition both for the suggestion and supervision of this project.

My dissertation (1967) represented my most ambitious effort to apply a conceptual model in the analysis of ethnographic data. My primary recollection of the dissertation experience was disappointment at being obliged to add a cultural summary to the analysis of Toba Pentecostalism. I felt that the coherence of the dissertation was disrupted by the addition of a superficial cultural summary, incorporated at the last instance into the introduction. It was my distinct impression that the late Professor John Gillin, who supervised the dissertation during his final years of declining health, recognized my arguments for letting the piece stand on its own, but acceded to pressure from other members of the department who insisted on its incorporation.

I often regret not having agreed to publish the dissertation with a publisher whom Gillin had found for me. By the time I came to revise the work for publication in Spanish, my thinking had changed significantly and the analytical model that had produced ethnographic insights was no longer pertinent. My major reason for refusing to publish the work in its original form was the presence of that cultural summary and my growing dissatisfaction with the model I had constructed from Wallace (1956) and Smelser (1962). An additional consideration was the awareness that it was written for my committee rather than for a more general audience. No thought whatsoever was given to the Toba reader, for example, nor to any other reader apart from the committee and other departmental faculty.

In order to understand my strong aversion to writing the cultural summary, it is necessary to recreate the context in which the requirement was made. In the midsixties at the University of Pittsburgh it was assumed that a dissertation in anthropology would include a general ethnographic account of the social group investigated, although it was recognized that major attention might be given to one aspect of culture over others. Thus, there was no problem with my focus on Toba religious revitalization, it was simply that a complete description of Toba culture was mandatory in a dissertation. Such attention to cultural description, criticized by fellow graduate students and younger professors, appeared to constitute a holdover from the

Human Relations Area Files and ethnographic atlas approach to ethnography, which many of us were in the process of rejecting.

In retrospect, I suspect that my perception of the debate was simplistic and to some extent misinformed. I identified with a younger generation that sought to break new ground where reliance upon outdated approaches to ethnography could be weakened and experimental ones explored. I felt that my dissertation represented an example of such an approach. Thus, to incorporate a descriptive cultural summary that had nothing to do with the body of the dissertation constituted a misrepresentation that I found hard to accept. Furthermore, it meant acceding to the authority of senior mentors, a sore point ever since my teenage rebellion against bishops.

I now acknowledge that the obligation to write that piece most likely was less politically motivated than I imagined. Furthermore, it had value in that I was forced to think about aspects of Toba life ignored in my analysis of the impact of Pentecostalism. At the time, however, it seemed like blind acquiescence to tradition and a means to keep the younger generation in line. Today I find it amusing that I, together with fellow students, considered the matter of such momentous import. Our intense reactions against what we considered the exercise of mentor power (a graduate student syndrome?) were no doubt intensified by the paradigmatic shift taking place in the discipline in the sixties.

What the dissertation did contain that I have not discussed since was a frank discussion of the strengths and weaknesses of the "participant observer" technique that I utilized to acquire the necessary insights for writing. Here as much as anywhere my notions about ethnographic practice were articulated. I distinguished two types of "informants": leaders and nonleaders. The first group was divided into traditional chief/shamans (*pi'oxonaq*) and contemporary religious leaders (*dirigentes*). Chief/shamans were further divided into those who participated in the *culto* under analysis, but not in a leadership capacity, those who converted to the movement and directed a congregation, those who did not join the movement and remained largely indifferent to it, and those who once participated but became disillusioned and largely abandoned their involvement.

The vast majority of my contacts were with several senior shamans, who kept a firm hand on the *culto* but did not direct it, and the Spanish-speaking church leaders whom I described as middle or younger generation men who spoke fairly good Spanish and who saw themselves in leadership opposition to traditional chief/shamans. Nonleaders were divided into regular participants, sporadic participants, and nonparticipants. Statements by informants were documented on the basis of this breakdown. Non-Toba informants included fellow missionaries and other Spanish-speaking Protestant pastors who had contacts with the Toba, *criollo* traders and cotton farmers whose interactions involved economic dealings, rural school teachers who taught Toba children, politicians who worked with indigenous organizations, and a variety of neighbors whose contacts were of a more informal nature.

I indicated the number of individuals with whom I worked in each category, so it became obvious that my description and analysis of Toba religious activities depended largely upon contacts with religious leaders and shamans active in the *culto*. No attempt was made to analyze the effect of such strong reliance upon religious leaders on the central thrust of the dissertation, which made religious action the center of community life and culture.

Clearly this represented a traditional realist approach to data that was less radical than I imagined at the time. While there was value in attempting to identify the source of information received, the relationship between source and conclusion in the text was seldom evident. Thus, what appeared to constitute a solid empirical technique, quantifying the basis of one's data, had no significant meaning in the text.

I found that Wallace's model of revitalization lacked teeth when it came to accounting for change. It neatly depicted a process of movement from one state of social equilibrium to another, but it didn't help to explain why the Toba indigenous churches took the particular form they did in the midtwentieth century. Consequently, I turned to Smelser's *Theory of Collective Behavior* (1962), which classified types of social movements and provided a model that enabled me to explicate better the social conditions that led the Toba to establish their own *cultos* throughout the Chaco. The approach was standard empiricism as I sought to order what I considered existing data into an explanatory model. The taken-for-granted generalization of a Toba Other that failed to account for regional variation and the presumption to speak on behalf of such an Other constitute serious problems from today's perspective that were simply not considered at the time.

My 1971 article on Toba church services entails a detailed description of the origin and character of the Pentecostalistic religious ceremony. It built upon materials I collected during the 1966 field trip, but also upon my experiences as a missionary. The idea was to provide an account of the religious ritual activity that could be called upon in subsequent writings. Professor Spoehr's comment that it was an easy article to edit encouraged confidence in my ability to write for professional journals. Writing this piece enabled me to conceptualize the order and structure of the *culto* still practiced in much the same manner described except for the addition of musical instruments and young women song leaders. The article reflects my contention that the *culto* is essentially of one character irrespective of denominational affiliation.

The 1973 paper proved to be of more interest to the Toba than any other item I have written. It identified traditional band names by ecological niche and the resources exploited. Subsequently I have come to view these names in more dynamic terms as well as to perceive the relationship between local bands and regional territories in more integrated fashion. During subsequent trips to the Chaco I discovered that young Toba are highly interested in these names and their meanings. While most names still persist in family lore, many young people, particularly in the southern region, are losing identification with them even while expressing nostalgia for their retention. While all senior Toba in the sixties could identify themselves by such kin group markers, this was no longer true in 1988 when young people at El Colchón and Castelli wanted to know more about the named groups and about the relationship between bands and regional categories. Unfortunately, my knowledge was too limited to fully satisfy their inquiries; thus, the discussion was less definitive than several of them would have desired.

Is it coincidental that of all my ethnographic productions, the one least acknowledged in the discipline is the one most valued as significant by the Toba? It is not difficult to recognize why this piece is of interest to young Toba seeking to know more about their cultural roots, yet it has found no comparable interest among colleagues, perhaps due partly to where it was produced. This observation raises the important question of for whom and for what purposes anthropologists write.

In preparation for the 1972 study leave, I began to rewrite my dissertation with the aim of publishing a revised version in Spanish for an Argentine reading audience. Most of the structural revisions were made prior to my arrival in Argentina, while the ethnographic content was developed and brought up-to-date in the field. As already indicated, I submitted the completed manuscript to Paidós before leaving Argentina in December 1972. The company promised to print it sometime the following year.

This trip coincided with President Perón's awaited return to his native country after nearly two decades of exile. It was a period of intense political and economic turmoil. The trauma of economic hard times faced by Paidós during the subsequent years caused my editor to recommend that I offer the manuscript to Siglo XXI when I arrived in Buenos Aires for the 1974 Social Articulation Conference. In fact, I arrived the very day Perón died and attended his massive funeral procession several days later in Plaza de Mayo.

A review of my passport entries shows that my visits to Argentina coincided with some highly significant political events: 1966, the military coup of Onganía, in which a tear gas bomb was thrown at my feet as I attempted to find out from a bystander what was going on in the Plaza de Mayo (my photograph of a burning automobile nearly resulted in confiscation of the film); 1972, the return of Perón; 1974, my arrival on the day Perón died.

Following Perón's death the political climate in Argentina turned increasingly reactionary. The publication headquarters of Siglo XXI, charged with publishing "leftist" material, was forcibly entered and the operation closed down. Eventually my manuscript, including the original maps and photographs, was tracked down through the persistence of Esther Hermitte and forwarded to Mexico City, where it was published by the same company (1979b). The English version, sans photographs, was made available to North American colleagues the following year under the title *Harmony and Dissonance in Argentine Toba Society* when produced by the Human Relations Area Files (1980c).

The musical metaphor of harmony and dissonance represented my attempt to reorganize the ethnographic material into a more coherent whole, even while relying less on the Smelser model I had constructed for my dissertation. Certainly Lévi-Strauss's *The Raw and the Cooked* (1969) and *Tristes Tropiques* (1955) were influential to my thinking at that time. Because of my singing experience, the music metaphor made a great deal of sense to me as a means to express the nature of Toba social transformation. It was my late colleague and close personal friend Abdul Hamid el-Zein's extensive knowledge and teaching of French structuralism that stimulated my interest in the subject and gradually changed the manner in which I conceptualized ethnographic endeavors.

A close examination of *Harmony and Dissonance* demonstrates the beginnings of this shift, which became more apparent by middecade. The structuralist impact on my notions of ethnography involved increasing awareness that anthropologists are produced by social context and circumstances rather than by mere individual will. In a word, I became sensitized to the notion of a decentered subject. At the same time, I also became increasingly attentive to the fact that my writings must pay more attention to the Toba reader. This was my first production that demonstrated at least a limited awareness of a Toba reading audience.

The fundamental problem with the book, however, was that I never quite got away from the Parsonian limitations of the Smelser model.[22] By postulating an original harmonious state, I projected an equilibrium model of the Rousseauan noble savage without intending to do so. The argument depicted the Toba's harmonious relationship with the social and physical environment that was disrupted by conquest, colonization, and missionization. In an effort to document what I still consider to be the enormous negative impact of European conquest, I overstressed the dissonance of contact and undervalued its original presence inherent in traditional social relations.

Toba life was not all peace and harmony before conquest, yet it was much more in tune with the natural habitat than it is today, and that was the point I sought to expound. The book did represent a social commentary on the ill effects of colonial domination, but it failed to acknowledge the tension and contradiction that already operated before the first Spaniard set foot in the Chaco. Robert Murphy's *Dialectics of Social Life* (1971) called my attention to the limitations of the functionalist equilibrium model underlying my ethnographic efforts up to that point. However, it was several years before I became sufficiently acquainted with his argument to recognize its significance for teaching and writing.[23] By this time I had begun to conceptualize cultural study in terms more in keeping with his argument.

My first publication subsequent to the dissertation, however, was not about the Toba per se, but rather about the missionary as an inadvertent conveyer of a naturalistic worldview, an idea expressed initially in two footnotes to my dissertation (1967:251–52). This article (1970) has been republished and cited more frequently than any subsequent one. It was my colleague Elisabeth Tooker who suggested that I had the makings of an article in the observation that missionaries tend to inadvertently serve as agents of secularization. At the time we were both teaching a course on religion in non-Western societies that attracted a large number of students. My lecture on missionaries piqued her interest and her enthusiastic response planted the seed for the article.

While the focus was on unintended consequences of missionary action, the article contained a great deal of ethnographic information as well. My observation that the Toba church tends to exclude economic concerns as part of its religious activities, in contrast to traditional shamanism where economics was clearly tied to shamanic dreams and control, was an important one that continued to inform my later writings. While the *culto* raises funds for its activities, as well as hopes for external support, it does not address concerns about subsistence practices in any significant manner. The notion (borrowed from Weber) of "disenchantment" with traditional means to cultural ends merited more attention than it received.[24] What the article failed to address, in retrospect, was the expectations about receiving cargo expressed by Nolasco Rodríguez on June 27, 1966.

The article appeared to stimulate a great deal of disciplinary interest in the investigation of missionary influence elsewhere in the world, a topic that had received surprisingly little professional attention previously.[25] As with many new ideas, however, it was soon overworked so that by the end of the decade research on missionary activity and reports on the tenuous relationships between missionaries and anthropologists became so commonplace that my interests shifted elsewhere. I did help to organize a session on the subject at the 1979 annual meeting of the American Anthropological Association in Cincinnati, where I read a paper subsequently published by *Anthropological Quarterly* (1981a). This piece sought to balance what I considered a myopic approach to the subject in which some anthropologists were too quick to judge missionary action in stereotypic terms, yet slow to recognize their own disenchanting influence among the people they studied. In the process I sought to blur some of the facile distinctions postulated between missionary and anthropological logic. This work reflects a significant shift in discourse in which the influence of structuralist thought is evident.

The publications on missionaries and anthropologists as agents of change, together with "Unintended Effects of Protestant Missions in the Gran Chaco," a paper read at the University of Wisconsin Tinker Lectures (1977b), tended to stereotype me in the discipline much as an actor gets identified with a particular role. Funding agencies and publishers continued to send manuscripts for review on the subject long after I had lost interest. The image of self projected by these professional agencies and colleagues surely had an influence on my notions of my own anthropologist self, if only in reaction to the stereotype. While intellectually I had resolved my ambivalence about missionary practice, the writings prompted professional colleagues to identify me with the subject, marginalizing me around a topic of problematic concern to the discipline and thus reinforcing my pilgrim sense of self.

Of particular interest to the theme under consideration here is the observation that my productions on unintended consequences of missionary activity served to bring closure to the doubting process involving mission activity. Confronting my own resolution in public affirmation, particularly at the 1977 Tinker lecture, concluded the inner struggle. Ironically, rather than cast out the "demon" of mission identity in my new profession, however, it served to reconfirm it for my colleagues for a long time. Furthermore, the missionary pieces clearly appealed to a broader disciplinary audience than did my more focused ethnographic productions.

Interaction with Latin American scholars during the early seventies, particular in Argentina, also had significant impact upon my professional self. I already described the dilemma I faced in 1972 over how to respond to Edgardo Cordeu and Alejandra Siffredi's book *De la algarroba al algodón*. Not only was I sensitive to their critique of my dissertation even while appropriating it, but I also felt strongly that they had overworked and exaggerated the social movement model for their analysis of aboriginal Chaco history. Furthermore, while I found some of their critical comments constructive, more represented misreading, even, it seemed to me, deliberate oversight of my analysis.

In a review article entitled "Los tobas y el milenarismo" (1972), I both documented the indiscriminate appropriation of my dissertation and criticized what I viewed as a too cavalier application of millennial modeling to events in Chaco history that did not appear to reach those proportions. While it might be argued that the disagreement depicted to some extent different research and writing styles in Argentina and the United States, the problem at heart was one of professional interaction. The relationship of mutual trust and respect that had been established with an older generation of Argentine scholars was seriously undermined by this experience.

The authors' response to my critique (Cordeu and Siffredi 1973) not only failed to clarify matters but raised the very specter of ethnographic imperialism that I had sought to overcome by revising my dissertation for publication in Spanish. It is unfortunate these exchanges were made in such confrontational terms that the professional and ethnographic issues involved tended to be ignored. I seriously regret the rupture in personal relationships that both their book and our commentaries produced.

The exchange did point to questions about how ethnographic data get collected and interpreted. My experience involved extended years with the Toba, learning the language and researching documents over more than a decade. Cordeu, in contrast, had spent only brief periods among the Toba in Miraflores, yet his work produced valuable data and theoretical insights (see Cordeu 1969, 1969–70). He had the advantage of access to Argentine literature and knowledge of historical events that provided a perspective that I could only partially acquire despite years of effort. Obviously length of time spent in the field does not in itself determine the quality of ethnographic reporting. The exchanges that Cordeu and I had begun in 1966 could have developed into meaningful stimuli and mutual benefit to our ethnographic productions had the door of communication not been closed. In the heat of battle our distinct perspectives on Toba history and culture were lost, yet it is these that might have been profitably pursued and discussed.

The interaction with Cordeu and Siffredi also had a significant impact on my professional self-image. Until 1972 I continued to imagine myself as an Argentinized American. I identified with Argentine colleagues interested in aboriginal populations and did not see myself as a Yankee writing about Argentina, but rather as an ethnographer with feet more solidly in Argentina than in the United States. My knowledge of South American ethnology, especially the Chaco, far surpassed any understanding of North America or any other continent. The break with Cordeu served to shatter this illusion at a time when I was in the process of establishing an identity with U.S. anthropology through efforts to develop our departmental program at Temple. In retrospect, the undermining of an "insider" sense of self in Argentina probably had a great deal to do with my intense reaction to Cordeu and Siffredi, a point I was not conscious of at the time.

During the three conferences of the Social Articulation Group in Buenos Aires an interesting and healthy debate developed concerning the relationship between theory and ethnographic data. My 1974 paper was data focused but contained the elements of a French structural analysis that I pursued in the following year's presentation entitled "The Interpretation of Signification: A Semiological Approach to the Study of Social Articulation." I wrote the latter partly in response to a discussion paper prepared by Leopoldo Bartolomé for the conference that attempted to elaborate the conceptual notion of social articulation.

Bartolomé identified five "principal dimensions" of social articulation processes found in the papers presented at the 1974 conference: interethnic, interclass, interregional, rural-urban, and symbolic or semiotic articulation, citing my paper. I argued that the first four, which Hermitte had originally proposed as possible thematic topics for our study of social articulation, were of a different order than the fifth. The fifth dimension, I insisted, constituted a radical alternative cross-cutting the first four more empirical approaches characterized by such concepts as status and role, integration and assimilation, equilibrium and homeostasis, brokers and networks. While such concepts contributed to our understanding of social articulation processes, I continued, they left us in the curious position of Alice and the Cheshire cat, wondering where to go from here.[26]

I suggested that the fifth dimension could systematize knowledge and organize our research in a much more theoretically coherent manner by taking us beyond the level of message to an underlying code that structures messages in particular ways. The intent was to search for this code in the deep structural arrangement of key symbols. I proceeded to illustrate the argument by proposing a tentative analysis of Toba symbolism as expressed in myth and ritual. This structuralist apologetic was later revised and included in a working papers series produced by Temple's Department of Anthropology (1981b). The shift in discourse to a search for meaning at the level of infrastructure is most clearly evident here for the first time. The break with a more empiricist approach to ethnographic production did not come easily, however, so that the genres became "blurred" during this period.

My final conference paper in 1976 on rethinking the peasantry concept criticized its construction and usage as ethnocentric and denigrating. The basic argument was that initial definitions of peasants as "part-societies with part-cultures" (Kroeber 1948:284) had instilled the concept with negative connotations, making it difficult to utilize the term in any positive manner. Foster's (1967:8) depiction of peasants as poor and powerless perpetuates the image found also in Redfield (1956) and Wolf (1966). Banfield (1958) even used the term *backward* in his title. The impression given is that peasants cannot be respected or admired because their political judgments and economic choices tend to be naive. They display stubborn traditionalist attitudes in the face of more enlightened alternatives. I concluded that a more classic case of ethnocentrism is difficult to find.

I cannot recall precisely what motivated me to write this piece, but it was a period when increasing attention was being directed toward peasant literature in the department at Temple. My negative response to the peasant category grew out of dissatisfaction with etic categories, the manner in which they shape ethnographic production, and, in turn, reader opinion. Perhaps of more interest to the theme under development here is the observation that my unwillingness, perhaps inability, to see the Toba as any less than fully human, intelligent, vibrant people with complete and holistic culture stems from my experiences with them as a missionary, *not* as an anthropologist. Obviously the relationship I had established with the Toba while a missionary was unlike the sort of relationships established by researchers who could write about part-societies with part-culture.

The marxists at the session responded that the term constituted an important analytic tool, even while acknowledging some of its problematic usages. Clearly they were not about to surrender it. Debate with the marxists over future topics and directions for the Social Articulation Group resulted in the group's disintegration and demise, much to the mutual frustration of the initial organizers, cutting off future cooperation and collaboration between Latin and North American colleagues.

The 1975 publication on Toba shamanism, a revised version of my 1974 Social Articulation Conference paper, sought to systematize understanding of Toba cosmology and the spiritual world of healing, which continued to play a dominant role in Toba social life. It represented my first attempt to clarify the confusing terms associated with Toba shamanic beliefs and actions. In an effort to explain the transformation of shamanic concepts and practices in the *culto*, I provided a history of Protestant missions that set the stage for the penetration of Pentecostal preaching and ideas during the 1940s. I also introduced the notion of ambiguity, in which the influence of an external symbolic system was shown to have its greatest impact where symbolic meanings lacked clear definition in the first place.

The juxtaposition of an analysis of Toba archaic terms for shamanic practices still in usage with a discussion of the history of Protestant missions among the Toba led at least one reader to ask why I had not published these topics in separate articles. The juxtaposition was intentional, however, as I sought to show how ideas penetrate a cultural system largely unconsciously. It is true that the article incorporates a wide range of materials that might well have merited further elaboration in separate articles (analysis of key shamanic terms, mythemes in folktales, history of missions, to name a few), but it should be noted that I was experimenting with a form of writing that would allow me to discuss history as process rather than event. By historically constituting the Toba shamanistic *culto*, I attempted to demonstrate the unity of mission activities and transforming shamanistic practices in a way that might point to processual analysis rather than description of fixed events. The 1974 paper on the interpretation of signification and this one marked most clearly my rejection of empiricist description in favor of a structuralist approach to ethnographic reporting.

My most ambitious and final effort at structuralist writing was "The Mennonites: The Sociology of Separation and Integration" (1985a). The article comprised a structuralist analysis of the Mennonite ideology of separation with which I was raised. I argued that the notion of a Mennonite identity linked to sixteenth-century Anabaptism was constructed by Mennonite scholars with special interests and motivations tied to specific temporal contexts. The fact that a particular view of Anabaptism was produced by certain scholars means that criteria of selection and rejection, of interpretation and emotion, entered into the resultant product. I went on to argue against the notion of a sixteenth-century Anabaptist *text* in any fixed historical sense. I also sought to demonstrate that no static notion of separation can be postulated for the entire period of Mennonite history.

The responses to that article were varied, but one in particular (Redekop 1986) seemed to imply that I was taking the soul out of believing, that I depicted Mennonite affirmations of identity as invalid. In my rejoinder (1986b), I asserted that the reaction demonstrated a misunderstanding of the structuralist enterprise, which I defined in the following terms:

> Structuralism is *not* an attempt to get at a hidden, invisible, mystical meaning. Rather, it is the analysis of a structuring process in terms of which reality is differentiated, cut, and mediated as signs that condition what, in lay terms, is misunderstood as a duality of form and content. By positioning the relationship of structure to event, the structuralist is analyzing the structuring process as conditioned by the symbolic function in terms of which the speaking subject is seen, *not as an object* but as an element, an instance, of collective symbolism. The nature of the relationship of the individual to the social, a central component of the French structuralist problematic, is perhaps least understood by the casual reader of the literature, thereby subjecting structural analysis to naive charges of reductionism that completely miss the point of the whole exercise.[27]

I went on to assert that the context in which an ideology gets produced is constantly changing. Thus, "since the context constitutes the structuring process, an ideology that served to mark identity in one generation necessarily undergoes transformation by means of the symbolic function." The result is that the basis for constituting themselves as "a people" may not always be what Mennonite ideologists affirm.

My experiences with the variety of affirmations defining Mennonite identity in college and seminary were surely at work here, but the structuralist model allowed the point to be made more dramatically. While reviewing this piece for discussion here, I was struck by the irony that my most articulate statement about structuralism was written at a time when the concept was losing salience for me. It was the last statement I would make on the subject, although the structuralist argument is perhaps more taken for granted than rejected in my later writings. The years in Italy had provided a new perspective on structuralist discourse that undermined my commitment to it as a research strategy.

In a paper on shamanic leadership (1977a), the emic approach to anthropological knowledge characteristic of my writing is most clearly articulated. I argued that the widely accepted distinction between religious and political leadership, between shaman and chief, misrepresented the ethnographic situation among foragers of the Gran Chaco. The assertion was not that such a categorical distinction was incomprehensible to the people concerned, but rather that no leader could be legitimated who had failed to demonstrate empowerment by a Companion Spirit of one sort or another. I suggested that the term *cacique* imposed on these populations by national agencies for purposes of governance was an empty title unless legitimated by some form of shamanic skill.

While this argument was based primarily upon extensive experiences with the Toba, I suggested that a closer analysis of leadership among hunters and gatherers in other parts of lowland South America reveals that such a distinction may often be imposed rather than elicited from ethnographic experience. I cited writings on lowland South American foragers that either overtly or inadvertently supported the thesis. I also noted that historical records demonstrate that leadership qualities change over time and depend to a considerable extent on external circumstances. The idea was to call attention to leadership as a dynamic rather than static category. The appeal was to search for categories in ethnographic context as ethnoscience and cognitive anthropology proposed rather than to impose them from without.

Two writing experiences for a nonprofessional audience taught me a great deal about the reproduction and transmittance of cultural knowledge. The first was a textbook in cultural anthropology (1979a). In the effort to illustrate conceptual arguments I incorporated many ethnographic details about Toba culture that have not been published elsewhere. In the classroom, however, I discovered that the Toba illustrations had little meaning to students until I described for them the larger context in which they operated and the manner in which they were obtained.

The other experience proved to be a lesson in humility that contributed to my growing dissatisfaction with an ethnographic style of presentation. Based on the recommendation of Robert Carneiro, National Geographic asked me to write a section for their book on aboriginal South America entitled *Lost Empires, Living Tribes* (1982a). While the focus was to be on the Gran Chaco region as a whole, the flavor that set the tone was to be based on personal experiences with the Toba. The society sent a photographer to the Chaco to provide illustrations. I was amazed at the variety and quality of prints he was able to produce based upon my recommendation of places and motifs that might best enhance the written text. The spectacular photographs of traditional fishing nets and of cotton fields were impressive, making me realize how primitive were my own feeble efforts at visual representation. The efficient editing of my initial submission that reduced the text without significantly changing its meaning was also an impressionable experience.

My second attempt to engage the growing marxist dialogue in our department was published in 1982 (see 1982b).[28] It was my clear intention to address concerns raised by contemporary marxist scholars without falling into what I considered the trap of dogmatism. I was intrigued with the notion of alienation and the connection between political economy and ideology. In discussions with my colleague Peter Rigby at the time, I envisioned a possible linkage of French structuralism and marxist analysis focused on infrastructural models that might provide fresh approaches to an analysis of my Toba materials.

As the article developed, however, I found myself increasingly affirming a Weberian position on a topic of vital concern to marxists. The argument was Weberian in that it aimed to make actions that were socially meaningful to the Toba comprehensible to a non-Toba audience. I argued that adoption of the Christian symbol Holy Spirit in its Pentecostalist version, where every individual believer had equal access to Companion Spirit power irrespective of position or place, enabled the Toba to move about in the labor market more freely than they would have been able to do without this symbol. I asserted, furthermore, that Marx's concept of alienation, tied as it was to the notion of a capitalist working class, proved surprisingly insightful for a comprehension of contemporary Toba sentiments that appear to have little or no association with a consciousness of class owing to the role of Pentecostalist ideology in reinforcing an ethnic sense of identity. I confess to having taken perverse pleasure in noting the disappointment on some faces when it dawned on them that my analysis was not leading in the direction anticipated.

This pleasure developed out of my frustration at the intellectual climate in my department. During the 1970s I had played a central role as department chair in the formation of a graduate program that offered training in most of the major contemporary trends in the discipline defined by Ortner (1984). However, owing to the premature deaths of two active colleagues and the departure of several others, I felt that the department was becoming too narrowly focused on marxist approaches to political economy. This admittedly paternalistic perception reflected my administrative self, which had previously tried to strengthen the department in this area. What I had not envisioned, however, was a monopolistic focus on marxist analysis that simply replaced the intellectual monopoly French structuralism had attained during the early seventies. My administrative-manager self-image was no doubt at work in the concern to open up options for graduate students rather than narrow them. In this article I sought to broaden the dialogue in directions that were less ideologically tied to the texts of Marx.

However, further investigation indicated that the intent to fuse structuralist models with marxism was highly problematic. The two discourses were simply too incompatible, despite the eloquent contributions of Sahlins (see, for example, 1976). Attention to administrative duties, including the move to Italy in June 1982, abbreviated my participation in the dialogue before it got off the ground. I have subsequently questioned the extent to which the Toba can be categorized as proletarian given the unique relationships they have established with the Argentine nation-state.

The influence of mentor Peter Berger on my thinking is most clearly evident in papers I read at two organized sessions on lowland South American Indians at the annual meetings of the American Association of Anthropology. Both sessions focused on concepts of self and person in the region. Following G. H. Mead (1934) as elaborated by Berger (1963), the first paper (1980a) aimed to show how personal identity is not only socially bestowed but also socially sustained by depicting the phenomenal world of rapidly changing lived experience in which contemporary Toba find themselves. I argued, further, that the notion of identity is devoid of positive content and only takes on meaning when contextualized; that is, relationally linked to the elements that constitute its meaning (the structuralist argument built upon Saussurean logic).

The major elements I identified included other aboriginal populations in the Chaco; white people, consisting of *criollos* (lower and lower middle-class Argentines who trace their origins neither to European nor indigenous North or South American roots) and *gringos* (Europeans); the animal kingdom; and a variety of power beings associated with a cosmographic map categorized into Sky, Earth, and Water beings. Additional elements included kinship terminology and a social identity that tends to underplay the notion of person, which we Westerners are inclined to conceptualize. I concluded that, while French structuralist thought argues for a decentered subject, the Toba ethnographic situation suggests that for them the subject has been decentered all along. This is to say that the idea of self that an anthropologist takes to a study of the Other may have little in common with social reality as that Other experiences it, a further emic argument of the sort now characteristic of my writings.

The second paper (1987) focused on Toba pronominal categories, kin terminology, and personal names with a view toward the dynamic processes that contribute to a transforming sense of Toba subjectivity. Calling upon Lacan's distinction (1977) between an "imaginary" and a "symbolic" order of self-recognition, I sought to elucidate contemporary Toba images of self in the terms *aŷim* (I and me) and *'am* (you) and in Spanish naming procedures that replace a less individuated approach to selfhood in the recent past. I concluded that the process of a growing sense of individuation is accompanied by an ever-increasing awareness of an alienated self. The alienated Toba self strikes me as a topic begging further elaboration and development.

During the sixties and seventies anthropological attention to self was practically nonexistent. The return to conceptualizations of self and personhood occurred in conjunction with the move toward reflexivity in the discipline. It also came at a convenient time for me as I reflected on my experiences in Europe and how they would impact upon reentry into the practice of anthropology in the United States.

In the summer of 1986 I read a paper entitled "Confessions of an Ethnographer" to professional colleagues working in lowland South America (1986a). This paper constituted my initial attention to reflexivity that led eventually to the present book. In fact, the fundamental theme in most of my subsequent writings was foreshadowed here. The late Robert Murphy's positive response to this original paper encouraged me to pursue further the reflexive mode.

How did this confessional stance came about? Why did I make the fundamental break with a transformed version of ethnographic realism to focus on the role of personal experience in the writing process, particularly since that version had been shaped by the structuralist emphasis upon a decentered subject?

Significantly, this was the first paper I wrote after my return from Italy and extensive travel in Europe and the Middle East. The extended hiatus and distance from my Chaco experiences enabled me to reflect on them with a new perspective. As noted previously, I had lost touch with the Toba component of my self-identity. When preparing to write something to present to colleagues working in the area, I was obliged to examine the inclination to write once again about the Toba. More than ever I was aware of a distance from my Chaco memories, yet I desired to return to them. The search for why and how led to the introspection expressed in that paper.

The shift from structuralist logic to an emphasis upon personal experience is not as contradictory as might first appear. To argue that the subject gets produced by a symbolic process involving systemic qualities is not to suggest that self-awareness should be ignored. Structuralism demonstrated how an act of self-recognition necessarily entails constitution of an Other and vice versa. Decentering the subject does not necessarily imply ignoring it. Yet structuralist logic *has* failed to confront the potential significance of unique experience, just as it has tended to sidestep the crucial ethical and moral questions of our time. It was this awareness that led me to abandon it as a research strategy even while the impact of structuralist thought on my notion of ethnographic practice continued to operate.

Curiously enough, I was unfamiliar with the emerging critique of ethnographic practice in the summer of 1986 that could have provided a context for what I sought to express. Although I attempted to maintain some contact with developments in American anthropology while in Rome, my activities and interests were directed elsewhere. Furthermore, when I wrote the 1986 paper I was newly ensconced in the dean's office, where my attention was directed toward curriculum development. Perhaps this distance from a disciplinary self was also at work in my introspection.

At any rate, self-reflection was enlightening in that I was able to articulate some concerns about the ethnographic enterprise that I had never expressed forthrightly. Shortly thereafter, while preparing to teach a graduate seminar in the department, I read Ruby's *A Crack in the Mirror* (1982), Marcus and Fischer's *Anthropology as Cultural Critique* (1986) and Clifford and Marcus's *Writing Culture* (1986), which put me in touch with a discourse about which I had been unaware, one to which I could relate, but not fully agree, at that point in time. It demonstrated for me the extent to which my move toward reflexivity was part of a larger dialogue initiated in the seventies and developed more fully in the 1980s. Once again it is apparent that my disciplinary work was less radical or original than I had imagined at the time.

The return to Argentina in 1988 reinvigorated my interest in prior Chaco experiences by jogging my memory. While investigating the mass migration of Toba families to major urban centers during that trip, I also gave four lectures throughout the country and one in Santiago, Chile, entitled "Hunter-Gatherers in the City: Urban Adaptations of the Argentine Toba." At each presentation I entertained responses that helped to reshape the following one.[29] The responses, as well as scholars in Argentina working with the Toba, led me to revise the lecture, upon my return to the States, for publication the following year (1989a).

The fundamental argument of the article was that foraging modes of subsistence do not disappear overnight when hunter-gatherers are pushed into an urban environment as a result of crisis in the hinterlands. I proposed that the philosophy of appropriating *from* nature, rather than one of *modifying* and *controlling* it, changes slowly. Furthermore, I suggested that paternalistic national policies toward aborigines often reinforce the sense of dependence upon external forces that characterized traditional life in the forest. I supported this argument with information about the kind of jobs to which the Toba are attracted in the city, along with some comments about practices of governmental and nongovernmental agencies that promote dependence rather than self-determination in urban settings.

The publication of "Women and Fire, a Toba Myth" (1988b) represented my effort to contribute to the growing folklore available in the Toba language. The diglot version of this central Toba myth allows the reader to see the literal translation of words and phrases into English, while the narrative translation provides a reading of the text that conveys the general plot. The subtleties of the story must be inferred since no commentary is provided.[30]

In 1989 I was pleased to be invited by Alejandra Siffredi to read a paper in a session on interethnic relations at the First International Congress of Ethnohistory held in Buenos Aires, which I later revised and read at the annual Bennington Conference on South American Indians, entitled "Why Do *Doqshi* (Whites) Always Tell Lies?" (1989b). This piece was prompted by the question I had been asked many times during my early years with the Toba but had long since forgotten until reminded in 1988. I cited it to demonstrate the one-sided nature of discourse on interethnic relations, pointing out that aboriginal populations are not *really* consulted about their views on interethnic communication. My suggestion was to listen to what the Toba say about the subject when left to their own initiatives, which is "Why do white people always tell us lies?" I suggested that whites sometimes lie to deceive, but more often they appear to lie because their intentions are misunderstood.

This appeal to engage the Toba themselves in direct dialogue about topics that affect them deeply was written at a time when I was not yet aware of the dialogic approach to ethnography in the literature (such as Tedlock 1972; Dwyer 1977, 1979; Webster 1982; Clifford 1988) that could have strengthened the argument. While my discomfort with speaking for an Other was stimulated by field experiences in 1988, particularly at El Colchón, rather than by scholarly debate, the growing literature on this topic demonstrates that what was once regarded as privilege and obligation, speaking on behalf of others presumably incapable of speaking for themselves, must now be acknowledged as naive, insensitive, and arrogant. Here a critique of standard ethnographic approaches to topics of concern to anthropology, in this case ethnicity, is most clearly evident.

An attempt to engage the Toba in dialogue about matters that concern them most deeply has been attempted at El Colchón by the United Missions (JUM) group stationed in Castelli and at Sáenz Peña, where the board of education established the Center for Bilingual Education, designed to train Toba teachers. Still another example involves the reorganization of the Indian Affairs Agency at Napalpí (IDACH) under indigenous leadership, although the extent to which indigenous input operates de facto remains in question.

In the *doqshi* paper I pointed out that dialogue can be a slow and painful process for those unaccustomed to listening to what indigenous people intend to say. The limited dialogue currently underway demonstrates the mistake of presuming to represent the Toba as one voice. It should not come as a surprise that, when given the opportunity, the Toba speak with many voices. Such a variety of expression not only calls into question conventional wisdom about Toba culture, a term found extensively in my writings, it also points to the limitations of a form of representation that presumes to speak with authority about an Other. In a word, the unity of such a constructed Other is both presumed and overstated. Keesing (1989:463) has noted that "the assumed sharing of meaning and the imputed omniscience of the 'native speaker' are heuristic myths of our [anthropologists'] own making that have retarded critical thinking about the dynamics and politics of cultural knowledge."

Greater attention *must* be paid to regional kin-based diversity in the Chaco that gets translated into political action, especially now that aboriginal groups participate directly in elections for regional public administrative offices. Precisely for whom a "native speaker" speaks is an issue of increasing relevance in the region. We need ethnographic genres that more effectively depict multiple social realities such as gender, class, ethnicity, and region than do the monolithic categories to which we have been accustomed.

• • •

In reviewing the developmental processes involved in these writings, what strikes me as perhaps most significant was my consistent effort to avoid attachment to any given discourse for extended periods of time. I seemed both willing and eager to experiment with new inventions in the discipline. In retrospect, it would appear that my intense struggle with the theologically conservative concept of revelation instilled at Youth for Christ while a teenager had an impact on the nature of my commitment to later discourses. The total commitment to a truth claim that subsequently proved untenable left its imprint. I knew what it meant to be a "true believer" (Hoffer 1951), just as I knew what it meant to truly disbelieve. The pain of that knowledge no doubt prompted my determination in seminary to pursue theological doubts to their logical and inevitable conclusions. It may very well also have inhibited my commitment to any one discourse in anthropology that would tie me dogmatically to its tenets, given the relationship already established with the Toba that did not fit neatly into any standard anthropological category/discourse. Obviously I have been nurturing doubt all of my adult life. This confession did not appear in the 1986 paper because the awareness only occurred to me while writing this scene. The capacity to engage newly developing conceptual positions in anthropology seems to have involved less emotional struggle than did my doubts about divine revelation and mission activity. Yet this conclusion overlooks the "leap of faith" associated with my move to anthropology and the need to cling to the security blanket of standard approaches, only questioning the authority of the ethnographer in print after it had become accepted discourse in the discipline. I did question my previous writings and sought to revise my perspective in newly designed ones, but the persistence of empiricist training proved difficult to shake. Having replaced religious/spiritual faith and hierarchies with scientific ones, I had an initial reluctance to question the latter as well.

Yet doubts about dogma clearly produced less stress, and even considerable satisfaction, once my appreciation for the doubting process became internalized. This same internalization made it more difficult to recognize my growing dissatisfaction with the practice of ethnography in terms of doubt, since the affirmation of doubt no longer represents the traumatic experience it did in my younger years.

While all my ethnographic accounts portray a culture in the process of transformation, nowhere do I provide insight into my own developing motivations for writing the particular piece I did at a given point in time. Certainly the model behind my formative writing in the discipline was standard ethnographic realism (Marcus and Cushman 1982) or what Spencer (1989:152) appropriately identifies as "ethnographic naturalism," so characteristic of anthropology throughout the first half of this century. The structuralist alternative, stimulated by discussions with my late colleague el-Zein and graduate students, provided the inspiration for much of my writing into the mideighties. In the transitional early seventies productions, however, the initial naturalism continued to inform my texts so that a structuralist "epistemological break" does not appear in any form that is neat and consistent. Similar reconstitutive processes, of course, characterize not only ethnography, but other forms of writing as well.

Rather than produce stress, shifting discourse in the discipline appears to have opened up new perspectives on my field experiences that enabled me to write about them from alternative perspectives. These writings, in turn, have generated responses from colleagues, and more recently from the Toba, that assuredly will shape the orientation of new texts. Hopefully this dynamic process will produce greater mutual understanding so that future texts might reflect more faithfully the interests of those whose lives are represented rather than primarily those of the context in which the ethnographer works.

Denouement

There is no Other, but multitudes of others who are all others for different reasons, in spite of totalizing narratives, including that of capital.

—Michel-Rolph Trouillot

The one constant throughout my adult years both as missionary and anthropologist has been an image of self closely identified with field experiences among the Toba. The we/they distinction characteristic of classical naturalist ethnography that depicts "natives" as objects of study is certainly inappropriate for depicting the nature of the interactions I experienced in the field. My relationship with the Toba is better characterized in Buberian I/Thou terms, but the style of writing pushed me into an I/them construction.[1] Thus, the style of representation obscured the real basis upon which my knowledge about the Toba was produced. This recognition led to a fundamental questioning of the manner in which ethnography has been practiced. Much of the effort here has been directed toward rectifying this deficiency by providing a clearer understanding of the processes whereby personal experiences get translated into scholarly productions.

However, the knowledge produced from these Buberian interactions appears to have had limited value as far as the Toba are concerned. On my most recent field trip in 1988 a "junior elder" from Castelli informed me that *Meguesoxochi* (a mythic figure whose name appears in Chaco history books) had informed him in a dream that I would have a message for his people. Since this message did not come through any channel I could recognize, I was unable, unfortunately, to enlighten anyone as to its content. This example of disjunction in a meeting of the minds illustrates well the limitations to which I refer. A different example was provided in the instance where my knowledge of named social categories extant in the 1960s was in demand among the people of El Colchón and the settlements in Castelli in 1988, but of limited value since I was unable to provide answers to specific inquiries.

In strictly personal terms, interactions with the Toba provided the opportunity to explore doubt and experience freedom from doctrinal constraints, enabling me to act upon my growing convictions concerning the nature of truth. Thus, engagement in Toba discourse both resolved a personal philosophical dilemma and established the basis for my professional identity as a Chaco ethnographer.[2]

The Toba, however, seem to have gained little from my scholarly productions, which would seem to justify their skepticism toward anthropological endeavors in the first place. Certainly individuals have expressed interest in my acquaintance with old-timers and my participation in the early development of the *culto*. Yet this interest is not a strong one urging me to write more for the sake of posterity. The attitude, rather, is one of tolerance toward my professional activities rather than any expression of mutual interest.

While several Toba individuals have expressed appreciation for my writings that document a period when now revered deceased elderly leaders practiced their shamanic powers, a period when Toba self-determination operated to a greater extent than it does today, it is clear that my ethnographic writings have been of primary concern not to the Toba but to scholars interested in lowland South America throughout North America, Argentina, and western Europe.[3] In this context there appear to be shared understandings amidst disagreements. But the purpose of this shared knowledge remains unclear. The role it plays for agencies intervening in Toba social life, for example, has not been investigated in any systematic manner. Also, the extent to which regional scholars gain or lose from this knowledge remains an open question.

At the heart of much contemporary criticism of traditional ethnography lies concern about the exercise of power. As I argued in the article on shamanism (1975), however, power only takes on meaning when contextualized, when the proper elements combine to make its exercise effective. Clearly my presence in the Chaco as a white man with financial support from the United States for a house and Jeep to transport me around, my knowledge of the Bible and familiarity with church liturgy and music, my contacts with Argentine authorities to assist Toba individuals and families with legal and health problems placed me in a greater position of power vis-à-vis the Toba during my missionary days than I was prepared to acknowledge. Attempts to downplay or equalize the position were only minimally successful as the Toba certainly recognized better than I.

Upon my return as an anthropologist I was in a less powerful position as far as the Toba were concerned. I rode buses or bummed rides much as they did and exercised no significant role in the community. But I did select the topics for discussion and determine the subjects for scholarly production, although the Toba gave no indication that they considered this power. They generally responded forthrightly and helpfully to my inquiries, giving the impression that they didn't expect the information to help or hurt them in one way or another. They did wonder why I had surrendered my position with the mission, which they admired and coveted.

Greater sensitivity to concerns about power and advantage has been a positive development in ethnographic endeavor. It has certainly contributed to the ongoing transformation of ethnographic practice. But arguments about power can be as ethnocentric and culture bound as any other. They can obscure the fundamental question of how anthropologists behave in the field or for whom and what purpose ethnographic texts are written.

In an analysis of Arctic ethnography undertaken since World War II, Charles Hughes (1984:24) affirmed that a major portion of Arctic research "was designed explicitly to be of use to the administrator, the policy maker, and the economic developer." The basic reason for this, of course, was that these were the agencies that funded much of the fieldwork in the first place.

In other words, anthropological productions constitute interested pictures that have been formulated not only by the personal experience of the ethnographer, but also by decisions about how research projects get funded. Graduate students and their advisors soon recognize that mainstream evaluators determine which project an agency might fund. Consequently, proposals must be written in such a manner as to be acceptable to those who make the funding decisions.[4] Precisely how those decisions are made, however, remains an enigma to many anthropologists and their students.

What knowledge about the Toba is most pertinent for the Western reader at this point in time and why? Such questioning strikes at the very heart of what anthropology is all about. Throughout its short history as a discipline (the majority of North American universities came to include it in the curriculum only after the middle of the twentieth century), practitioners have provided a variety of responses to this inquiry. The most consistent response has been that in the process of studying another culture we learn important things about ourselves. Certainly this book demonstrates how important my relationships with the Toba were for self-growth, both emotional and intellectual. By extension, to put it in contemporary jargon, cultural study enlarges our discourse of understanding about the human condition. But what specific knowledge accomplishes this objective, how the desired effect is produced, and for whom, merits greater attention than awarded thus far in the discipline.

Certainly the Toba provide an excellent example of cultural persistence amidst pressure for absorption by the nation-state. They demonstrate how a foraging ideology can persist amidst the encroachment of capitalist economy. This knowledge certainly has curiosity value if nothing else. But the question persists. Why is this knowledge significant? For purposes of domination and control? In other words, does the knowledge produced benefit the Toba in any apparent manner or does it primarily contribute to more effective implementation of administrative nation-state policies that the Toba continue to regard as exploitative rather than philanthropic? In our attempt to understand the human condition generally, as distinct from this specific case, do we reinforce dominant hierarchies that inhibit or preclude emancipation from power relations?

Throughout the 1980s anthropologists have demonstrated increasing sensitivity to their motivations for writing. They also show greater awareness of the audience to whom their texts are directed. Such sensitivity does not solve the problem of unanticipated utilization of ethnographic accounts for purposes beyond what the author could have imagined. It does make one aware that ethnography is not the innocent activity of simple documentation that a poorly informed readership might imagine. Attention to such concerns has contributed to improved forms of ethnographic reporting.

It is not yet clear what forms the creative ethnography of the 1990s will take, but for the time being a number of experiments are being tested. We can expect to see less reliance on literary criticism for conceptual input and more attention to processes of intersubjective understanding that call into question established categories of knowledge as well as how they get produced and distributed. Thus far, no convincing model has emerged to point the way. We are likely to see further experimentation and critiques involving particular cases rather than totalizing efforts that provide models for all time and place.

Based upon the experiences discussed here, I would argue that experimentations need to place greater emphasis on the actual practice whereby field experience gets translated into ethnographic texts. This will require increased attention to unique personal history and transactional analysis of interpersonal relationships in the field with an ongoing critical eye (the doubting process), together with a closer examination of changing professional discourses both within and beyond anthropology that shape ethnographic production. Precisely such attention has been offered here. If the introspection contributes to ethnographic endeavor, it will have been worth the effort.

The astute reader will have recognized an attempt here to obliterate the notion of a distant Other that my earlier depictions of a world of spirits and foraging mode of production tended to invoke. At question are discursive practices of the profession that unwittingly support self-definitions by providing descriptive accounts of an exotic

Other. Alternative discursive forms must be pursued that better serve people such as the Toba, whose lives have changed mine forever.

Doubting *is* the "philosophical attitude par excellence." It *must* become a way of life that tempers response to conflicting as well as contradictory discourses in a multicultural world. This attitude should govern all knowledge held with regard to people and ideas constituted as Other. In its absence dogmatism gets entrenched, crimes are committed, and wars are fought all in the name of unquestioned truth. Here is where the image of pilgrim can play a significant role. Pilgrims know that they are not fully at home in their physical and intellectual surroundings and, consequently, are never in full control. Such awareness modulates their responses to persons and ideas recognized as different from their own. This modulation, in turn, enhances the possibility of constructing the more sane and safe societies to which Mack alluded.

Notes

Overture

1. A version of this and the following episode were reported in Appell (1978:21–22).

2. See, for example, Asad (1973), Fabian (1983), and Trouillot and Abu-Lughod in Fox (1991).

Act 1: Ethnic Discourse, Seeds of Doubt

1. I use quotes throughout this act to signify catch words and phrases that carry special meaning for Mennonite community participants.

2. Mennonites trace their roots to the Reformation period when Anabaptists broke with Zwingli over infant baptism and the nature of the church. They do not consider themselves Protestants, but rather, contemporary Anabaptists who stress a believers' church and a strong sense of community. Of course, there are major divisions among Mennonites who practice their faith differently, not only in the United States, but also around the world. For an introduction to Mennonite beliefs and practice as distinct from the Amish, see, for example, Hostetler (1983), Dyck (1981), Klaassen (1971), Kauffman and Harder (1975), and Kauffman and Driedger (1991). Major concentrations of Mennonites are found in Pennsylvania, Ohio, Indiana, Iowa, Kansas, Oregon, and in the Canadian provinces of Ontario, Manitoba, and Saskatchewan. Today some of the largest denominational membership is located in Africa and India.

3. The notion of plenary verbal is that every word of the Bible is inspired by God and is intended to communicate divine purpose and will for humankind. *Premillennial* refers to a belief that Christ will return to earth and take away his chosen people prior to a "tribulation period" and subsequent "thousand-year reign" depicted in the book of Revelation. These are some of the teachings still held firmly by fundamentalist Christians. For a discussion of the emergence and presence of fundamentalism in twentieth-century Protestantism, see, for example, Marsden (1980) and Blumhofer and Carpenter (1990).

4. Social science studies of religion have tended to stress belief and ritual, but as Lewis (1971:11) points out there is a third "cornerstone" of religion, spiritual experience, that tends to get ignored, owing perhaps to the difficulty of documenting subjective experience. Throughout college, seminary, and early fieldwork I have had numerous experiences that I credited to

divine intervention of one sort or another. They provided stability and direction in my life at a time when I needed them. While the symbolic meanings I associate with these experiences today are conceptualized differently, I do not discredit the meanings I attached to them during that period in my life nor the intensity and profound nature of those experiences.

5. Ironically, this test was designed to permit soldiers returning from the war to enter college.

6. The film was produced by the minister's daughter, Joyce Keener.

7. See Gingerich (1970) for a discussion of Mennonite attire in historical context.

8. Throughout I will be using the term *Toba* to refer to the dominant aboriginal population of the Argentine Chaco. Small, historically isolated groups with the same name and similar language are found also in Paraguay and Bolivia. This term was bestowed almost certainly by the neighboring Guaraní. Their name for themselves is *qom* or *nam qom* (the people), which I utilized to set the boundaries for my study of Toba bibliographic materials (1964, 1980b). However, from the earliest point of contact in the sixteenth century until today, historical records identify these people as Toba and they have come to accept the name as appropriate. Consequently, I conform to general usage rather than introduce an unfamiliar term.

9. After arriving in Argentina, I continued the search in museum and university libraries in Buenos Aires, particularly at El Museo Etnográfico and in the Jesuit Collection at Colegio del Salvador, as well as in the Congressional Records dealing with aboriginal affairs; in La Plata at the university and museum libraries; in Córdoba and Tucumán at the university libraries; and in Resistencia at the university museum library, the Historic Archives, the Land Office and Office of Aboriginal Affairs, and at the public library, particularly in their good collection of local newspapers no longer published.

10. There are a number of mission boards in the Mennonite church representing different denominational bodies. The one at Elkhart represented a broad spectrum of Mennonites and was more culturally and theologically liberal at that time than the Eastern Mission Board located in Salunga, Pennsylvania, identified with the Lancaster Conference. Elkhart began its work in the late 1800s in India and expanded to Japan and Latin America, although it currently has representatives all over the world. Salunga was initially strong in Africa, but it, too, has representatives scattered throughout the world today. Currently the various Mennonite mission boards communicate and cooperate with one another to a greater extent than they did during the period under consideration here; theological differences are also less apparent.

Act 2: First Field Experience, Maturation of Doubt

1. J. W. Shank (1951) described the mission's formative years. For a discussion of the Protestant mission mandate and the socioeconomic and political context in which it developed, see Hutchinson (1987); see Bastian (1986) for a treatment of its impact in Latin America.

2. See Miller (1970).

3. The result of that study was published in a small booklet by William Reyburn (1954b). He also left a grammar that served as the basis for later language learning, literacy, and Bible translation in Toba (1954a).

4. The term *Gran Chaco* refers to a region involving northern Argentina, Paraguay, and eastern Bolivia. The same term applies to the province in which we lived. *Chaco* and *Argentine Chaco,* of which the Chago province is a part, are used interchangeably to denote the Argentine portion of the Gran Chaco.

5. See Braunstein (1992).

6. I recall that my mother was concerned about my Spanish accent when Lois and I returned in 1963. She wanted to know if the accent would persist or whether my original speech would return after some time in the States.

7. The inclusion of this lore demonstrates my early interest in topics of an ethnographic nature.

8. For a discussion of *maté* history and culture, see Barreto (1989).

9. See Miller (1967, 1971, 1979b). See also Loewen, Buckwalter, and Kratz (1965); Reyburn (1954b); and Wright (1990).

10. By now I had become accustomed to loud unison praying in churches, but I was not prepared to have my early morning sleep interrupted with the same loud, lengthy prayers. My emotions were no doubt mixed because, while I was impressed with Toba piety, I also wanted another hour of sleep.

11. These two hardwoods have profound practical and symbolic meaning in Toba culture. The *algarrobo* tree produces a sweet-tasting pod that forms a staple in the Toba diet. It was also brewed in ancient times to form a beer, fermented during the *algarroba* bean harvest festivals. Its wood was utilized to construct ancient housing. The red *quebracho* is an extremely hard and heavy wood that produces tannin, which has been a major Chaco industry, but also has other commercial value. The Toba select it for firewood because it burns slowly and generates intense heat.

12. Written in jest.

13. Aurelio's role as chief healer made demands on him at all hours of the day or night. No wonder he thought the people owed him something. He was the prime mover, as always, in the services during the following day as well.

14. The mosquitoes were an ever-present pest whether in country or town. In time we learned to judiciously swat them away in slow sweeping gestures rather than hack and squirm as we did initially. In town we used screens with some success.

15. This was our only trip with the Cressman sisters to a Toba community. They retired from the mission and returned to their native Canada shortly thereafter.

16. This was my first visit to the Mocoví, a small population in the southern Chaco with a language closely related to Toba. The Mocoví are generally more acculturated than the Toba to the white world. However, in the La Reducción area Mocoví and Toba interact and occasionally intermarry.

17. For a discussion of denominational groups working with the Toba, see Miller (1967, 1975, and 1979b), Cordeu (1984), and Wright (1983, 1988, 1990). The major Protestant denominations that have established missions

of one sort or another in the Argentine Chaco over the years include the British Emmanuel Mission, which was obliged to abandon its efforts in 1951, the Church of God Pentecostal, which has maintained ties with only a few congregations over the years, the Baptists, which worked mainly in La Pampa and Zapallar areas, the Foursquare Gospel (curiously translated Iglesia Cuadrangular in Spanish), which maintains congregations in both the Chaco and Formosa provinces, the Grace and Glory and Go Ye Missions, which were among the original missions in the Resistencia area, and the Mennonites, which have worked within the IEU since the late 1950s.

18. The exclamation point signals surprise; this was the first Sunday school hour we had experienced in a Toba church. It will be recalled that this congregation was affiliated with the Pentecostal Church of Buenos Aires, which provided support for the preacher Sánchez.

19. The brick house had been a sore spot with José Durán for many years. He coveted it. Neither the Buckwalters nor we planned to sleep there on any regular basis, nor would we attend the sick in the tradition of the Cressman nurses. It, therefore, seemed appropriate to hand the building over to Durán, who had been associated with the old Mennonite mission and made certain claims to the place. He was sufficiently trained in the uses of the stored medicines to dispense them properly. This action also closed the book on mission commitment to medical treatment. It meant that the Toba of Legua 15 would need to rely on regional clinics in the future.

20. See Metraux (1946) and Karsten (1932).

21. A *torta* is a pancakelike batter fried in grease, which I found tasty but difficult to digest.

22. Before leaving the Chaco I tape-recorded another account of Aurelio's conversion to Christianity, which complements interestingly this longer version. Anthropology classes at Hartford had introduced me to the value of life history material. Furthermore, the Toba always wanted to give their "testimony" on the tape recorder when they visited us in town. Chief Juan Alegre, Soria's competition in Miraflores, once spoke for over three hours, filling up all the tape I had available at the time.

23. This was my first taste of fresh fish roasted over an open fire. It was delicious despite the bones.

24. A drastic drop in temperature was not uncommon during the winter months, but 50 degrees in one night was a record. Fortunately, our sleeping bags were sufficiently thick to provide the protection we needed.

25. For a discussion of the Emmanuel mission and why it was obliged to dissolve, see Sockett (1966).

26. I have described the nature of this obligation in a paper (1989b) in which I point out that the Toba project a perception of the white person as a deceiver, one who fails to fulfill commitments.

27. Note the argument that even as the Toba adopt the rhetoric and rituals of Christianity, their own epistemology remains to shape and interpret what is being adopted.

28. In my dissertation (1967) I referred to this articulation as structural conduciveness, a notion borrowed from Neil Smelser (1962).

29. See Miller (1975, 1979b, 1980b, 1985b).

30. The difference in interpretation was not a theological issue, but rather a cultural one. For the Toba the sign was iconic whereas for me it was metaphorical. I read the Scripture as I had been trained, with all my subsequent experiences underscoring metaphorical meaning rather than undermining it. The Toba, in contrast, were accustomed to direct contact with the powers that shape life and death.

31. For an introduction to Old Testament notions of a separate people of God, see, among others, Smith (1956), Frazer (1918), Douglas (1966), and Leach (1983).

32. For an understanding of the notion of consciousness under consideration here, see Lévi-Strauss (1971:629ff.).

33. This observation was suggested to me by Jon Church.

34. Palavecino wrote more than a dozen reports on his brief excursions to the Chaco. See 1955, 1958–59, and 1965 for his latest summary contributions. For a more complete listing, see Miller (1980b).

35. He also provided me with a generous sample of his own writings.

36. Tovar's major contribution was his catalogue of South American languages (1961). His 1951 publication is also of interest to Chaco scholars.

Act 3: Professional Discourses and the Doubting Process

1. The social movement literature is full of examples such as this where tradition is rejected and the new order is upheld. Following Lowie (1957), Cordeu and Siffredi (1971:147f) refer to this rejection of the past as iconoclasm. It is of interest to note that traditional tales are now being reinstilled with value by many Toba leaders to the extent that one prominent leader has published a series of them (Sánchez 1987) with the support of JUM, a united Protestant mission organization in Argentina.

2. The one exception was preacher José Durán on the visit to Legua 15 on October 24, 1959, when I was unaware of the significance of what I was hearing.

3. I refer to the discussion with Antonia Cabrera in the subsequent diary entry of July 5, 1966.

4. The diary fails to mention this shock, indicating once again the extent to which deeply personal experiences affecting my missionary role were repressed there.

5. Until reviewing this diary I had forgotten that I was pursuing the role of the Pentecostal evangelist John Lagar at this early stage of the research.

6. The decision by Kratz to invite me along was courageous and earned my highest respect, given my criticism of mission philosophy and activity, together with the uncertainty of how our new relationship would impact upon their work with the Toba.

7. Marriage of Toba males and white females was practically unheard of during my stay in the Chaco. Recently two European mission workers married Toba women.

8. The number of whites and aborigines killed varies enormously in the

telling, but the official records indicate two whites and an unknown number of "Indians."

9. Cordeu and Siffredi (1971:155f) criticized this belief contrast as a fundamentally "psychological" dialectic of "deception-failure/success-truth" that did not incorporate both internal and external structural factors of an "objective" rather than subjective nature. Their critique ignored completely both the fact that the distinction was made by the Toba themselves rather than by the ethnographer and the structural analysis described subsequently.

10. The smooth ferry ride contrasted dramatically with the excitement of our first crossing in 1959.

11. It was on this occasion that I learned that Cordeu and Siffredi had written a book on the Chaco; they offered me a copy in the museum with the inscription, "With affection and apologies for whatever misinterpretations."

12. At this point nothing whatsoever was said about their book and I had no idea what was in store for me later in the evening when I started to read it.

13. It was during this visit with Rex that I informed him of my critique of the Cordeu and Siffredi book. He requested a copy when it was completed and subsequently saw to its publication.

14. Experiencing this trauma with the Miranda family bound us to them and made us a stronger component of the local white community.

15. Chase-Sardi had just published a book on the indigenous people of Paraguay (1972). Our paths crossed again in 1977 when we both spoke at the University of Wisconsin Tinker Foundation Lectures.

16. Subsequently, the Buckwalters established contact with the mission brothers, and there has been travel back and forth between the Toba of Formosa province and the Paraguayan mission Emok Toba ever since.

17. This is the same person Albert and I visited in Legua 7 on November 14–16, 1959.

18. The efforts to assist the Belli Lawyer Group proved to be in vain when they later made their own arrangements.

19. See, for example, Crapanzano (1977), Marcus and Cushman (1982), Marcus and Fischer (1986), Clifford and Marcus (1986), Geertz (1988), Clifford (1988), and Fox (1991).

20. An *emic* approach seeks to discover categories of cultural understanding as articulated from a native point of view. *Etic* refers to the predetermined conceptual toolkit the researcher takes to the field.

21. See Van Maanen (1988), who compares the realist tale with other genres of ethnographic writing.

22. I refer to Talcott Parsons's theory of social action (Parsons, Shils, Naegele, and Pitts 1961) underlying Smelser's study of collective behavior.

23. Pablo Wright has pointed out that Cordeu and de los Ríos (1982) made a similar critique of the harmony and dissonance conceptual model.

24. The relevance of Weber's notion of disenchantment to my argument was suggested by Richard Barrett, another Temple colleague at the time (see Gerth and Mills 1958:139).

25. Perhaps one reason the topic attracted the interest it did was due to a

discourse shift in the 1970s that required anthropologists to examine more critically their role as agents of change among the people they studied.

26. Bartolomé himself had proposed this metaphor.

27. Two of my graduate students, Ali Kleibo and Elena Kogan, contributed to the wording of this response.

28. The first attempt, of course, was the peasant paper in 1976.

29. In response to a comment at Comahue University in Neuquén about why I criticized governmental policy in Argentina when the United States Indian policies have failed so miserably, I assured the respondent that anthropologists are, indeed, critical of U.S. policy, which certainly does not provide a model for other nations to follow. The circumstances surrounding my involvement with the Toba do merit explication, of course, which is what this work is all about.

30. A transcription problem occurred in that the Toba $\hat{y}$, pronounced as English *y* in *yes*, was not distinguished from the Toba *y* pronounced as English *g* in *gin*. See Karsten (1932), Lehmann-Nitsche (1923), Metraux (1946), Cordeu (1969), and Fernández Guizzetti and Bigo de Pérez (1985) for other published versions of this myth.

Denouement

1. The reference here is to Martin Buber's *I and Thou* (1958) subjective relationship, which leaves little space for an objective Other.

2. My colleague John Hostetler, the communal societies scholar, posed many of the questions that shape the discussion here after he read an earlier version of this manuscript, such as who gains what from the production of ethnographic knowledge or what is worth knowing about a society.

3. See Pablo Wright (1992), who discusses the discursive space established by my notion of Toba Pentecostalism (1967).

4. In my own case, the funding for my original stay with the mission certainly influenced my activity. For example, I did not record and transcribe more Toba folklore because I felt a degree of guilt about dedicating too much time and effort toward the collection of tales that had very little to do with mission goals. I also limited the amount of time I spent at university libraries in the search for sources. My subsequent research trips were funded by Wenner-Gren and the Universities of Pittsburgh and Temple, none of which exerted ostensible influence on my actions. The one funded project I did for the Inter-American Foundation involved a report on their projects that was never published (1988a).

References Cited

Appell, George N., ed.
  1978   *Ethical Dilemmas in Anthropological Inquiry: A Case Book.* Waltham, Mass.: Crossroads Press.
Asad, Talal
  1973   *Anthropology and the Colonial Encounter.* London: Ithaca Press.
Banfield, Edward C.
  1958   *The Moral Basis of a Backward Society.* New York: Free Press.
Barreto, Margarita
  1989   *El maté.* Buenos Aires: Ediciones del Sol.
Bastian, Jean Pierre
  1986   *Breve historia del protestantismo en América Latina.* Mexico City: Casa Unida de Publicaciones.
Berger, Peter
  1963   *Invitation to Sociology.* New York: Doubleday.
Blumhofer, Edith L., and Joel Carpenter
  1990   *Twentieth Century Evangelicalism: A Guide to the Sources.* Hamden, Conn.: Garland.
Braunstein, José
  1992   *Hacia una nueva carta étnica del Gran Chaco.* Las Lomitas, Provincia de Formosa, Argentina: Centro del Hombre Antiguo Chaqueño no. 4.
Buber, Martin
  1958   *I and Thou.* 2d ed. New York: Scribner.
Censo Indígena Nacional
  1987   *Censo indígena nacional de la provincia del Chaco.* Resistencia: Provincia del Chaco.
Chase-Sardi, Miguel
  1972   *La situación actual de los indígenas del Paraguay.* Asunción: Escuela Ténica Salesiana.
Clifford, James
  1988   *The Predicament of Culture.* Cambridge, Mass.: Harvard University Press.
Clifford, James, and George Marcus, eds.
  1986   *Writing Culture: The Poetics and Politics of Ethnography.* Berkeley: University of California Press.
Cordeu, Edgardo
  1969   "La comunidad toba de Miraflores: Materiales para el estudio de un proceso de cambio." MS. Buenos Aires.

1969–70 "Aproximación al horizonte mítico de los tobas." *Runa* 1–2:67–176.

1984 "Notas sobre la dinámica socio-religiosa toba-pilagá." *Suplemento Antropólogico* 19 (1):187–235.

Cordeu, Edgardo, and Miguel de los Ríos

1982 "Una enfoque estructural de las variaciones socioculturales de los cazadores, pescadores y recolectores del Gran Chaco." *Suplemento Antropológico* 17 (3):1–2.

Cordeu, Edgardo, and Alejandra Siffredi

1971 *De la algarroba al algodón.* Buenos Aires: Juarez Editor.

1973 "Réplica a Miller." *Etnía* 1:14–18.

Crapanzano, V.

1977 "On the Writing of Ethnography." *Dialectical Anthropology* 2:69–73.

Douglas, Mary

1966 *Purity and Danger: An Analysis of Concepts of Pollution and Taboo.* London: Routledge and Kegan Paul.

Dwyer, Kevin

1977 "On the Dialogic of Fieldwork." *Dialectical Anthropology* 2:143–51.

1979 "The Dialectic of Ethnology." *Dialectical Anthropology* 4:105–24.

Dyck, C. J.

1981 *Introduction to Mennonite History.* Scottdale, Pa.: Herald Press.

Fabian, Johannes

1983 *Time and the Other.* New York: Columbia University Press.

Fernández Guizzetti, Germán, and Margot Bigot de Pérez

1985 "Those Who Come from the Sky: A Toba Myth about the Origin of Women and the Humanization of Men." *Latin American Indian Literatures* 7 (2):123–33.

Foster, George

1967 "Introduction: What Is a Peasant?" In *Peasant Society: A Reader,* ed. J. M. Potter, M. M. Díaz, and G. M. Foster. Boston: Little, Brown.

Fox, Richard G., ed.

1991 *Recapturing Anthropology: Working in the Present.* Santa Fe, N.M.: School of American Research Press.

Frazer, Sir James G.

1918 *Folk-lore in the Old Testament: Studies in Comparative Religion, Legend, and Law.* 3 vols. London: Macmillan.

Gerth, H. H., and C. Wright Mills

1958 *From Max Weber: Essays in Sociology.* New York: Oxford University Press.

Geertz, Clifford

1973 *The Interpretation of Cultures.* New York: Basic Books.

1988 *Works and Lives: The Anthropologist as Author.* Stanford: Stanford University Press.

Gillin, John

1955 "Ethos Components in Modern Latin American Culture." *American Anthropologist* 57:488–500.

Gingerich, Melvin
1970   *Mennonite Attire through Four Centuries.* Breinsville, Pa.: Pennsylvania German Society.
Gleason, H. A.
1955   *An Introduction to Descriptive Linguistics.* New York: Henry Holt.
Griva, Edelmi, and Maricel Stroppa
1983   (1977) *Yo Montiel Romero de raza toba.* 2d ed. Mexico: Editorial Mar de Cortes.
Hermitte, Esther, and Leopoldo Bartolomé, eds.
1977   *Processes de articulación social.* Buenos Aires: Amorrortu Editores.
Hoffer, Eric
1951   *The True Believer.* New York: Harper and Row.
Hostetler, John
1983   *Mennonite Life.* Scottdale, Pa.: Herald Press.
Hughes, Charles
1984   "History of Ethnology after 1945." In *Handbook of North American Indians,* vol. 5, *Arctic,* ed. D. Damas. Washington, D.C.: Smithsonian Institution.
Hutchinson, William R.
1987   *Errand to the World.* Chicago: University of Chicago Press.
Karsten, Rafael
1932   *Indian Tribes of the Argentine and Bolivian Chaco.* Helsingfors: Akademische Buchhandlung.
Kauffman, J. Howard, and Leo Driedger
1991   *The Mennonite Mosaic: Identity and Modernization.* Scottdale, Pa.: Herald Press.
Kauffman, J. Howard, and Leland Harder
1975   *Anabaptists Four Centuries Later.* Scottdale, Pa.: Herald Press.
Keesing, Roger
1989   "Exotic Readings of Cultural Texts." *Current Anthropology* 30 (4):459–79.
Kinsey, Alfred C.
1948   *Sexual Behavior in the Human Male.* Philadelphia: W. B. Saunders.
Klaassen, Walter
1971   *Anabaptism: Neither Catholic nor Protestant.* Waterloo, Ontario: Conrad Press.
Krieg, Hans
1939   "Indianerhunde im Gran Chaco." *Physis* 16 (48):153–58.
Kroeber, Alfred L.
1948   *Anthropology.* New York: Harcourt, Brace.
Lacan, Jaques
1977   *Écrits.* New York: Norton.
Leach, Edmund R.
1983   "Anthropological Approaches to the Study of the Bible in the Twentieth Century." In *Structuralist Interpretations of Biblical Myth,* ed. E. R. Leach and D. A. Aycock. Cambridge: Cambridge University Press.

Lederer, William J.
   1958   *The Ugly American.* New York: Norton.
Lehmann-Nitsche, Robert
   1923   "La astronomía de los tobas." *Revista del Museo de la Plata* 27:267–85.
Lévi-Strauss, Claude
   1955   *Tristes Tropiques.* Paris: Librairie Plon.
   1969   *The Raw and the Cooked.* New York: Harper and Row.
   1971   *The Naked Man.* New York: Harper and Row.
   1976   "The Scope of Anthropology." Chapter 1 in *Structural Anthropology II.* New York: Basic Books.
Lewis, I. M.
   1971   *Ecstatic Religion.* Baltimore, Md.: Penguin Books.
Loewen, Jacob, A. Buckwalter, and J. Kratz
   1965   "Shamanism, Illness, and Power in Toba Church Life." *Practical Anthropology* 12:250–80.
Lowie, E.
   1957   "El mesianismo primitivo y un problema etnológico." *Diógenes* 5 (19):87–100.
McGavran, Donald A.
   1955   *Bridges of God.* New York: Friendship Press.
Mack, Burton L.
   1993   *The Lost Gospel: The Book of Q and Christian Origins.* San Francisco: Harper.
Malinowski, Bronislaw
   1922   *Argonauts of the Western Pacific.* London: Routledge and Kegan Paul.
Marcus, George E., and Dick Cushman
   1982   "Ethnographies as Texts." *Annual Review of Anthropology* 11:25–69.
Marcus, George E., and Michael Fischer
   1986   *Anthropology as Cultural Critique.* Chicago: University of Chicago Press.
Marsden, George M.
   1980   *Fundamentalism in American Culture.* New York: Oxford University Press.
Mead, George Herbert
   1934   *Mind, Self, and Society.* Chicago: University of Chicago Press.
Metraux, Alfred
   1946   *Myths of the Toba and Pilagá Indians of the Gran Chaco.* Philadelphia: American Philosophical Society.
Miller, Elmer S.
   1961   Seeing Christ through Toba Eyes. *Christian Living* (June):8–9, 44.
   1964   "A Critical Analysis of Toba Bibliographic Materials." M.A. thesis, Hartford Seminary Foundation.
   1966   "Toba Kin Terms." *Ethnology* 5 (2):194–201.
   1967   "Pentecostalism among the Argentine Toba." Ph.D. diss., University of Pittsburgh.
   1970   "The Christian Missionary: Agent of Secularization." *Anthropolog-*

ical Quarterly 43 (1):14–22. Reprinted in *Missiology* 1 (1):99–107, 1973; and in *Native South Americans*, ed. Pat Lyon, Boston: Little Brown, 1974, republished by Waveland Press, 1985.

1971   "The Argentine Toba Evangelical Religious Service." *Ethnology* 10 (2):149–59.

1972   "Los tobas y el milenarismo." *Actualidad Antropologica* 11:17–20.

1973   "The Linguistic and Ecological Basis for Argentine Toba Social Categories." Paper presented at the Ninth International Congress of Anthropological and Ethnological Sciences, Chicago.

1974   "The Impact of Pentecostal Symbolism upon the Concept of Power among the Argentina Toba." Paper presented at the meeting of the Anthropology Working Group of CLACSO, Buenos Aires.

1975   "Shamans, Power Symbols, and Change in Argentine Toba Culture." *American Ethnologist* 2 (3):477–96.

1976   "Rethinking the Concept 'Peasantry.'" Paper presented at the meeting of the Anthropology Working Group of CLACSO, Quito.

1977a   "Shamanism and Leadership in the Gran Chaco: A Dynamic View." Paper presented at the annual meeting of the American Anthropological Association, Houston. Available in *Working Papers on South American Indians* no. 4, ed. K. Kensinger. Bennington, Vt.: Bennington College, 1992.

1977b   "Unintended Effects of Protestant Missions in the Gran Chaco." Tinker Foundation lecture at the University of Wisconsin, Madison.

1978   "The Efficacy of Faith Healing." In *Ethical Dilemmas in Anthropological Inquiry: A Case Book*, ed. George N. Appell. Waltham, Mass.: Crossroads Press.

1979a   *Introduction to Cultural Anthropology.* New York: Prentice-Hall.

1979b   *Los tobas argentinos: Armonía y disonancia en una sociedad.* Mexico City: Siglo XXI.

1980a   "Contexts that Confer Individual Identity: An Example from the Gran Chaco Toba." Paper presented at the annual meeting of the American Anthropological Association, Washington, D.C. Available in *Working Papers on South American Indians* no.4, ed. K. Kensinger. Bennington, Vt.: Bennington College, 1983.

1980b   *A Critically Annotated Bibliography of the Gran Chaco Toba.* 2 vols. New Haven, Conn.: Human Relations Area Files.

1980c   *Harmony and Dissonance in Argentine Toba Society.* New Haven, Conn.: Human Relations Area Files.

1981a   "Great was the Company of the Preachers: The Word of Missionaries and the Word of Anthropologists." *Anthropological Quarterly* 54 (3):125–33.

1981b   "The Interpretation of Signification: A Semiological Approach to the Study of Social Articulation." *Working Papers in Culture and Communication* 3 (2):39–62. Department of Anthropology, Temple University.

1982a   "The Chaco Indians." In *Lost Empires, Living Tribes.* Washington, D.C.: National Geographic Society.

1982b   "Pentecostalist Contributions to the Proletarianization of the Argentine Toba." In *Culture and Ideology: Anthropological Perspectives*, ed. Jean Barstow. Minneapolis: University of Minnesota Press.

1985a   "Marking Mennonite Identity: A Structuralist Approach to Separation." *Conrad Grebel Review* 3 (3):251–63.

1985b   "Poder y cosmos." *Uno Mismo* (special ed.):32–39.

1986a   "Confessions of an Ethnographer." Paper presented at the Tenth Lowland South American Indian Conference, Bennington College, Vt.

1986b   "Elmer Miller to James Juhnke and Ben Redekop." *Conrad Grebel Review* 4 (2):162–65.

1987   "On the Transforming Nature of Toba Subjectivity." Paper presented at the annual meeting of the American Anthropological Association, Chicago. Available in *Working Papers on South American Indians* no. 3, ed. K. Kensinger. Bennington, Vt.: Bennington College, 1993.

1988a   Report on Chaco Indian Study to Inter-American Foundation.

1988b   "Women and Fire: A Toba Myth." *Latin American Indian Literatures Journal* 4 (1):42–60.

1989a   "Argentina's Toba: Hunter-Gatherers in the City." *The World and I* (June):636–45.

1989b   "Why Do *Doqshi* Always Tell Lies?" Paper presented at the I Congreso Internacional de Etnohistoria, University of Buenos Aires.

Murdock, George P.
1961   *Outline of Cultural Materials*. New Haven: Human Relations Area Files.

Murdock, George P., and Alexander Spoehr, eds.
1965   "Ethnographic Atlas." *Ethnology* 4 (4):448–55.

Murphy, Robert
1971   *Dialectics of Social Life*. New York: Basic Books.

Nida, Eugene
1960   "Report on Toba Program." MS. Sáenz Peña, Argentina.

Ortner, Sherry
1984   "Theory in Anthropology since the Sixties." *Comparative Studies in Society and History* 26:126–66.

Palavecino, Enrique
1955   "Las culturas aborígenes del Chaco." In *Historia de la Nación Argentina*, vol. 1, ed. R. Levene. Buenos Aires: El Ateneo.

1958–59 "Algunas notas sobre la transculturación del indio chaqueño." *Runa* 9:379–89.

1965   "Introducción al problema indígena chaqueño." *Informe Final de las Primera Convención Nacional de Antropología*. Resistencia: Universidad Nacional del Nordeste.

Parsons, Talcott, Edward Shils, Kaspar D. Naegele, and Jesse R. Pitts
1961   *Theories of Society*. 2 vols. New York: Free Press.

Redekop, Ben
1986   "Reader Response to Elmer S. Miller." *Conrad Grebel Review* 4 (1):60–63.

Redfield, Robert
   1956   *Peasant Society and Culture*. Chicago: University of Chicago Press.
Reyburn, William
   1954a   "A Toba Grammar." MS. Sáenz Peña, Argentina.
   1954b   *The Toba Indians of the Argentine Chaco: An Interpretative Report*. Elkhart, Indiana: Mennonite Board of Missions.
Royal Anthropological Institute of Great Britain and Ireland
   1951   (1894) *Notes and Queries on Anthropology*. 6th ed. London: Routledge and Kegan Paul.
Ruby, Jay, ed.
   1982   *A Crack in the Mirror: Reflexive Perspectives in Anthropology*. Philadelphia: University of Pennsylvania Press.
Sahlins, Marshall
   1976   *Culture and Practical Reason*. Chicago: University of Chicago Press.
Sánchez, Orlando
   1987   *Togueshic l'aqtaxanaxac na qompi: Antiguos relatios tobas*. Buenos Aires: Junta Unida de Misiones.
Shank, J. W.
   1951   *We Enter the Chaco Indian Work*. Elkhart, Indiana: Mennonite Board of Missions.
Smelser, Neil
   1962   *Theory of Collective Behavior*. London: Free Press.
Smith, Robertson W.
   1956   (1894) *The Religion of the Semites: The Fundamental Institutions*. 2d ed. New York: Meridian.
Sockett, B.
   1966   *A Stone Is Cast*. Birkenhead, Cheshire: Wrights' Ltd.
Sotelo, R. J., and A. Burlli
   1963   "Informe sobre la Colonia Aborigen Chaco." MS. Quitilipi, Chaco, Argentina.
Spencer, J.
   1989   "Anthropology as a Kind of Writing." *Man* (N.S.) 24:143–64.
Susnik, Branka J.
   1962   "Estudios emok-toba." *Boletín de la Sociedad Científica del Paraguay y del Museo Etnográfico*, vol. 7. Asunción.
Tedlock, Dennis
   1972   "The Analogical Tradition and the Emergence of a Dialogical Anthropology." *Journal of Anthropological Research* 35 (4):387–400.
Tovar, Antonio
   1951   "Un capítulo de lingüística general." *Boletín de la Academia Argentina de Letras* 20 (77):369–403.
   1961   *Catálogo de las lenguas de américa del sur*. Buenos Aires: Editorial Sudamericana.
Trouillot, Michel-Rolph
   1991   "Anthropology and the Savage Slot: The Poetics and Politics of Otherness." In *Recapturing Anthropology: Working in the Present*, ed. Richard Fox. Santa Fe, N.M.: School of American Research Press.

Van Maanen, John
1988   *Tales of the Field.* Chicago: University of Chicago Press.

Wallace, Anthony F. C.
1956   "Revitalization Movements." *American Anthropologist* 58:264–81.

Webster, Steven
1982   "Dialogue and Fiction in Ethnography." *Dialectical Anthropology* 7 (2):91–114.

Wolf, Eric
1966   *Peasants.* Englewood Cliffs, N.J.: Prentice-Hall.

Wright, Pablo
1983   "Presencia protestante entre aborígenes del Chaco argentino." *Scripta Etnológica* 7:73–84.

1988   "Tradición y aculturación en una organización socio-religiosa toba contemporánea." *Cristianismo y Sociedad* 95:71–87.

1990   "Crisis, enfermedad y poder en la Iglesia Cuadrangular Toba." *Cristianismo y Sociedad* 105:15–37.

1992   "Toba Pentecostalism Revisited." *Social Compass* 39 (3):355–75.

Index

ELMER S. MILLER has been studying the Toba for thirty-five years. He has published *Introduction to Cultural Anthropology, Los Tobas Argentinos: Armonía y disonancia en una sociedad, Harmony and Dissonance in Argentine Toba Society,* and *A Critically Annotated Bibliography of the Gran Chaco Toba,* as well as numerous articles on missionaries, anthropology, and the Toba. He is a professor of anthropology at Temple University.